The Habsburg Monarchy, 1490

European History in Perspective
General Editor: Jeremy Black

Benjamin Arnold *Medieval Germany*
Ronald Asch *The Thirty Years' War*
Christopher Bartlett *Peace, War and the European Powers, 1814–1914*
Robert Bireley *The Refashioning of Catholicism, 1450–1700*
Donna Bohanan *Crown and Nobility in Early Modern France*
Arden Bucholz *Moltke and the German Wars, 1864–1871*
Patricia Clavin *The Great Depression, 1929–1939*
Paula Sutter Fichtner *The Habsburg Monarchy, 1490–1848*
Mark Galeotti *Gorbachev and his Revolution*
David Gates *Warfare in the Nineteenth Century*
Martin P. Johnson *The Dreyfus Affair*
Peter Musgrave *The Early Modern European Economy*
J. L. Price *The Dutch Republic in the Seventeenth Century*
A. W. Purdue *The Second World War*
Christopher Read *The Making and Breaking of the Soviet System*
Francisco J. Romero-Salvado *Twentieth-Century Spain*
Matthew S. Seligmann and Roderick R. McLean
Germany from Reich to Republic, 1871–1918
Brendan Simms *The Struggle for Mastery in Germany, 1779–1850*
David Sturdy *Louis XIV*
Hunt Tooley *The Western Front*
Peter Waldron *The End of Imperial Russia, 1855–1917*
James D. White *Lenin*
Patrick Williams *Philip II*

European History in Perspective
Series Standing Order
ISBN 0-333-71694-9 hardcover
ISBN 0-333-69336-1 paperback
(*outside North America only*)

You can receive future titles in this series as they are published by placing a standing order. Please contact your bookseller or, in the case of difficulty, write to us at the address below with your name and address, the title of the series and the ISBN quoted above.

Customer Services Department, Palgrave Ltd
Houndmills, Basingstoke, Hampshire RG21 6XS, England

The Habsburg Monarchy, 1490–1848

Attributes of Empire

PAULA SUTTER FICHTNER

palgrave
macmillan

First published 2003 by
PALGRAVE MACMILLAN
Houndmills, Basingstoke, Hampshire RG21 6XS and
175 Fifth Avenue, New York, N.Y. 10010
Companies and representatives throughout the world

PALGRAVE MACMILLAN is the global academic imprint of the Palgrave Macmillan division of St. Martin's Press, LLC and of Palgrave Macmillan Ltd. Macmillan® is a registered trademark in the United States, United Kingdom and other countries. Palgrave is a registered trademark in the European Union and other countries.

ISBN 0-333-73727-X hardback
ISBN 0-333-73728-8 paperback

This book is printed on paper suitable for recycling and made from fully managed and sustained forest sources.

A catalogue record for this book is available from the British Library.

Library of Congress Cataloging-in-Publication Data
Fichtner, Paula S.
     The Habsburg Monarchy, 1490-1848 : attributes of empire / Paula Sutter Fichtner.
     p. cm. – (European history in perspective)
     Includes bibliographical references and index.
     ISBN: 978-0-333-73728-6
     1. Habsburg, House of. 2. Austria–History–1519-1740.
3. Austria–History–1740-1789.   4. Austria–History–1789-1900.
5. Austria–History–1867-1918.   6. Nationalism–Austria.
7. Austria–Ethnic relations.   8. Holy Roman Empire–History.   I. Title.
II. European history in perspective (Palgrave (Firm))

     DB36.3.H3F53 2003
     943.6'03–dc21
                                                             2002044804

10   9   8   7   6   5   4   3   2   1
12   11   10   09   08   07   06   05   04   03

Transferred to Digital Printing 2012

For Fritz Fellner

Contents

Chapter 3: Creating a State 59

Chapter 4: Holding the Center 89

Chapter 5: Revolution: Text and Subtext 113

Chapter 6: From One to Many 139

A Summary Afterword 167

Acknowledgements

I am grateful for the opportunity to thank the several people whose patient reading of this manuscript reminded me once again how much scholarship is a collegial enterprise. The insightful suggestions of Katie Arens, Karin MacHardy, Miriam Levy, Peter Judson, and Gabor Vermes improved the book in countless ways. As always, Edward Fichtner was generous in both scholarly and technical advice and supremely tolerant of an often-distressed author. Whatever flaws the book has are my responsibility and mine alone.

The author and publishers also wish to thank the following for permission to use copyright material:

University of Washington Press, for the three maps from *Historical Atlas of East Central Europe* by Paul Robert Magocsi, © 1993. Reprinted by permission of the University of Washington Press.

Every effort has been made to trace the copyright holders but if any have been inadvertently overlooked the publishers will be pleased to make the necessary arrangement at the first opportunity.

A Note on Style

Dates of important figures in the history of the Habsburg empire appear after the first mention of their names. In the case of cities, countries, and other geographic locations, contemporary names are used, often followed by earlier designations that still appear in some of the literature. Commonly recognized English spellings – Vienna, Tyrol, Bavaria, for example – have been preferred to their German equivalents.

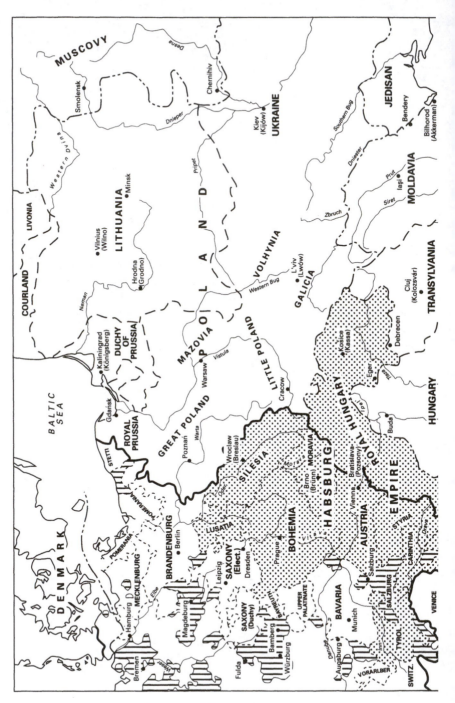

Map 1: East central Europe, c.1570

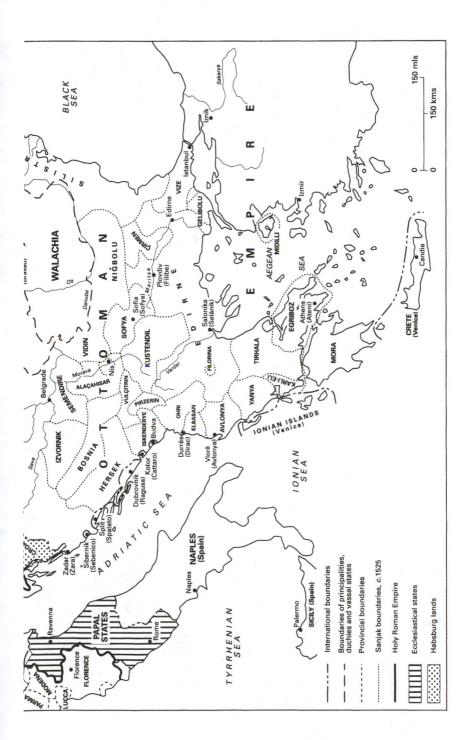

BLACK SEA

WALACHIA

Olt

(Erdel)

Danube

Belgrade

Morava

Sava

Ravenna

FLORENCE
Florence

PARMA
LUCCA
MODENA

PAPAL
STATES

Rome

T Y R R H E N I A N
S E A

Palermo

SICILY (Spain)

Naples

NAPLES
(Spain)

A D R I A T I C   S E A

Zadar
(Zara)
Sibernik
(Sebenico)
Split
(Spalato)

Dubrovnik
(Ragusa)

Kotor
(Cattaro)
Budva

ISKENDERYE

HERSEK

BOSNIA

IZVORNIK

SEMENDIRE

VIDIN

Nis

ALAÇAHISAR

VULÇITRIN

PIZERIN

KUSTENDIL

SOFYA

Sofia
(Sofya)

Maritsa

Plovdiv
(Filibe)

NIĞBOLU

ÇIRMEN

Edirne

E   D   I   R   N   E

O   T   T   O   M   A   N

Vardar

FLORINA

OHRI

ELBASAN

Durrës
(Dirac)

Vlorë
(Avlonya)

AVLONYA

YANYA

TIRHALA

Salonika
(Selânik)

KARLI-ELI

I O N I A N
S E A

IONIAN ISLANDS
(Venice)

MORA

EGRIBOZ

Athens
(Atení)

A E G E A N

S E A

MIDILLI

Izmir

E   M   P   I   R   E

Istanbul

Iznik

Sakarya

VIZE

GELIBOLU

SILISTRE

CRETE
(Venice)

Candia

150 mls

150 kms

0

0

International boundaries

Boundaries of principalities,
duchies and vassal states

Provincial boundaries

Sanjak boundaries, c.1525

Holy Roman Empire

Ecclesiastical states

Habsburg lands

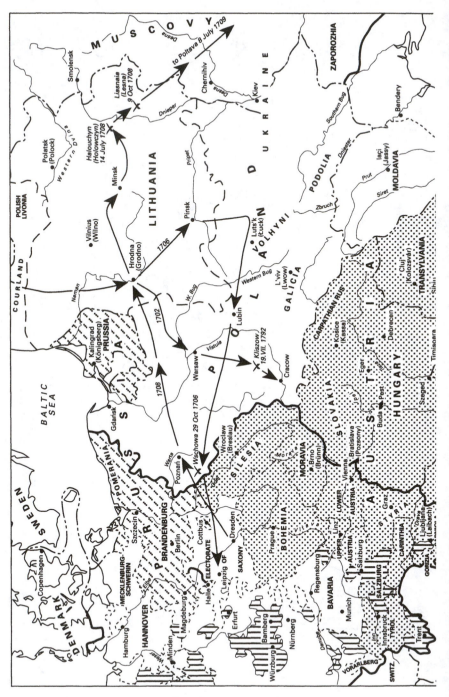

Map 2: East central Europe, c.1721

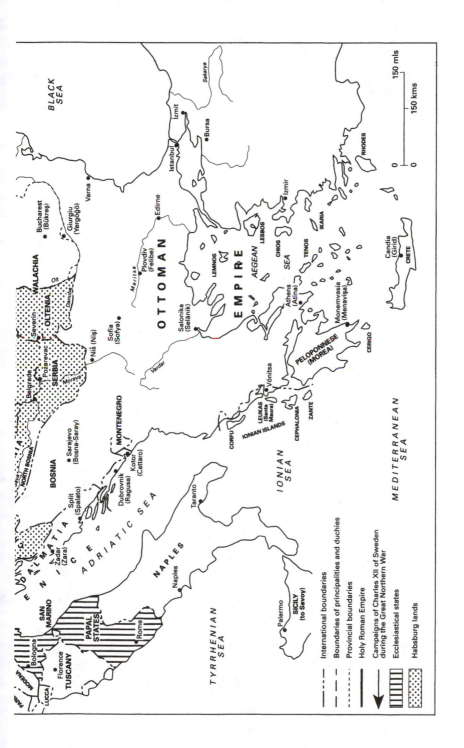

BLACK SEA

Sakarya

Izmit

Bursa

Istanbul

RHODES

Varna

Edirne

Bucharest (Bükreş)

Giurgiu (Yergögö)

WALACHIA

Izmir

OLTENIA

Olt

Maritsa

IKARIA

Danube

Plovdiv (Felibe)

OTTOMAN

LESBOS

CHOS

Severin

AEGEAN

TENOS

Candia (Girid)

CRETE

Sofia (Sofya)

Pozarevac

Vardar

LEMNOS

EMPIRE

Salonika (Selânik)

Niš (Niş)

Belgrade

SERBIA

Morava

Athens (Atina)

Monemvasia (Menavişa)

CERIGO

NORTH BOSNIA

MONTENEGRO

PELOPONNESE (MOREA)

Vónitsa

Sarajevo (Bosna-Saray)

BOSNIA

Kotor (Cattaro)

LEUKAS (Santa Maura)

ZANTE

Dubrovnik (Ragusa)

CORFU

IONIAN ISLANDS

CEPHALONIA

Split (Spalato)

DALMATIA

Zadar (Zara)

ADRIATIC SEA

Taranto

IONIAN SEA

MEDITERRANEAN SEA

NAPLES

Naples

SAN MARINO

PAPAL STATES

Rome

Palermo

SICILY (to Savoy)

TYRRHENIAN SEA

MODENA

Bologna

Florence

TUSCANY

LUCCA

PARMA

International boundaries

Boundaries of principalities and duchies

Provincial boundaries

Holy Roman Empire

Campaigns of Charles XII of Sweden
during the Great Northern War

Ecclesiastical states

Habsburg lands

0   150 mls

0   150 kms

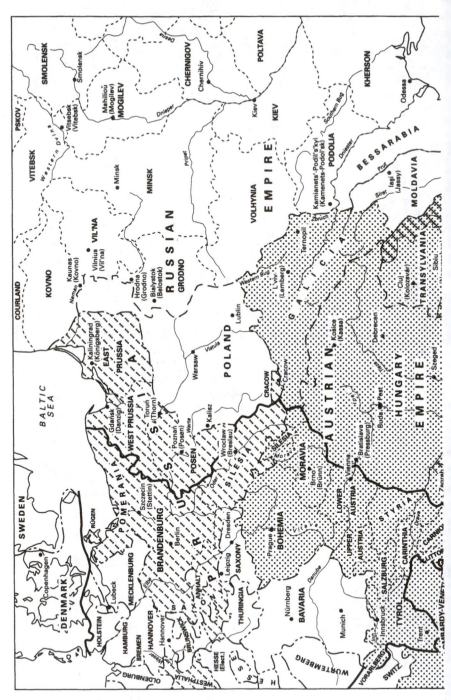

Map 3: East central Europe, c.1815

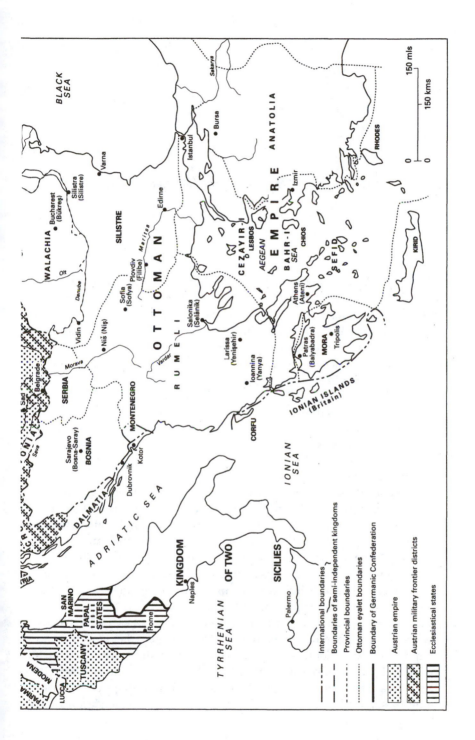

Some Introductory Considerations

Along with the rulers of England, France, and their soon-to-be relatives in Spain, the Habsburgs of central Europe began acquiring lands far beyond their traditional domains in the late fifteenth century. They continued on this path in fits and starts for the next 300 years. Eventually administered out of Vienna, the empire never went overseas as did its western counterparts. Nevertheless, it covered a great deal of territory and ruled a very diverse populace. By the final decades of the eighteenth century the Habsburgs held sway over lands that dominated Europe's east–west axis. To their modest hereditary patrimony of Upper and Lower Austria, Carinthia, Styria, and the Tyrol, now in today's Austria, along with bits and pieces of land in southwestern Germany, the Habsburgs added the crowns of Bohemia and Hungary and the various lands attached to them, parts of what are modern Poland and Ukraine, a substantial portion of northern and eastern Italy, and a sliver of the Istrian coast that is now Slovenia. In the west there were the Austrian Netherlands. A territorial ruler in all of these places, the dynasty became a major player in Europe's international affairs and shaped in significant ways the lives of a large and exceedingly heterogeneous population. The Habsburgs' impact on the continent, therefore, shared many features with Spanish, French, and British colonial imperialism abroad, as well as with Russian and Ottoman expansion closer to home.[1]

Until the beginning of the nineteenth century, members of the dynasty also acted as emperors of Germany. Often called the Holy Roman Empire, this was a loose assemblage of city-states and territorial principalities, the German-speaking Habsburg lands among them. Some of these areas were ruled by high clergymen such as bishops and abbots, some by secular figures who carried titles such as duke, landgrave, and the like. Seven of these figures also acted as electors, empowered to choose the man who would serve as their emperor. Large or small, the self-referential agendas of these polities often thwarted the ambitions of their nominal sovereign. Habsburg emperors, however, drew just enough support and resources from Germany's princes to justify maintaining close connections with them. Moreover, until Napoleon Bonaparte wiped the venerable empire off the map of Europe altogether at the beginning of the nineteenth century, its titular ruler enjoyed a measure of international prestige that the Habsburgs turned to good use, especially in moments of crisis.

Both in Germany and in their non-German dominions, Habsburg purposes and constitutional strategies were often as 'foreign' to the outlook of their subjects as the world-view of the Spanish conquistadors was to natives of South and Central America. East central and southeastern Europe also had its exotic side for the house of Austria, a term commonly used only during and after the reign of Emperor Frederick III (1415–93). The Czech and Hungarian languages were as strange to the early Habsburgs and those who served them as were Native American tongues to the first Europeans in the New World and Indic idioms to the first English speakers who arrived in the Asian subcontinent.[2] The Ottoman Turks, the most formidable foe that the Habsburgs faced in the early modern era, were also objects of general curiosity in central Europe. Visits of envoys from Constantinople were both public entertainment and acts of state.

There were, of course, some striking differences between the Habsburg *imperium* and the worldwide British, French, and Spanish empires of the early modern era. Central, east central, and southeastern Europe were overwhelmingly Christian in faith and white in complexion. Such lands were therefore less prone to the glaring cultural polarities created by the intrusion of the Old World on the New, or on the yet older worlds of Asia, the Middle East, and Africa. The Habsburgs, by and large, did not intrude as conquerors. Indeed, their armies did much to liberate Hungarians, Transylvania's Romanians, and several branches of Balkan Slavs from Ottoman Muslim occupation. Again in contrast to their Spanish, French, and British counterparts, the Habsburgs did not initially turn their multi-ethnic acquisitions into mercantile colonies to enrich the imperial treasury; the dynasty's efforts to reorganize and improve revenue flows from Hungary, Bohemia, and the Netherlands were little more than examples of policies European monarchs had applied to their holdings on and off over the centuries.

The political, social, and economic infrastructures of the Habsburg lands were also far more similar to one another than were the overseas outposts of France, Great Britain, and Spain. The economies of the dynasty's holdings from west to east differed in natural resources, modes of production, and general complexity. Nevertheless, the prevalent quality of material life was much the same. Like every other European state well into modern times, the Habsburg holdings lived largely from agriculture and animal husbandry. Serfs, whose labor obligations did vary from region to region, along with some free peasants, especially in the empire's western lands, were the rural workforce everywhere. The size and importance of urban centers fell off the farther east one traveled in the monarchy. Large and small, however, such places housed a mix of social classes familiar to Europe generally: middle classes of varying degrees of wealth and local importance; artisans and their assistants; and people of no social standing whatsoever, but on the lookout for employ-ment, charity, or simply a place to hide from whom, or whatever, they wanted to escape.

Political factors often shaped economic life in the Habsburg lands. Lower Austria, and the city of Vienna in particular, had been an impor-tant mercantile stop on the Danube river that ran through almost all the Habsburg lands. Local territorial conflict in the late Middle Ages and the Ottoman incursion from the southeast had lessened considerably the entire region's commercial attractiveness. But the condition of agricul-ture and the activities associated with it determined the economies of towns even more. Hungary was the least urbanized sector of the early Habsburg empire, Bohemia and its crownlands the most, but in both realms the prosperity of even the more developed towns depended heavily upon the output of each kingdom's agrarian and mining enterprises.[3]

The political styles of the various Habsburg lands followed European patterns of monarchy as well. The Habsburg hereditary Austrian hold-ings had no kings – the German emperor had titular sovereignty over them, but Habsburg territorial rulers and their predecessors, the Baben-bergs, had long governed these provinces as they pleased. The kingdoms of Hungary, Bohemia, and Poland were formal monarchies, though not hereditary as they were in western Europe. Like the German emperors, rulers in east central Europe were elected by the so-called estates of those kingdoms – nobilities both great and small, high clerical officials, and spokesmen for the important towns. In practice, the crown normally passed from one generation of a dynasty to another; nevertheless, the electoral process was usually a bargaining session between the king and these notables over their respective constitutional privileges and responsibilities, with the latter often holding the upper hand. Should the reigning dynasty die out – Hungary, Bohemia, and later Polish Galicia were ruled by 'foreign' houses long before the arrival of the Habsburgs – the negotiations between estates and the candidates for royal office were particularly intense.

Nobles as a group, or order, had, by the sixteenth century, become entrenched parts of the political, social, and economic systems that would be incorporated into Habsburg central Europe. At a time when most people lived from the land, the practical source of an aristocratic family's power was its territorial demesnes, which varied considerably in size and quality of ownership. Some were available for simple purchase, but others carried titles and legal status that limited ownership to noble houses. The comparatively few families who held vast properties were called magnates in Hungary and often in Bohemia, but lords (*Herren*) in the Austrian provinces. Imitating their counterparts in the west, these people would later adopt titles such as baron or count. New members could be admitted to their ranks, but only when they were sufficiently wealthy and had enough marital connections with the high nobility to merit formal elevation in their status.

The Austrian lands, Bohemia, and Hungary all had a more numerous lesser nobility as well, generally referred to as gentry or petty nobility, once again on French and English models. In the Austrian lands and Bohemia they were called knights (*Ritter, rytíř*). Some of these people were very well-to-do, others no more comfortable than prosperous peasants. Many of them had descended from erstwhile bondsmen or servants of higher nobles or even rulers themselves, who had become free when their masters endowed them with small grants of land. Minor nobilities were always wary of the lords and magnates, who often satisfied their political and proprietary ambitions at the expense of their lesser brethren. The latter, however, were always eager to upgrade their titles when they could. And all nobles, petty or great, clung fiercely to whatever preferred status they had, for it exempted them all from regular tax contributions to the territorial ruler.

The other important privileged group was the Catholic clergy, especially major officials such as bishops and abbots of rich monasteries. The rule of celibacy made it difficult for them to turn church properties into hereditary holdings in the manner of lay aristocracy. Nevertheless, the sizeable revenues these men drew from the lands attached to their offices occasionally equalled the income of great lords. In Bohemia and its crownlands and in the Austrian provinces, some members of the high clergy were virtually absorbed into this class by the beginning of the sixteenth century. Though in Hungary royal restrictions on clerical patronage curbed the influence of that kingdom's major ecclesiastical officers a bit, the political influence of those at the pinnacle of the Catholic hierarchy and the secular magnates was equally great, especially in territorial affairs.[4]

The middle-class town culture of the Habsburg empire, preoccupied with trade and manufacture, was also dominated by elites: property owners and legally recognized residents of these municipalities. Decades could go by before new arrivals and their families were accepted as free townsmen. But throughout the empire as a whole, the central points of contact between the elites and the common mass of humanity were the rural properties of ecclesiastical officials and lay nobles. Landlords gave small plots of land to peasant cultivators who fed themselves as best they could from what they raised and also handed over a certain amount of produce or income to the proprietor as rent or dues.

As a money economy spread throughout Europe generally in the thirteenth and fourteenth centuries, outright bondage to the land was disappearing from what would become the Habsburg domains. But forced labor (*Robot*), in which a peasant gave over a certain amount of his time involuntarily to tasks assigned by his landlord, persisted.[5] Indeed, during the general prosperity of the late fifteenth and early sixteenth centuries, landowners began wringing even more unpaid work from their tenants, a cause for much agrarian discontent throughout central and east central Europe. The manorial lord was also judge and jury in most criminal and civil cases that affected peasants on his properties.[6]

Thus, for all their linguistic and historic diversity, the Habsburg lands were recognizably European in ways that Europe's colonial subjects in the New World, Asia, and Africa were not. Nevertheless, finding ways to keep these holdings together, particularly persuading the elites of their various territories that they had sound reason to support Habsburg rule, was as much a problem for the central European Habsburgs as it was for their cousins in Spain, and for the royal governments of Great Britain and France.[7] The Habsburgs, as we shall see, were survivors. The narrative that follows analyzes the techniques that helped the dynasty to get its empire underway and encouraged its perpetuation until the middle of the nineteenth century, when radically new social, political, and economic circumstances demanded very new approaches to governing.

From it, a reader will learn both some general principles about the growth and development of imperial structures along with important specifics about the strategies of Habsburg rule and its impact on central and east central Europe. He or she should also come away from this book with a clearer understanding of the roots of a culture that, while part of the past, still tantalizes imaginations throughout the world.

Habsburg Family Tree

This tree shows only the major (ruling) branches of the family during the period of their unbroken tenure of the empire, namely from 1452 on. Family members not mentioned in the present work are omitted. Emperors' names are given in **bold**.

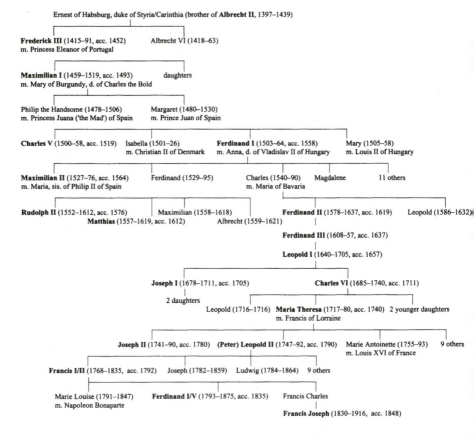

Ernest of Habsburg, duke of Styria/Carinthia (brother of **Albrecht II**, 1397–1439)

Frederick III (1415–91, acc. 1452)   Albrecht VI (1418–63)
m. Princess Eleanor of Portugal

Maximilian I (1459–1519, acc. 1493)   daughters
m. Mary of Burgundy, d. of Charles the Bold

Philip the Handsome (1478–1506)   Margaret (1480–1530)
m. Princess Juana ('the Mad') of Spain   m. Prince Juan of Spain

Charles V (1500–58, acc. 1519) Isabella (1501–26) **Ferdinand I** (1503–64, acc. 1558) Mary (1505–58)
    m. Christian II of Denmark m. Anna, d. of Vladislav II of Hungary m. Louis II of Hungary

Maximilian II (1527–76, acc. 1564) Ferdinand (1529–95) Charles (1540–90) Magdalene 11 others
m. Maria, sis. of Philip II of Spain   m. Maria of Bavaria

Rudolph II (1552–1612, acc. 1576) Maximilian (1558–1618) **Ferdinand II** (1578–1637, acc. 1619) Leopold (1586–1632)
    Matthias (1557–1619, acc. 1612) Albrecht (1559–1621)

Ferdinand III (1608–57, acc. 1637)

Leopold I (1640–1705, acc. 1657)

Joseph I (1678–1711, acc. 1705)   **Charles VI** (1685–1740, acc. 1711)

2 daughters   Leopold (1716–1716) **Maria Theresa** (1717–80, acc. 1740) 2 younger daughters
m. Francis of Lorraine

Joseph II (1741–90, acc. 1780) **(Peter) Leopold II** (1747–92, acc. 1790) Marie Antoinette (1755–93) 9 others
    m. Louis XVI of France

Francis I/II (1768–1835, acc. 1792) Joseph (1782–1859) Ludwig (1784–1864) 9 others

Marie Louise (1791–1847) **Ferdinand I/V** (1793–1875, acc. 1835) Francis Charles
m. Napoleon Bonaparte

Francis Joseph (1830–1916, acc. 1848)

Chapter 1: The Pattern of Empire

From Petty Princes to European Rulers

The Habsburgs were not supposed to amount to much in central Europe. When the princes of the German Holy Roman Empire named Rudolph of Habsburg (1218–91) their king in 1273, they thought that they had a sovereign who would respect their territorial freedoms, not one who would advance his family's fortunes through his office. They badly misjudged the relatively obscure count from southwestern Germany. Though never crowned emperor, a title that the German kingship allowed him to claim and that in theory made its holder the secular champion of Christendom, he proved himself to be ambitious, energetic, and resourceful. Beating back Přemysl Otakar II (1233–78), the aggressive Bohemian king who had invaded Austria above and below the River Enns and Styria, today in eastern Austria, Rudolph endowed his family with these provinces. Rudolph's heirs added the county of Tyrol, along with an assortment of lands in southeastern Europe along the Istrian coast, to the Habsburg central European patrimony. The family also retained ancestral holdings in southwestern Germany into modern times.

Rudolph's new position brought other advantages as well. Even as he waited in Basel for news of his election, he already saw that his improved status opened the way to prestigious marriages for his daughters.[1] The princesses, six in all, found husbands in Bavaria twice and Brandenburg, Saxony, Bohemia, and Hungary, all of which were strategically central to the defense of Rudolph's newly acquired lands. The long-celebrated Habsburg success in marital politics has made historians sometimes forget that these alliances would never have come about unless other dynasties had taken an interest in close relationships with what would

1

become the house of Austria. That Rudolph's heirs through the centuries seemed to profit from these contracts disproportionately was as much an accident as the result of a plan.[2] Nevertheless, their illustrious ancestor's attentiveness to marital politics set a pattern followed consistently throughout the 600-odd years of their family's history.

The road to Habsburg preeminence in Europe, however, was neither smooth nor direct. Conspicuous beneficiaries though they were of European proprietary dynasticism (the notion that the families of rulers in some sense owned the lands they governed), Rudolph's male heirs did not use their legacies to best advantage. Well into the seventeenth century, the Habsburgs, like most German territorial rulers, divided their lands among their legitimate sons. The practice generally weakened the economic and political power of any single one of them; fratricidal quarrels over these partitions sometimes lasted for decades. The dukes of Austria – after the middle of the fourteenth century archdukes – were frequently rivals and even enemies.

Indeed, the Habsburgs emerged in 1463 as a more or less unified house only following the extinction of competing lines and a last vicious intradynastic conflict between Emperor Frederick III and his younger brother, Albrecht VI (1418–63). About the only political card the former had to play was his imperial title, conferred in 1452. Indeed, he would be the last of his line to be crowned by the pope in Rome, though, except for a brief break in the eighteenth century, members of his house would hold both titles until the empire came to an end in 1806. Frederick could be cunning: he came to very favorable terms with the papacy concerning his rights and those of his heirs to revenues from ecclesiastical establishments in Habsburg territories. He also avoided the worst vices of his age. Though he enjoyed a hearty meal, Frederick drank sparingly, a sharp contrast to many of his German colleagues. But his overall record as a ruler was dismal: he spent much of his time on the run from sovereigns more aggressive than he – King Matthias Corvinus (1440–90) of Hungary being perhaps the most bothersome – and he clearly preferred spending his intermittent bursts of energy on his collections and pseudoscientific activities rather than on governing his endangered lands.[3] But, episodic though his appearances in Vienna were, he showed that the Habsburg imperial court had great potential for drawing a variety of people into its orbit of power. On the lookout for privileges and patronage, local nobility as well as their counterparts from other areas of Germany found it increasingly worth their while to spend some time at Frederick's Habsburg establishment. The city changed as well. Nobles brought with them servants, and the presence of wealth lured a motley assortment of hangers-on, so that by 1460 anywhere from 1800 to 3000 souls may have been living in and around the imperial residence, the *Hofburg*.[4]

Like Rudolph I, Frederick wielded his imperial title shrewdly to advance his family fortunes. It was a marriage promoted by Frederick for his only son, Archduke Maximilian (1459–1519), that gave his family major standing not only in Germany, but in Europe as a whole. Following more than ten years of negotiations between the emperor and Charles the Bold, the Valois duke of Burgundy (1432–77), Frederick manipulated the latter's quest for the imperial title and a military setback Charles suffered in Germany in 1475 into a consequential marital union. Archduke Maximilian was betrothed to the duke's only apparent legitimate heir, Duchess Mary (1457–82). The actual nuptials took place in 1477, after Charles himself died in combat at Nancy. The Habsburgs thus found themselves with a significant foothold in one of Europe's richest territorial complexes. They also had more borders to defend. The kings of France would be especially eager to recover several sections within the Burgundian patrimony that had once served as a royal French appanage, lands given by rulers to junior sons from which the latter could supposedly support themselves in a style that befitted their status.

Dynastic Marriage: Its Uses and Limitations

Even in an age of unusually dynamic rulers, Maximilian stood out. An indifferent, sometimes belligerent student, he was as outgoing and reckless as his father was introverted and timid. Dislike of formal education did not keep Maximilian from becoming one of the most sophisticated patrons of art and literature of his age; his musical tastes were exquisite, and he indulged them generously. Some of Germany's finest composers and instrumentalists – Ludwig Senfl, Paul Hofhaimer, Heinrich Isaac – wrote both secular and liturgical works for him; it was Maximilian who began his family's close association with music that would make their court in Vienna Europe's center of the art by the late seventeenth century. History fired his political imagination: becoming emperor in 1493, he believed that his dynasty would rise to the eminence of the Romans, Carolingians, and Ottonians. With the imperial title went theoretical responsibility for all of Christendom; Maximilian took that charge seriously, especially when others did as well. Publications forecasting that the Habsburgs had come to vanquish the invading Ottoman anti-Christ began appearing around 1496. Once Maximilian recaptured Jerusalem, the Day of Judgment would be underway.[5]

But Maximilian was far too ambitious to await the outcome of prophecies. His Burgundian marriage was a much quicker opening to the career for which he was supposedly destined. When Mary of Burgundy died unexpectedly from a hunting accident in 1482, her husband took the opportunity to announce himself as the heir to his wife's patrimony. He now had a major foothold in western Europe, though persuading local authorities in these lands to accept his claims was a tedious and costly task.[6] As territorial rulers, Maximilian and generations of Habsburgs to come were only one element in the interactive machinery of government that oversaw the polities of Europe by the end of the fifteenth century. Burgundy was a conspicuous example of how troublesome this dynamic could be. Provincial estates – territorial aristocracies, high clerical officials such as bishops and abbots, and other local notables – along with powerful municipalities such as Bruges and Gent were aggressive advocates of their constitutional prerogatives and interests. They boldly criticized even the foreign policies of rulers whose military undertakings abroad became overly expensive.[7] King Louis XI (1423–83) of France had already lured domestic rebels to his side in nasty skirmishes with the archduke that had been going on since 1477. Maximilian and Mary had themselves added an additional complication to the situation by producing a son, Archduke Philip (1478–1506), and a daughter, Archduchess Margaret (1480–1530). Many notables of the Burgundian lands now felt even more secure in rejecting Maximilian as their territorial overlord; the Burgundian Valois line, they argued, had passed unbroken from the much-mourned Mary to her son.

Maximilian was intellectually prepared to use armed force whenever necessary against either rebellious subjects or foreign invaders. Indeed, warfare and its technologies fascinated him, and reforming the quality of German mercenary troops, the *Landsknechte*, was one of his lifetime projects.[8] While such ventures were expensive, he had hoped that taxes from the Netherlands would improve his finances generally. The outcome of his military efforts in the Netherlands, however, was ambiguous at best. The Habsburgs retained most of the Burgundian patrimony, but permitted important exceptions. In 1482 France reacquired the duchy of Burgundy, with Dijon as its center, as part of the two-year-old Archduchess Margaret's dowry to King Charles VIII (1470–98) in a ritual betrothal agreement attached to one of the several peaces that temporarily lulled hostilities. Though the marriage never took place, Charles held on to the land, to Maximilian's deep fury. The province of Guelders to the north, a relatively recent acquisition of Charles the Bold, returned to autonomous status as well.

Furthermore, though the combatants began an extended armistice in 1489, the Netherlands were less prosperous. They had also to be reconciled to Habsburg rule. Major municipalities of the area had rebelled against the role Maximilian had assigned them in his fiscal plans, and he had retaliated in kind. In 1483 he had the mayor of fractious Antwerp executed. With revenues running even lower, however, the Habsburg quickly saw that such harshness would be counterproductive. His decision to accommodate his interests to those of the region's nobles and urban oligarchs set a pattern for Habsburg rule in the Low Countries and most of the other territories they acquired in the early modern era. In return for reasonable cooperation when taxes were called for, Maximilian left many of the political traditions and socioeconomic institutions of the Netherlands intact.

The losses he sustained in the Netherlands, however, and the threat of more to come – the Habsburg–Valois Wars would endure into the second half of the next century – shifted Maximilian's priorities from simply acquiring more territory to defending the perimeters of what he had. Unable to enlarge his sources of funding, he turned to creating claims for himself and his family to most of the important thrones of Europe and some secondary ones as well. His personal gains through marriage and succession agreements, in which dynasties pledged their thrones to one another should either of them die out, were actually atypical of these arrangements. More often than not, generations went by before the stipulations of these compacts became operative, and even then in compromised form. The Netherlands was only one among many political arenas in Europe where local political institutions and customs carried as much weight as did bargains that monarchs struck among themselves. Nor did cadet lines of ruling houses abandon their claims lightly. Thus, in negotiating such arrangements, Maximilian probably hoped to forestall unwanted military confrontations as much as he did to expand his holdings. Even one of his more extravagant schemes, in which the Yorkist pretender to the English throne, Perkin Warbeck (d. 1499), signed over his claims to France, England, and Scotland to Maximilian should the former die without legitimate male heirs, addressed the practical problem of defending the new Channel coastline of the Habsburgs.[9] He was also taking advantage of a very favorable diplomatic climate, for by the end of the fifteenth century Spain, England, and Burgundy all saw France as their natural enemy.

Maximilian's pursuit of defensive marriage alliances was underway years before he accepted his Burgundian standoff in 1489 with Charles VIII. Archduke Philip had scarcely been born before his father was thinking of the infant as a husband for Anne of York, a daughter of Edward IV (1442–83) of England. The Iberian peninsula was another jumping off point for the maritime provinces of the Netherlands, particularly Portugal, to which Maximilian had a tie through his mother, Empress Eleanor (d. 1467), a Portuguese princess. France was to be kept from establishing any footholds here as well.[10]

By the last decade of the fifteenth century, anxiety about Portugal and Aragonese interests in Italy also troubled the rulers of Spain, Isabella of Castile and Ferdinand of Aragon. In 1494 Charles VIII invaded the Italian peninsula, occupying Spanish holdings and fiefs of the Holy Roman Empire alike. Ferdinand of Aragon was especially eager for tighter links with Burgundy and the empire; it was in good part his persistence that brought about the dynastic unions that placed the house of Habsburg squarely astride the west–east axis of the European continent until the beginning of the eighteenth century. In November 1495 the Castilian–Aragonese and Austrian houses committed themselves to a double marital bond which joined Maximilian's still-single daughter, Archduchess Margaret, and Ferdinand and Isabella's son, Prince Juan (1478–97); one of the Spanish rulers' daughters, Princess Juana (1479–1555), was to be the wife of Archduke Philip, known as Philip the Handsome, not so much for his appearance but for his free and easy ways.

Two years later, the imagined and the real intersected, at least for Maximilian.[11] An improbable series of deaths of both her elder siblings and their male offspring made Princess Juana and her husband the claimants to the Spanish crowns once King Ferdinand (1452–1516) and Queen Isabella (1451–1504) died. It was their male offspring, to the great distress of Ferdinand of Aragon, who fell heir to the massive Habsburg patrimony. The eldest, Charles (1500–58), became Charles I of Spain in 1516 and Emperor Charles V of Germany in 1519. He also retained control of the Burgundian lands that his grandfather had so ardently protected. His younger brother, Archduke Ferdinand (1503–64), gradually took over the central European holdings and responsibilities of his house after 1521.

Young Ferdinand was also part of yet another bizarrely productive marital scheme of Maximilian I, this time much closer to the Habsburg

Austrian lands. The older man's great worry here was the Jagellonian kingdom of Poland, whose rulers had for some time been trying to extend their lands westward. Maximilian insisted on his rights to the Polish province of Masovia, the homeland of his paternal grandmother. The marriage of Maximilian's granddaughter Isabella (1501–26) to King Christian II (1481–1559) of Denmark, Norway, and Sweden was designed to mount a counterweight to Poland on its Baltic front. As the French began exploring a Polish alliance to help them to encircle the Habsburgs in the east, the need to keep Hungary and Bohemia closely connected to the Habsburgs became more pressing as well. Both of the latter were elective monarchies, in which the estates of the realm formally chose their ruler, though usually from the same house until it died out. Both kingdoms had suffered episodic succession crises since the fourteenth century, compounded in Bohemia by religious civil war. Indeed, since 1471 Bohemia had had a Jagellonian ruler, Vladislav II. Feeble though he was, or perhaps for that reason, he was also chosen King Ladislas II (1456–1516) of Hungary in 1490. Maximilian concluded arrangements with Vladislav in 1491 that called for mutual succession should either line die out in the Austrian lands or in the Hungarian–Bohemian complex. The capstone of this scheme, however, fell into place with a double marriage compact in 1515 between two of his grandchildren, Archduke Ferdinand and Archduchess Mary (1505–58), with the daughter and son respectively of King Vladislav. Unlike the Spanish arrangement, Maximilian would never live to see the fruits of his central European marriage policy. It would, however, yield a bountiful harvest not too long after his death.

Attempting an Empire

Maximilian himself played a relatively subordinate role in Burgundy in the last 20-odd years of his career. The estates wanted their governor to be Archduke Philip, and after 1494 the emperor complied. His attempts to exercise some supervision over the personnel in his son's government and the region's fiscal affairs were regularly frustrated. The taxable wealth of the Netherlands, therefore, was not to be his, even though he needed it desperately to cover other responsibilities. The Ottoman empire threatened to overrun the eastern borders of his Austrian patrimony; as emperor he had a host of obligations in Germany, several of which, such as maintaining internal peace and protecting imperial claims in northern Italy, required military intervention.

Maximilian attacked these issues with the mixture of flamboyance and hardheadedness he brought to his challenges in the Netherlands. Though he talked fervently about heading a vast crusade to drive the Ottoman Turks from Europe and the Mediterranean, his rhetoric had a very specific target. This was the papacy, which historically had contributed major financing to such ventures and whose support Maximilian thought would rescue him from his worst fiscal embarrassments. He also understood that lofty language was no substitute for effective government, without which he would not realize his greater goals.

The Austrian Habsburg patrimony, which had been divided in the middle of the fourteenth century, was his alone to rule after 1490, when his distant cousin, Archduke Sigismund (1427–96), ceded him the Tyrol. Around 1500 these territories taken together held between 1 and 1.5 million people. While around 80 percent of the population of the Austrian lands lived directly or indirectly from agriculture, that figure had dropped considerably from the 93 percent of 200 years earlier. Lower Austria, a comparatively wealthy region in the Middle Ages, had suffered considerably during Frederick III's wars with Matthias Corvinus of Hungary. Nevertheless, the rest of Maximilian's central European holdings at the outset of his reign were enjoying something of an agricultural boom. Even more remunerative for him were mines, which employed perhaps a quarter of his subjects. Significant veins of silver ran through the Tyrol, where a soaring population, a key indicator of economic vitality, rose from 70,000 in 1427 to around 150,000 in 1630.[12] A central location on the trading route over the Brenner Pass further enhanced the province's importance. Maximilian therefore protected it as intensely as he did Burgundy; to secure Tyrolean borders against Bavaria and Italy he acquired several small territories to the north and south of the region.[13]

To have title to such wealth was one thing; to actualize it, however, was quite another. Like many rulers of his time, Maximilian was eager to control his lands as directly as he could, a first step in gaining access to resources that could rescue him from the financial pressures that beset him. Hoping to administer both his patrimonial holdings and the fiscal affairs of the empire from Innsbruck, he took his model from the Burgundy of his late father-in-law, who occasionally calculated his revenues at a table with the treasury clerks hired for the job. From roughly 1491 to almost his death, Maximilian devoted himself in fits and starts to fashioning offices that would further efficient government and fiscal stability. By 1518, three major sectors were in place. The court council (*Hofrat*) advised him generally and was often called upon for opinions in both local disputes and imperial ones, particularly quarrels between individual German territories. The court chancellory (*Hofkanzlei*) generated state documents and correspondence; and the court treasury (*Hofkammer*) oversaw finances. Imperial business and the affairs of the Habsburg dynastic patrimony were handled by the same personnel on a case-by-case basis.

Maximilian clung stubbornly to his visions. The estates in the Netherlands stifled any attempts to harmonize their fiscal operations with those of the empire and Habsburg Austria, and Germany stymied his efforts to create the forerunner of an imperial standing army. Nevertheless, the emperor did not abandon transterritoriality in his own holdings. His officers in Innsbruck were instructed by Burgundians, bankers from mercantile Augsburg, and Saxons and Swabians. Tyroleans themselves would be sent to Lower Austria to instruct officials there in their territorial overlord's administrative methods.

Persuading his subjects to accept tighter princely control of their lives and livelihoods was, however, exceedingly difficult. Maximilian's lands in central Europe observed a common Christianity, at least up to 1517 and the onset of the Protestant Reformation. Beyond that, however, there was little to bring them together. Each of these lands had well-developed identities and were jealous of their historical prerogatives, especially where revenues and properties were concerned. The regional influence of local estates and the aristocrats who dominated them had, if anything, expanded during the chaotic decades of Maximilian's predecessors. Should a territorial prince threaten their privileges, these men were very quick to defend them.

Estates in Austria did not welcome tutelage from Innsbruck on financial matters or other subjects. Though Maximilian left the superstructure of a centralized administration, its effectiveness was heavily qualified by the many concessions he had to make to local sensibilities. After 1502, Lower Austria had a subsidiary administration and treasury which, while theoretically subordinate to the Habsburg government in Innsbruck, kept as distant from Tyrolean oversight as it could. The estates were also accustomed to dealing with their territorial ruler personally when important financial and legal issues were at stake. Maximilian's efforts to use his officers and their subordinates as his negotiators aroused great hostility as well. The grotesque sums of money that Maximilian spent in realizing his pan-European ambitions, even in fulfilling his conventional responsibilities, antagonized a broad spectrum of his subjects, from officers of local estates to peasants, who bore the brunt of taxation.

Denied direct access to the resources of Burgundy, Germany, even his own lands, Maximilian fell back on customary taxes and tolls for cash, thereby putting himself even more at the mercy of his Austrian lands, the only place from which he drew such incomes regularly. What revenues these imposts generated, he used profligately. Over 70 percent of Maximilian's income in 1508 went to a war with Venice; armed intervention between 1508 and 1516 to uphold imperial rights in Italy forced him to mortgage almost all of his regalian incomes, anticipated duties on imports and exports, and rents from various properties. The cost of winning the support of the German electors for naming his grandson Charles V as his successor in 1519 added up to around a million gulden, much of which Maximilian borrowed from the Augsburg banking house of Fugger. Once again, the Austrian lands and their revenues served as collateral. As one of Europe's habitual borrowers and mortgagers of regalian properties, Maximilian was versed in the dangers of over-extended credit. But faced with the need to protect his borders, defend imperial prerogatives, and advance the interests of the house of Habsburg, all three of which were tightly linked in his thinking, he was in no position to internalize the fiscal discipline that his half-realized administrative reforms were supposed to promote.[14]

But even if Maximilian had launched his administrative agenda in less pressured times, his subjects would have been no more receptive to them. While his public never rejected him as a man – he was a master of self-presentation, personally engaging, and could offset dignity with self-deprecating humor – the intermediate authorities in the lands he ruled, in Burgundy, then in Austria, and less directly even in Germany, had little sympathy for the grander ambitions of the house of Habsburg and were willing to use whatever legal power they had to keep it within bounds. Maximilian had no alternative other than to compromise with them. Furthermore, in his own way he was just as rooted in conventional political assumptions as were the estates. Major administrative offices were created more as matters of ad hoc challenges than as part of a total concept. Burgundian centralization and the larger administrative apparatus that went with it attracted him as a means to a very specific end – improving his finances. His understanding of government remained as personal as was that of his estates. Only when his health began to fail badly in 1518 did he set up the *Hofrat* with 18 nobles and jurists from both the empire and his Austrian lands to relieve him of responsibilities that he admittedly was no longer strong enough to handle.[15]

Thus Maximilian had written a basic but imperfect script for the organization of a Habsburg government now charged with administering a territorial complex that extended far beyond the dynasty's medieval patrimony in central Europe. Though he preferred to leave the give and take of ruling his Austrian patrimony to the more detached management of councils staffed with his stand-ins, he continued to personalize his own role in his lands. He was the final voice of authority. He had rethought the structure through which he exercised his power, but only under the pressure of necessity. He had also made plain that the defense of that complex, along with the other titles that he held in Germany, was central to Habsburg policy. Maintaining the integrity of his borders, by wars, by alliances – marital, military, diplomatic – even by further territorial expansion, was his first priority. If cooperating with local estates and interests was the only way he could realize these goals, he was ready to do so.

Ferdinand I and the Construction of Habsburg Central Europe

The late emperor's testament ordered the division of the Habsburg Austrian patrimony between his two grandsons, Charles and Ferdinand, whose territorial position had yet to be fixed. Maximilian and Ferdinand of Aragon had discussed the younger archduke's future often, but inconclusively; the partition of the Austrian lands was solely the emperor's initiative. By 1522, however, Charles's and Ferdinand's spokesmen had agreed to assign most of the Austrian lands to Ferdinand to govern; after 1525 he held them all. Ferdinand had also been the male Habsburg beneficiary of the double marriage compact of 1515. Husband since 1521 of Princess Anna (1503–47), the daughter of Vladislav II of Hungary and Bohemia, he had entered into a rewarding union, both materially and emotionally. The Hungarian and Bohemian estates insisted that Anna's consort have princely holdings of his own, an argument that helped move Charles's advisers into allowing Ferdinand's installation as territorial ruler over most of Austria. By the time Anna died in 1547 – a devastating blow to her spouse – she had given birth to 15 children who supplied their father with more than enough resources to whet his skills as a marital politician.

Ferdinand owed his position in Austria to his grandfather, but the failures of the elder Habsburg's policies soon challenged the young archduke sorely. The fault lines running through Maximilian I's administrative structure were opening even before the young archduke had permanently relocated to central Europe. Maximilian's incessant requests for funding, his disregard for local prerogative and custom, his willingness to mortgage some of his richest assets to 'foreigners', such as the Fuggers who were now profiting from some of his mines in the Tyrol, had enraged commoners and nobles alike in provincial estates. Discontent ran perhaps highest in Vienna and Lower Austria, in which the city was territorially embedded, and organized opposition sprang up throughout the region. The presence of key advisers from Spain and the Netherlands at Ferdinand's court irritated his new subjects even more.[16]

By 1525, Ferdinand had forcibly subdued his mutinous peasants and mine workers. In Vienna itself he had appointed a judicial commission that in 1522 ordered the execution of major conspirators, including the mayor, Martin Siebenbürger. From then until well into the nineteenth century, the territorial ruler of the Austrian lands had close oversight over the political life of the city. With the exception of the Tyrol after 1525, however, the provincial estates of all the Habsburg domains would resist the dynasty's control. Their position received reinforcement from two developments which, though independent in origin, intersected during the sixteenth century in central Europe and gave the Habsburg enterprise much of its peculiar character.

One was the Protestant Reformation. Spreading rapidly to the Austrian lands after Martin Luther's (1483–1546) excommunication in 1520, it came in many forms. Most important were the doctrines that Luther and his followers developed and incorporated into the Augsburg Confession of 1532. Calvinism, named after the French cleric who settled in Geneva and challenged Luther on basic issues such as the meaning of the sacrament of communion, put in an appearance somewhat later. More troublesome yet for their reluctance to engage in secular warfare were the political and spiritual radicals who have historically, though inaccurately, been gathered under the rubric of Anabaptism. Confessional diversity bespoke a divided polity and, worse yet, imperfect authority; all were anathema to Europe's rulers. Though he soon found ways of making necessary compromises with Luther's partisans who acknowledged the legitimacy of civil authority, Ferdinand was deeply uncomfortable with a sundered Christendom and would work very hard to reknit it.

His other, and more frightening, problem was the steady progress of the Ottoman Turks through southeastern Europe. Their chief line of march had followed the course of the Danube, a river that ran through

Serbia and Hungary on to Austria above and below the Enns. Carinthia and Styria to the south were frontally exposed to attack from Constantinople as well. The Ottoman offensive had been underway since the latter third of the fourteenth century; while often interrupted, it had unfailingly resumed at times when the sultan was free from problems on his other borders.

The key to keeping the Turks out of the Austrian lands was a militarily strong Hungary, which ran along most of the eastern and southeastern border of the Habsburg lands. The house of Austria had long been sensitive to the vital strategic roles of that kingdom, and of Bohemia to the north as well. No effective natural boundaries separated the three territorial complexes; the Danube, the preeminent topographical feature of the region, all but invited the invasion of Hungary or Lower Austria rather than discouraged it. Before his sudden death in 1490, Matthias Corvinus had been on the way to enlarging his realms westward at the expense of Frederick III. The Bohemian crownlands and northeastern Austria above the Enns had a seamless boundary through heavily forested but generally penetrable terrain. From King Otakar, vanquished by Rudolph I, to Hussites, followers of the early fifteenth-century Czech reformer Jan Hus (*d.* 1415), Bohemian armies had marauded in the eastern Habsburg lands.

For almost two centuries the Habsburgs had been securing their northern and eastern borders by nuptial compacts with the kings of Hungary and Bohemia and by mutual succession agreements. The latter, while rarely enforced, did address the real problem of maintaining the friendship of neighboring rulers over time. Each generation of the house of Austria from Rudolph I until Frederick III married into the royal families of those two kingdoms; one Habsburg, Albrecht V (1397–1439), did actually rule the two countries from 1437 until his death. He was followed by a posthumous son, Ladislas I (1440–57).

As long as the fundamentals of those agreements stood undisturbed, the dynasty seemed in no hurry to force its rights of succession in Bohemia and Hungary. Wishing to concentrate on western and imperial affairs, Frederick III had not pressed his claims in Bohemia when that throne briefly fell vacant in 1439.[17] The Habsburg–Jagellonian succession treaty of 1491 was worded to perpetuate itself, and not to accelerate a shift of power. Particular attention was paid to guaranteeing the fidelity of Hungarian regencies should a minor become king to the larger agreement. Nor, should the Habsburgs actually take over Hungary, did they want to look like conquerors. They would not enter the kingdom with an army until they had received a proper welcome at the border from the prelates and notables of the realm. The sensibilities of the Bohemian estates were also considered: Vladislav II vowed in 1491 that he would try to win their assent to the arrangement.[18]

But the intrusion of the Turks into central Europe brought an element of stark urgency into Ferdinand I's relations with the two kingdoms on his eastern borders. The lands of the Crown of St. Stephen had valiantly withstood Ottoman expansion for more than a century. But those days were over by 1521. Ruling Hungary was now the feckless, even childish Louis II (1506–26), who had married Archduchess Mary, Ferdinand's younger sister. Turmoil dominated the kingdom's politics; landed magnates with enormous properties and more modest country squires struggled to influence the crown, or, in some cases, to capture it for themselves.

Ferdinand at first tried to persuade his brother-in-law to manage his resources in ways beneficial to Hungary's self-defense. Louis responded tepidly at best. All such policies, however, became irrelevant in 1526 when Sultan Suleiman the Magnificent (d. 1566) launched a massive invasion of central Europe which ended with the death of Louis while fleeing from a crushing defeat at Mohács in southwestern Hungary. Ferdinand lost no time in gaining the Hungarian and Bohemian crowns for himself, tasks that he completed at least formally by 1527. He had to move fast. Sigismund I (1467–1548), the Jagellonian ruler of Poland, was the uncle of the late King Louis and the erstwhile brother-in-law of John Zápolya (1487–1540). The latter was *voivode*, or duke of Transylvania, a quasi-autonomous principality of the Hungarian crown; he had been named king of Hungary by a faction of the Hungarian estates before Ferdinand's selection by yet another group. Sigismund had already hinted that he was willing to cooperate with the Turks, the last thought Ferdinand wanted in the mind of any ruler ensconced on Habsburg borders.

Thus, even with his new titles, Ferdinand's hold of his new kingdoms was initially precarious; he spent much of his life making the Habsburg position in both of these kingdoms more secure. Zápolya was subdued, though not decisively vanquished, during the summer of 1527. In the Treaty of Nagyvárad of 1538, Ferdinand acknowledged his rival's right to rule in Transylvania. Furthermore, the *voivode* had put himself under the protection of the sultan in exchange for tribute, thus giving Suleiman and his immediate successors considerable power over Habsburg policy in Hungary. Transylvania would remain a weak point in the dynasty's military defenses to the end of the seventeenth century and even beyond. Ferdinand never would control more than the western third of Hungary; by the middle of the sixteenth century, vast portions of the central part of the kingdom would fall under the sway of the sultans in Constantinople.

Equally problematic were Ferdinand's relationships with the Hungarian and Bohemian estates. From the outset of his career, Ferdinand was acutely sensitive to the role that these bodies, particularly membership from the high nobility, played in the kingdoms. As soon as he came to the Austrian lands, he began developing contacts with leading Bohemian aristocratic families such as the Rožmitals and the Pernštejns.[19] Though he insisted that Bohemia and Hungary were hereditarily his through his relationship to his wife, he did allow the estates to go through the mechanics of their electoral process in both realms. In bargaining with the estates over the conditions of his rule, however, he made it plain that he would raise the issue again. Nevertheless, both sides needed one another, and, as long as the threat of Ottoman conquest was on everyone's mind, for somewhat similar purposes.

Control of Hungary was essential to Ferdinand's defense of his Austrian holdings. The Hungarians, for their part, were interested in his resources. The aristocracy, particularly its heavily propertied segment, clearly expected the Habsburgs to reconquer those parts of the kingdom lost to the Turks and, once that mission had been accomplished, restore newly freed lands to their former occupants. Such men wanted Ferdinand as their king, not for his character and talents but for his close relationship to Emperor Charles V, who they thought would contribute German resources to their cause.

In return for a crown, the new king was prepared to respond in the desired way. He, too, certainly wanted to drive the Ottoman occupation from central Hungary. Illustrious names such as Thomas Nádasdy, who campaigned actively for his election, even some who bargained with all sides in the divided kingdom, were generously rewarded with the lands that were his to distribute. The fortunes of noble families who held on to their huge estates down to the end of World War I soared in the sixteenth century. At its end the nobility in the Habsburg portion of Hungary had oversight of almost 80 percent of all peasant households in the region. Magnates continued to support private armies – something of a necessity under the constant threat of Turkish invasion – and supplying them was a profitable enterprise for landowners. Although some of the great Hungarian houses that supplied the officers of the crown had died at Mohács, Ferdinand and his successors replaced them with other families.[20] Perhaps the most fortunate of all were the Esterházy, whose origins were in the country gentry but whose wealth grew to colossal proportions in the seventeenth and eighteenth centuries. The greatest hopes of the Hungarian nobility were, however, sadly misplaced for decades. Spanish–Burgundian concerns preoccupied Charles V far more than did the problems of central Europe, where he would go to war with Suleiman only if the Ottoman army truly threatened Germany. Such a situation seemed to be developing in 1532, and the emperor did assemble a massive force with which Ferdinand and Habsburg supporters in Hungary hoped they could begin the reconquest of the kingdom. But the sultan unexpectedly pulled back, and the emperor, to his brother's dismay, withdrew as well, thus aborting any larger enterprises.

Ferdinand, moreover, did no better when acting on his own initiative. Two campaigns in 1541 and 1542 to retake Buda and Pest on either side of the Danube ended only in entrenching Ottoman government in both places; efforts to dislodge John Zápolya's widow and son from Transylvania in the 1550s also came to naught. Habsburg failure to meet the expectations of their noble collaborators in Hungary thus left the latter always open to the blandishments of others who promised to further their goals – the dukes of Transylvania, even the sultans themselves. Outright bribery was Ferdinand's only way of retaining Hungarian loyalty, but it cost him dearly. He began complaining bitterly about the fickleness of his support early in his career, but had no alternative but to accept the situation and the dictates it imposed on him as best he could.[21]

Matching Ferdinand's purposes with those of the estates in Bohemia, less directly threatened by Ottoman offensives, was even harder. The kingdom had one of Europe's most diverse and developed economies and important natural resources, especially the silver mines of Jachýmov and Kutná Hora. The new king was very eager to get his hands on these revenues, in part to defray his expenses in Hungary. The estates, dominated by a relatively small number of landed magnates, were just as keen on controlling this wealth and their monopoly over the high administrative offices of the realm. The lethargic rule of Ferdinand's immediate predecessors had only encouraged the ambitions of these men and their families. What they expected from the Habsburg was a better government but one that respected their long-standing privileges. In return for their support, Ferdinand also had to rescue at least some of them from financial embarrassments. Lev Zdeněk of Rožmital, the high burgrave of the kingdom and the preeminent officer of the crown, needed around 50,000 florins to satisfy his creditors. The Šliks, another leading family, wanted Ferdinand's promise that he would not touch incomes which they drew from the royal mines at Kutná Hora. Like the Hungarians, most members of the Bohemian estates also hoped that Ferdinand's connections with Charles would supply the young monarch with funds to pay off the debts of his last two predecessors.[22]

Religion complicated Bohemian affairs as well. The estates wished their kings to guarantee the position of the Hussite or Utraquist church, which permitted the laity to take both the bread and the chalice at communion in both kinds and was unique to the kingdom since the fifteenth century. Ferdinand's most persistent competitor for the throne had been the Wittelsbach dukes of Bavaria, whose rigid Catholicism had ultimately worked against them in Prague. Here, too, opponent of evangelical reform though he was, Ferdinand dealt with the Bohemians very circumspectly. While he promised to protect the Utraquist faith, his construction of that confession was very narrow. He, and his immediate successors, would publicly combat inroads Luther's doctrines made in the Hussite credo, as well as offshoots of that movement, most importantly the Czech Brethren. The stance, while perhaps technically correct, did please conservative Utraquists, but practically no one else, Catholics included. It did not, however, in Ferdinand's time, provoke religious rebellion.

Even when the opportunity to alter his relationship to the Bohemian estates came his way, Ferdinand did not attack the magnate class nor the religious constitution of the realm systematically. During the 1540s, the kingdom's nobles and cities had begun to put aside traditional differences in a loose coalition against Ferdinand's relentless efforts to tax them more heavily. The situation reached crisis proportions in 1547 during the Schmalkaldic war, Charles V's military campaign against German Protestantism. As the emperor drew further eastward, many of Ferdinand's opponents in Bohemia supported the Lutheran Elector of Saxony, John Frederick. The Habsburgs, however, prevailed. Four Bohemian nobles did lose their heads for their treachery, but as a group they did not suffer. Aristocratic high officials from the crownland of Moravia were members of the court that handed out these penalties, and their political and social perspectives may have influenced these decisions. Important Bohemian magnate families, most notably the Rožmberks and the equally wealthy Pernštejns, had supported their king unwaveringly. They and other loyalists among their colleagues profited from the land Ferdinand confiscated from the dissidents, as did those cities which remained in his camp. The heaviest penalty fell on disloyal townsmen, especially in Prague. Cities alone now shouldered three months of his war expenses; they were also obligated to pay a perpetual beer tax that generated vast future revenues for the crown. As in Hungary, Ferdinand clearly wanted more cooperative estates, not a kingdom minus estates altogether.[23]

Administering an Empire

Though no military leader, Ferdinand, like Maximilian I, was administratively imaginative and eager to turn his ideas into tools that would give him better control over his lands. Even before he fully pacified his Austrian patrimony in the early 1520s, he had established a makeshift *Hofrat* for Lower Austria to carry on judicial and government business in his absence. He also set up a collections office, a *Raitkammer*, to gather his ordinary revenues – tolls, tariffs, income from mines and the like – in the province. By 1525, Ferdinand, having put down the most seditious elements among his Austrian subjects, was ready to reintroduce some of his grandfather's major innovations under more favorable circumstances. Presiding in his brother's stead over the German diet, a gathering of the emperor along with Germany's territorial secular and spiritual rulers and representatives of major cities, Ferdinand received a delegation from the estates of his Austrian lands themselves, who urged the young Habsburg to create a permanent *Hofrat*. They had a program of their own: to dilute the influence of Ferdinand's Burgundian and Spanish advisers, particularly that of an ambitious man named Gabriel Salamanca, who ran Ferdinand's treasury and his chancellery with little regard for the sensibilities of either greater or lesser nobility throughout the entire Habsburg Austrian patrimony. Therefore, any offices in this body were to be staffed with men of distinction, by which they meant notables indigenous to the Austrian lands like themselves. They also wanted the young archduke to bring order into his treasury and government offices generally. The price of these demands was financial aid which Ferdinand desperately needed at that moment: Suleiman the Magnificent was preparing the westward drive which culminated in the Hungarian disaster at Mohács.

Thus, his own interests as well as those of his estates dictated that Ferdinand add a chancellery and a treasury to the court council, establishing a structure fully described in his Court Executive Order (*Hofstaatsordnung*) of 1 January 1527.[24] Unlike the prototype of Maximilian I, it would remain in effect with only minor changes until the large-scale reform of Habsburg government undertaken by Empress Maria Theresa (1717–80) and her advisers in the eighteenth century. Ferdinand apparently also consulted a smaller advisory body, a privy council, though there is no evidence that he formally assigned it any function.

Ferdinand also granted his estates' request that he appoint natives of the Austrian lands or people closely associated with those lands as his high court and government officials. The outstanding exception was his high equerry, the Spanish poet Don Pedro Laso de Castilla, who held the position until 1548.[25] Nevertheless, his administrative structure, like that of Maximilian I, operated only at the will of the prince. Relations between territorial ruler and estates in the Austrian lands therefore remained tense, even competitive. Ferdinand's efforts and those of his immediate heirs to improve the administration of their lands faltered for want of large pools of administrative talent among their subjects. The need of his estates for people with the same skills in local offices made a general shortage all the worse.[26] But the outlines for a pattern of mutual accommodation between two constitutional entities in the Austrian lands had been drafted.

Extending this organizational model to Hungary and Bohemia was his next task once Ferdinand acquired these lands in 1526, but also a very problematic one. His informal efforts to make the political classes in these lands Habsburg partners were quite successful. Turning the young aristocrats of one's realms into courtiers was becoming a familiar technique for curbing noble independence, and Ferdinand did what he could in this vein. To help his three sons, Archdukes Maximilian (1527–76), Ferdinand (1529–95), and, somewhat later, Charles (1540–90), acquire some grasp of the languages of the peoples that they would eventually rule, he brought young noblemen from all corners of his realms to be schooled at the court. There they would babble at the Habsburgs who, in time, were to pick up what was being said and reply as best they could.

True structural integration of his lands, however, eluded Ferdinand. Initially he hoped to use the court council, the treasury, and the privy council as the highest administrative offices for all his lands. He even reserved places for Hungarians and Bohemians in the *Hofrat*. Fearing that such a move would erode the identity that gave them most of their own power and influence, the estates of his new kingdoms would not cooperate. For the rest of the sixteenth century and well into the seventeenth, Hungarian and Bohemian affairs were dispatched in separate chancelleries; in Bohemia local crown officers such as the high burgrave exercised extensive administrative control over the realm. Hungary's regional counties remained largely apart from direct royal authority. Ferdinand's estates, moreover, retained substantive fiscal powers. Their agents collected revenues from even such key imposts as the Bohemian beer tax; such men did not overly bestir themselves to see that monies were delivered promptly, especially in Ferdinand's last years.[27] Nor did Ferdinand make much effort to restrain any of his nobilities from adding to the labor requirements of peasants and serfs in a time of rising prices for agricultural products. In 1563, a year before his death, he agreed upon petition from the estates of Lower Austria to refrain from fixing a maximum for servile labor (*Robot*) on noble domains. On regalian properties, however, a maximum of 12 days a year was to be the rule. He did ask that nobles continue to follow tradition and local custom when setting such duties, but this was more suggestion than policy. The nobles throughout the Habsburg lands would continue to have wide discretion in managing their agricultural labor force well into the eighteenth century. Serfdom as an institution would endure down to the revolutions of 1848.[28]

Given the military and political pressures he faced, Ferdinand's administrative compromises in Hungary and Bohemia were all but a foregone conclusion. Nevertheless, the successful refusal of Bohemians and Hungarians to join the central institutions of his government was a clear sign that the Habsburg modus vivendi with the notables of these lands was a work in progress in which the dynasty had yet to develop even an equal role. With the exception of the Bohemian uprising in 1547, which positioned him to exploit its tax revenues more favorably, Ferdinand was a perpetual supplicant in his own dominions, as were his immediate heirs.

Thus, the territorial complex that Ferdinand put together in central and east central Europe, while impressive in outline, was not a functional unit. Its administrative reach was too compromised, and even its expanded form after 1526 fit Habsburg purposes less effectively than had prior arrangements used to protect the Austrian lands. A real buffer state between Ottoman and Habsburg holdings, even one ruled as ineptly as Hungary, was preferable to defending yet more territory with essentially the same resources. Cooperation of local intermediary powers was in some ways far more crucial for the Habsburgs than for those whom they ruled.

Moreover, even had the privileged nobilities of the Habsburg lands been more docile, is it likely that Ferdinand and his immediate heirs could have administered their lands any better than they did? In practice, Ferdinand I and his son Emperor Maximilian II insisted on approaching state management as personally, and therefore as inconsistently, as had Maximilian I. At his death Ferdinand I divided his lands among his sons, thereby undermining both the spirit and the letter of reforms he had worked a lifetime to establish. Furthermore, the clarity on paper of his and Maximilian II's administrative agendas lost much of their resolution as decisions were being made, especially about personnel. Whom to hire, whom to dismiss, whom to repay, whom to put off – these decisions were often shaped by the moral values of the family and the household rather than by calculations of cost and benefit which members of the dynasty understood, but did not accept as an absolute priority.[29] When cash flow was a problem for the government, the impoverished servant was paid because of his or her needs and not because of job performance or the importance of what they did. Household personnel and court functionaries were kept on staff only because of the financial hardship dismissal would bring to them. Salaries, even for crucial positions, were paid irregularly and were hardly commensurate to the responsibilities of the men who received them. Even though they deplored the practice, Ferdinand and Maximilian distributed huge sums of money as special grants to their employees, particularly toward the end of their reigns. Indeed, one could argue that without the financial restraint that their estates imposed on the Habsburgs in the sixteenth century the dynasty would have had no frame of reference beyond its own definition of need for evaluating the costs of political and military policies.[30] The house of Habsburg thus depended upon its estates not only for funds but for discipline.

Religious Divisions

Ferdinand's efforts to impose a uniform administrative structure on his new lands were not the only reason for his troubles with his estates. The Protestant Reformation gave him even greater problems. Like many devout Catholics of his time, he thought that reform of the Church of Rome was needed. The process, however, had to follow the moderate lines of Christian humanists such as Erasmus of Rotterdam (d. 1536), whose influence was strong not only on Ferdinand, but on Charles V. Neither brother, however, wanted to break with the papacy, politically or theologically. And, once again, Ferdinand did not want to antagonize his estates any more than he had to.

Developing a religious policy to satisfy various popes, a confessionally ·divided central Europe, and Charles and Ferdinand's genuinely sensitive consciences was a tricky matter. As holders of multiple crowns, the Habsburgs often found themselves in situations where measures useful to them in one realm were disadvantageous in another. Estates, on the other hand, were quick to demand equal treatment when they saw something positive in procedures that their territorial ruler was following elsewhere. In dealing with Luther's reform and its offshoots, the Habsburgs would come close to undoing all that they had put together in the fifteenth and early sixteenth centuries.

The dynasty's relationship to Germany was an important part of the problem. Since the time of Rudolph I, the house of Austria had recognized the value of the imperial crown. At the very least, Rudolph and Frederick III had shown that the prestige associated with the office opened the way for territorially strategic marriages. Though the powers of the emperor had dwindled over the centuries, he still had a few that were exceedingly important. Chief among them was his right to assign titles in Germany, confer fiefs, and enforce observation of testaments made by the empire's territorial rulers. The last of these was very important, for it allowed an emperor to resolve disputed inheritances and, in so doing, to obligate to himself families who benefitted from his decisions, at least for a while. The imperial princes were also happy to leave defense of their territorial integrity to their sovereign, since they themselves, singly or even allied, were usually unable to command the wherewithal required for such undertakings.

Nevertheless, by the beginning of the sixteenth century the locus of political authority in Germany had decidedly shifted to its many territorial rulers, some of whom commanded substantial holdings. The dukes and electors of Saxony and the electors of Brandenburg, so-called because they and five other colleges had the right to vote for the emperor after the middle of the fourteenth century, were conspicuous examples. Others had their seats on very sensitive boundaries: the lands of the Elector Palatine ran along the Rhine, making them the first in the line of march of armies leaving France. The Wittelsbach dukes of Bavaria had a history of contesting Habsburg ambitions in central and east central Europe, including the imperial succession itself.

Habsburg borders, especially after the acquisition of Bohemia, could be attacked through or from all of these territories; therefore, the dynasty had all the more reason to hang on to the imperial crown. Other rulers wanted the job. When Francis I (1494–1547) of France offered himself as a candidate for imperial office in 1519, the entire house of Austria shuddered. The seven imperial electors voted for Charles V only upon receipt of lavish emoluments from Maximilian I, whose already frayed credit rating disintegrated completely with this new borrowing. The empire was also a potential source of significant military aid for its emperors.

The imperial diet, which spoke for both the spiritual and the secular princes of Germany as well as certain categories of cities, came together periodically with the emperor, as did a council of the electors. Spokesmen for the regional administrative districts, called circles (*Kreise*), met with him irregularly as well. All of these bodies fulfilled agreed-upon obligations slowly, if at all, and with ill-paid and unreliable mercenaries, but they could, on occasion, be generous. Even as the Germans became increasingly skeptical of requests for funding the reconquest of Hungary in the sixteenth century, they rarely refused any aid at all, especially when Ottoman armies drew uncomfortably near.

Thus, Habsburg interests mandated cooperation from both Germany's princes and estates in the Austrian lands, Hungary, and Bohemia. The Protestant Reformation strained all of these relationships to the utmost, especially after 1526. Meeting that year with the imperial diet in Augsburg and desperate for aid to counter the Turkish attack that ended with the death of Louis of Hungary, Ferdinand I agreed to allow the German princes who had adopted the Lutheran reform to require that their subjects follow suit. Catholic territorial rulers had the same privilege. Ferdinand meant this as a temporary concession – he revoked it in 1529 – pending a final resolution of the controversy by a church council, be it solely German or one called by the pope himself.[31]

Though this formula eased Ferdinand's immediate problem, his exchange of military aid for religious concessions set a precedent that the house of Habsburg would regret, especially after 1555 when he re-endorsed the division of Germany between Catholics and Lutherans in the Peace of Augsburg. Almost every time the dynasty faced an Ottoman offensive, appeals for aid were met with demands from one or the other of their own estates or the imperial diet for changes in religious policies. Protestants wanted greater freedoms for their creeds, Catholics wanted to preserve the status quo or to see the evangelical movements eradicated altogether. One or the other religious side always had objections to the terms of these bargains, and the network of cooperating noble elites and clerical officials that the dynasty required to further its own political and military concerns remained in a state of flux.

Estates in the Habsburg lands mobilized this strategy even when the dynasty's appeals for funds were not directly linked to imminent invasion from Constantinople. In 1568, Emperor Maximilian II extended far-reaching freedoms to Luther's followers in Lower Austria. For their part, the estates promised to take over his vast debts, many of them inherited from his father, and to support work on a creed that all of his peoples could adopt. He carefully avoided the formal establishment of an evangelical church in his Austrian lands, a concession to Catholics. Nevertheless, he opened a path that, by 1571, led him to formal recognition of the rights of Lutherans to exercise their faith in the province. Though only nobles received the privilege – cities and market towns were expressly ruled out – his action infuriated the loyal Catholics among his subjects, his Spanish relatives in Madrid, and the popes in Rome. In 1578, a similar measure was introduced in Inner Austria, made up of Styria, Carinthia, and Carniola, along with the Dalmatian lands of Gorizia, Istria, and Friuli and the port of Trieste at the head of the Adriatic, now governed by his youngest brother, Archduke Charles.

A variant of this scenario unfolded in the kingdom of Bohemia in the 1570s. Here Maximilian II was eager before his death to have the estates of the kingdom acknowledge his son Rudolph as his successor. Grievances against tax rates were mounting in the estates; spearheaded by William of Rožmberk, whose family had once looked to the Habsburgs for strong leadership, a new generation of spokesmen were asking for fiscal relief and for changes in the religious profile of the kingdom as well. Their most serious demand was for the recognition of a Lutheran-oriented wing of the Utraquist church. Maximilian resisted the introduction of a synthesized Bohemian Protestant confession which incorporated Lutheran, Calvinist, and Utraquist elements. He did, however, informally acknowledge Protestant rights to worship in the kingdom, in return for the Bohemians' recognition of his son Rudolph (1552–1612) as their next ruler.

Catholics Rearm

The Peace of Augsburg of 1555 did relieve some of the tension between Luther's evangelicals and traditional Catholics in Germany, and between Emperor Ferdinand I and Maximilian II and the Protestant princes of the Holy Roman Empire. Reconciling the two confessions still seemed possible to many, the two emperors included. The accord did nothing, however, to resolve religious problems in the Habsburg domains themselves. Neither man dared offend the large numbers of Protestants in their estates by taking the opening given them in the Augsburg formula to enforce Catholic uniformity where they ruled. Only in the Tyrol, governed until the end of the sixteenth century by the impeccably orthodox Archduke Ferdinand II (1529–95), did Catholicism remain firm. In the lands not subject to imperial jurisdiction – Bohemia since the fourteenth century and the third of Hungary that was Habsburg territory – religious pluralism prevailed as well. The upper chamber of the Hungarian royal estates remained under Catholic control because of the bishops who were entitled to seats in it.[32] Nevertheless, even a shared confession did not lead to consistent cooperation between Hungary's great lords and the Habsburgs. Moreover, in the eastern regions of the kingdom, especially near and in Transylvania, Calvinism, along with several smaller groups such as the Unitarians, had an important presence in the estates that caused much trouble between them and Vienna until into the eighteenth century.

The court in Vienna was, however, Catholic in name – indeed, somewhat more than that under Ferdinand I. Even as the fate of the Church of Rome in central Europe seemed ever more uncertain, he was preparing the way for its vigorous defense.[33] In 1551 Ferdinand brought a new order, the Jesuits from Spain, to energize the Catholic renewal to which he had always been deeply committed. He opened the University of Vienna to them immediately. They quickly installed themselves in schools throughout the Austrian provinces – Innsbruck in the Tyrol in 1562, Graz, in Styria, ten years later, and in Linz around 1600. The Jesuit University of Graz was founded in 1586. Maximilian II's attachments to Rome were far weaker, but his wife, Empress Maria, was a one-woman redoubt of Catholic orthodoxy; and her brother, Philip II of Spain, did all he could to promote her activities. She was an especially enthusiastic patroness of the Jesuits, as were a couple of Maximilian's sisters who were cloistered near Innsbruck in the Tyrol. Indeed, one of them, Archduchess Magdalene, all but bankrupted herself in her profligate support of the order. Jesuits would remain very close to the ruling house; they educated many of its members and heard their confessions well into the eighteenth century.

Organized in 1534 by St Ignatius Loyola, a one-time Spanish soldier who came to his religious vocation on the mend from a serious injury, the Jesuits quickly became missionaries and pedagogues to central Europe. In some ways they were religious modernizers: they respected the classical scholarship of Renaissance humanists and realized that they would have to incorporate it into their own language pedagogy to win the minds and souls of their public. A Netherlander, St Peter Canisius, the first member of the company in Germany, was the author of a revised Catholic catechism sponsored by Ferdinand I. It proved to be a crucial element in the pedagogical mission of the order. They also installed themselves in a number of German universities just north of the Austrian lands – Bavaria especially – where they would play an important role in the education of young noblemen from the Habsburg lands who would later become officials of a militantly Catholic imperial court. Emperor Ferdinand II (1578–1637) was a student at the Jesuit university in Ingolstadt, the sole member of his house to receive something resembling a public education in early modern times. The Jesuits went to Hungary in 1561 where they would become central to higher education in the kingdom for the next two centuries.

The order came even earlier to Prague, where it made the church of St. Clement its headquarters in 1555. Jesuit colleges had spread to the cities of Bohemia and Moravia as well by the end of the sixteenth century. Their theater became, as it would in the Austrian provinces, the official stage of the land. Their works, often written by teachers in their schools, had a strong moral content in which the salvation of the soul was the central issue. But their presentations also had an engagingly artless quality about them, blending as they did the mythical, the historical, and the specifically biblical. Above all, they made heavy use of spectacular stage effects and dizzying interchanges between this world and the one beyond to hold the imaginations of their audiences, who came from all classes of society. The order wrote for everyone – plays celebrating the coronations of rulers, for weddings of noble families. They also matched their auditoriums to the social and political station of their viewers. When playing before the court and the nobility in Prague, they performed in the royal castle, the *Hradčany*, which looms above the city of Prague itself. When townspeople came to their plays, they came to the courtyard of their college.[34] Such work would be crucial both for the restoration of Roman Catholicism in central Europe and for the philosophical validation of Habsburg rule itself.

Conflict in the House of Habsburg

The Peace of Augsburg could not permanently smooth relations between Catholic Habsburg emperors and German Protestant princes. The success of Calvinism during the 1550s in the lands of Elector Palatine Frederick III (1515–76) made it ever more difficult for the house of Austria and the imperial estates to accommodate one another's interests. The Augsburg formula made no room for Calvinism, and neither Catholic nor Lutheran wanted to add it to Germany's confessional alternatives. Fearing, however, that an attack upon one Protestant confession would be a prelude to an attack upon all, Protestant electors grew exceedingly wary of Emperor Maximilian II's determination to eradicate this new direction in Christendom.

That Maximilian II was both cousin and brother-in-law of Spain's Philip II, who, as duke of Burgundy, sent a Spanish army in 1568 under the duke of Alba to quell a rebellion in the Netherlands, undermined the Habsburg position in Germany even further. Many regions of the Low Countries were technically part of the empire, and Germany's Protestant princes believed that Philip had gone to war to destroy the reformed confessions there. Philip II, a Spaniard in German eyes regardless of his Burgundian title, backed his generals even when they mobilized against German princes, particularly around Frisia, who were Calvinist sympathizers and supporters. Lutherans and Calvinists alike had talked on and off since 1562 about developing their own foreign policy, particularly toward France, where Calvinist Huguenots had also challenged the crown.[35] Ignoring all of Maximilian's arguments not to do so, the elector palatine funded troops who in 1568 went to the aid of fellow Calvinists in the Netherlands and of French Huguenots. The Habsburg worst-case scenario – a breaching of the empire's borders by foreign powers – appeared to be unfolding when the kings of France threatened invasion.

Cautious and consensus-driven though they were, Germany's princes were drifting even further from the Habsburg camp in the final decades of the sixteenth century.[36] Protestants were even more uneasy about Maximilian's successor, Rudolph II, than they had been about his father, even though that relationship had also deteriorated considerably. The new emperor had spent his formative years in Spain at the court of his uncle, and Lutherans and Calvinists expected him to favor the Catholic cause more openly than had his predecessor. It took all of Maximilian II's powers of persuasion to get the electors to accept the young man; only the three spiritual princes, the archbishops of Trier, Mainz, and Cologne, really approved of him as emperor. In truth, while Rudolph as a young man gave great public show of his Catholic orthodoxy, he was quite flexible when forced to choose between political advantage and personal religious conviction. As was the case with Maximilian II, extremes of any kind disturbed him.

But it was the estates throughout the Habsburg lands, taking advantage of discord between Rudolph and his brothers, who turned religion into a dangerous political weapon against the house of Austria in the early years of the seventeenth century. For reasons not quite clear, Rudolph moved his court and the administration of the Holy Roman Empire from Vienna to Prague after 1583. There he became more and more preoccupied with reclusive studies that turned his establishment into a center of late humanist learning and art but marginalized him politically. Prone to the dark moods that afflicted several in his family, especially in moments of crisis, he may have tried to commit suicide in 1600.[37] Though Rudolph never lost his aura of dignity, the administration of his own lands and of German affairs drifted erratically into the control of advisers and other intimates.[38] Eagerly waiting to step in for his brother was the younger Archduke Matthias (1557–1619), a man as frenetically ambitious as the emperor was lethargic. On the lookout for a political role appropriate to his outsized self-image, Matthias persuaded Rudolph to make him governor of the two divisions of Lower Austria, Austria above and below the Enns.

From 1591 to 1606 the Habsburg lands were once again at war with the Ottoman armies. Rudolph seemed incapable of controlling troops whose rampaging in the eastern reaches of Hungary and Transylvania turned the estates of the latter into rebels. Between 1604 and 1606 they would go to war against the Habsburgs under the leadership of the duke of Transylvania, Stephen Bocskay (1557–1606). The management of the conflict and its funding fell largely to Matthias. He began his tenure in the province by intensifying efforts already underway to promote Catholicism as a way of asserting the rights of the territorial ruler. The estates were not inclined to protest too loudly. From 1595 to 1597 peasant uprisings raged throughout Austria above and below the Enns, fueled by anger over increases in forced labor requirements and the efforts of noble landlords to deprive rural workers of what few legal rights they had. The nobles, Catholic and Protestant alike, would have preferred to settle the conflict without the intervention of their territorial overlord, but in the end had no choice but to call upon him. Matthias was gratifyingly sympathetic to their cause and the punitive measures of the commander of the Lower Austrian militia, Wenzel Morakhsy, who summarily ordered the noses and ears of thousands of peasants to be cut off for their sedition.[39]

But to deal with the larger Turkish conflict, Matthias had to throw himself upon the mercies of various estates for extraordinary aid, thereby handing Protestants yet another opening to condition their aid on the rights to worship freely. He yielded, as had his father and grandfather before him. Moreover, where religious pluralism was the price of satisfying his personal ambitions, he gave in there as well. Given Rudolph's distant ways and rapacious army, Matthias was well situated to offer himself as an acceptable alternative to both the Austrian and Hungarian estates. In 1608, representatives of the Austrian estates met with the Hungarian royal diet in Bratislava. There, in return for permission to worship as Protestants, they announced their support for Matthias as their territorial ruler and king. With the archduke's army marching on Prague in 1609, Rudolph capitulated. He turned over the crown of St. Stephen to Matthias and the right to act as territorial ruler in Lower Austria and Moravia, one of the lands of the Bohemian crown. The Bohemian estates remained true to Rudolph, but on negotiated terms. The hapless king had to sign the Letter of Majesty in 1609 in which he recognized the religious rights of Lutherans, Calvinists, Utraquists, and, to a limited extent, even the much-persecuted Czech Brethren in the kingdom. To become king of Bohemia in 1611, Matthias not only confirmed these concessions but allowed the nobility of the realm powers they had not enjoyed since the advent of Ferdinand I. In the short time remaining to him – he died in 1612 – Rudolph would hold only the title of emperor, theoretically the greatest of his dignities, but in fact the least.

The success of these machinations clearly encouraged the estates of the Habsburg lands to regard their territorial rulers as figures to be used, even as their creatures. 'Homage belongs to him who occupies and possesses the fatherland with the will of its general representatives. . . . The people elects for itself its princes and can also reject them,' wrote George Tschernembl (1567–1626), a leading Calvinist nobleman in Austria above the Enns sometime between 1608 and 1610.[40] Like the Habsburgs themselves, who preferred to work with compliant estates rather than eradicate them, Tschernembl did not intend to wipe out princely rule. The terms on which he had come to think that they governed, however, were very far from the way that the Habsburgs had once constructed their role.

Religion had clearly become a serious impediment to the Habsburgs' government of their lands and all the peoples whom they ruled. As long as the sultan could be counted on to reappear from the east, Protestant nobles in the estates could manipulate their rulers in ways that made a mockery of princely authority. Equally dangerous was the failure of the dynasty to resolve antagonism between Protestant and Catholic in its lands. While Protestantism seemed the more vital of the two confessions, the Church of Rome still had significant support. Important noble houses in the Austrian lands, Hungary, and Bohemia still remained loyal to the papacy, and the Habsburg courts themselves, especially in Inner Austria and the Tyrol, were centers of Catholic practice. Even in Vienna, there had been signs that the latitudinarian policies of Maximilian II could be reversed. Before Archduke Matthias had moved decisively to seize power for himself in Lower Austria, the bishop of Vienna, Melchior Khlesl (1552–1630), had started a vigorous program to recatholicize the city and its surrounding countryside. A resolution of the religious issue that took the faith and the interests of the dynasty into account would go far to reestablish the position of the Habsburgs in their own lands. The opportunity to do this, however, had yet to present itself.

Chapter 2: An Empire Takes Hold

The Habsburgs, Ferdinand of Styria, and the Counter-Reformation

Rudolph II never married, and Emperor Matthias produced no heirs. In 1617, their remaining and also childless brothers, Archdukes Maximilian (1558–1618) and Albrecht (1559–1621), and a young cousin from Styria, Archduke Leopold (1586–1632), had agreed that age, frailty, or other interests precluded any of them from governing the entire Habsburg patrimony and holding the imperial crown. Leopold's elder brother, Archduke Ferdinand, had already sired a son. He therefore seemed a far better prospect for the long-term interests of the dynasty. His religious views, as well as those of his parents, were more attuned to the dynasty's confessional preferences as well. Though both nobles and towns in Inner Austria had embraced Protestantism as warmly as their counterparts in Austria above and below the Enns, Ferdinand had grown up a dedicated Catholic. Archduke Charles, his father, while eventempered and cautious, was eager to restore the Church of Rome to preeminence throughout his provinces. In 1578 he did agree, orally, though not in writing, to the Pacification of Bruck that allowed both the Lutheran nobles and the townsfolk of the region to practice their faith freely. A year later, however, he, his brother Archduke Ferdinand of the Tyrol, and their Wittelsbach nephew in Bavaria Duke William V (1548–1626), resolved to stop trimming their policies to accommodate the new confessions. Almost immediately thereafter, Archduke Charles took advantage of the questionable legality of his assent to the Pacification of Bruck to begin curbing Protestant freedoms in his lands.[1] His Bavarian wife, Archduchess Maria (1551–1608), was also an exceptionally devout Catholic and influenced her son greatly, especially after his father

31

died in 1590. Ferdinand himself studied at the University of Ingolstadt where the Jesuits had settled to indoctrinate as well as to instruct young Catholics, especially the aristocrats among them.

Archduke Charles's testament ordered that the government of Inner Austria be turned over to his eldest son at the age of 18. Once in power, Ferdinand made clear that the days for compromise with the evangelicals of Inner Austria were at an end, even when war with Ottoman forces loomed. In 1596 he demanded an oath of fealty from the Carinthian and Styrian estates without reciprocating with a promise to observe the religious freedoms stipulated in the Pacification of Bruck. This agreement, Ferdinand said, had no bearing on the profession of loyalty itself. The estates themselves were badly factionalized among Catholic prelates, nobles for whom legitimacy was the sole issue in succession questions, and Protestants fearful of losing their right to worship altogether. Without a viable bargaining position they reluctantly, but unambiguously, recognized Ferdinand as their territorial ruler.

Convinced that a prince's highest calling was to further the true faith in his lands, Ferdinand and like-minded advisers redoubled the ongoing effort to reestablish Catholicism throughout the archduke's southeastern domains during the next few years. In 1598 all evangelical pastors had to leave the cities and regalian properties in Styria. Local Protestant nobles protested, but did not convert words into action. The passive imperial regimes of Maximilian II and Rudolph II had left the responsibility for defending Inner Austria largely to its resident prince. Withholding funds from their territorial ruler, particularly in wartime, put the lands and livelihoods of members of the estates in peril as well as their confession. Such weakness encouraged Ferdinand's ruthless program of eradicating religious differences between himself and those whom he governed, august aristocrat and humble peasant alike.[2]

A kind of state church, protected and supervised by Ferdinand and his successors, slowly took shape in his domains. A Reformation Commission, similar to earlier ecclesiastical visitations that took place under Ferdinand I and Maximilian II, started work throughout Inner Austria in 1599. Headed by one or two major court officers along with a high ecclesiastical figure such as a bishop, they appeared at their chosen sites with a contingent of troops to protect them if necessary. Their presentations combined religious exhortation with pointed assurances that conversion to Catholicism was one way of acknowledging the authority of the territorial ruler. Non-Catholics had to decide by a fixed day whether to join the Church of Rome, or to go into exile. Many left quickly; in 1600 11,000 townsfolk had already emigrated.[3]

Ferdinand also realized, however, that he did not have to threaten Protestant nobles or make distasteful religious compromises with them in order to win their support. Large land grants went from the archduke to intimates such as Johann Ulrich von Eggenberg (1568–1634), who had renounced his family's Lutheranism for the Church of Rome to smooth his career at the court in Graz.[4] Catholic preferment had taken hold in the governments of Emperors Rudolf II and Matthias and at the Habsburg court in Innsbruck as well. Where there were not enough local aristocrats to fill its new confessional requirements in Prague and in Vienna, the dynasty recruited nobles from elsewhere in Germany and even granted titles to commoners. That the nobles were on the whole better educated than their immediate forebears improved their chances for employment. Some families eagerly sought these jobs, especially in Lower Austria, for birth rates among them soared during the late six-teenth and early seventeenth centuries. While the province's aristocracy did not routinely observe partible inheritance, office at court supported surplus sons appropriately, whatever their birth order. Such positions also brought noble houses closer to the ear of their territorial prince, an advantage few among the Austrian nobility would scorn. They also pro-vided opportunities to school young aristocrats in courtly behavior, an increasingly crucial requirement for anyone who wished to advance himself with his prince in the seventeenth century.[5] The dynasty ben-efitted from surrounding itself with Catholics too. Solidly orthodox Habsburg households and administrations reassured many of the great prelates in the dynasty's lands. The more Catholics there were in secular institutions, the stronger the position of the Church of Rome would be.[6]

By 1618, with Catholics predominating among both chief and lesser offices at Habsburg establishments, the dynasty had begun to fashion a strategy for working with the nobility of the Austrian lands while at the same time regaining lost preeminence. In tying court preference to re-ligion, Ferdinand of Styria and other members of his family forged ties to men likely to serve the house of Austria well and at the same time advanced the cause of religious uniformity that would make governing much easier. Some Lutheran nobles of Lower Austria began to object to the court's confession-driven appointment practices at the beginning of the seventeenth century. But many Protestants assimilated the message and switched confessions accordingly. In Lower Austria, the size of the

Catholic nobility grew steadily, though from a very low number, while the evangelical roster began to contract.[7]

Crisis, Conflict, and Dynastic Opportunity

The outline of the Habsburg model for control of their lands first appeared in their Austrian patrimony. It was in Bohemia, however, that Ferdinand of Styria got the chance not only to recast a nobility to his confessional liking, but to introduce constitutional and religious changes that his dynasty had long regarded as essential for effective rule. Elected Emperor Ferdinand II in Germany in 1619, he had been elected king of Bohemia in 1617 and ruler of Hungary a year later. Nevertheless, the process had not been free of controversy. His aggressive pro-Catholic agenda in Inner Austria worried the Bohemian estates greatly. In May of 1618 a group of them met in Prague, marched to the royal compound, the Hradčany Palace, and hurled three of their monarch's representatives from a window into a moat around 60 feet below. Contemporaries, particularly Catholics, called the men's survival miraculous; modern historians have put more credence in a dung heap that cushioned their fall. A little over a year later a Protestant army, led by a Bohemian nobleman, Count Matthias von Thurn, marched on Vienna where it almost captured the new emperor in June.

In August of 1619, the normally particularistic lands of the Bohemian crown established a confederation and deposed Ferdinand as their ruler. As his replacement they called upon the German elector palatine, Frederick V (1596–1632), a Calvinist more ambitious than politically astute. He was, however, married to the daughter of James I of England, who (or so the rebels hoped) might aid his son-in-law on the continent. Worse yet for the Habsburgs, the estates in Austria above the Enns and a Protestant faction of the estates in Austria below the Enns joined in support of the Bohemians. Eager to pick up any territory in Hungary free of Ottoman control that he could, the *voivode* of Transylvania, Gábor Bethlen (1580–1629), also sided with the dissidents. The Thirty Years War was underway; it embroiled the Habsburgs both in their patrimonial lands and in the larger Germany. Though the conflict began very badly for the dynasty, it would end by giving its empire in central Europe a territorial focus to which it would hold until it collapsed forever in 1918.

Ferdinand II's first task was to quell the uprising in Bohemia. This, thanks to important aid from his cousins, Duke Maximilian I (1573–1651) in Bavaria and King Philip III (1578–1621) of Spain, he managed to do early in the conflict. In November of 1620, the Habsburg forces decisively defeated the rebellious confederates, who included dissidents from Lower Austria, outside Prague at the Battle of the White Mountain. The dissidents in Lower Austria were brought under control shortly afterward. Duke Maximilian directly occupied Austria above the Enns in the summer of 1620: he did not leave until he had Ferdinand's promise to reward him with an electoral title for his pains. The emperor himself, once again king of Bohemia, and after his death in 1637 his son Ferdinand III (1608–57), set to aligning the religious, social, administrative, and political constitutions of Bohemia and the Austrian lands more closely with the dynasty's interests.

More centralized government was one of their goals. In 1620, Ferdinand II created a separate Austrian chancellery to handle his dynasty's business, leaving a parallel, but increasingly marginalized, imperial chancellery to deal with German affairs. The Bohemian chancellery was transferred to Vienna in 1624; its affairs, including those that touched on the several Bohemian crownlands such as Moravia and Silesia, were now run directly from what was becoming the monarchy's capital. Ferdinand and his advisers argued that both Bohemia and Austria above the Enns had forfeited their constitutional rights altogether by rebelling against their territorial ruler. Both lands had no choice but to accept his reconfiguration of their relationship to him and his government. Some ringleaders of the rebellion were executed, and Protestant nobles went into exile along with lesser folk who shared their faith. The crown seized vacated lands and would put it to its own uses. The Bohemian Renewed Land Ordinance of 1627, which summarized the institutional changes taking place in the kingdom, made the Bohemian crown hereditary in the house of Habsburg. The monarch also won complete control over regalian lands and incomes in the realm. Crown-appointed governors appeared not only in Bohemia, but throughout the Habsburg lands. Ferdinand II laid the groundwork for a standing army directly under his command. The role of the estates and independent recruiters in Habsburg military undertakings and campaigns diminished accordingly.[8]

Ferdinand II and his seventeenth-century successors were not averse to placing political considerations before religious ones. Where estates remained largely loyal to him at the outset of the Thirty Years War, he temporarily ignored confessional niceties. In July of 1620 he reaffirmed the rights of Lower Austria's nobility to follow their faith. Catholics, whose ranks were growing, and several Protestants swore their fealty to him along with military and financial support. Furthermore, they renewed this pledge again and again until the conflict ended. But where politics and the restoration of the Church of Rome could be harnessed in the dynasty's interests, Catholicism was slowly established as the religion of the land. The demographic changes that this process had brought to Styria at the beginning of the seventeenth century took place elsewhere throughout much of the century. Between 1620 and 1680, almost 200,000 people left Bohemia. Not all of them were religious refugees; other areas of Germany were offering greater economic opportunity. Aside, however, from Protestant pockets in remote areas of the Austrian lands and in eastern Hungary, confessional uniformity prevailed in the Habsburg domains by 1700. The Habsburg government took an especially direct interest in parish activity, so much so that in 1659, the church itself protested.[9]

The Terms of a Modus Vivendi

However vigorously Ferdinand II reasserted his dynasty's authority in his domains, his absolutism fell considerably short of despotism. Though closely associated with military enterprises, he was not depicted as a man of arms during his lifetime. An influential tract on princely rule circulating at his court, *Princeps in compendio*, pointed out that the first duty of divinely chosen monarchs was to be just; his treatment of the clerical and noble estates of his domains often exceeded that obligation.[10] While the balance of power between territorial ruler and intermediate bodies might have shifted with the Thirty Years War and its aftermath, mutual interest continued to govern a relationship between crown and estates that the dynasty had no serious reason to alter. The Habsburgs consistently used some members of the middle classes in their administrations, but they did not employ them in the numbers to be found at the courts of other German territorial princes. Many of the dynasty's bourgeois subjects were Protestants and leaving the house of Austria's lands in large numbers, so they may not have been available for service at all.[11] But whatever the reason, Catholic nobles had good reason to ingratiate themselves with the court. Positions were to be had there, particularly for those of them who had the legal training that the dynasty welcomed.[12]

Furthermore, while Habsburg religious policies would change the names of Bohemia's nobility, they did not alter the economic position or social preeminence of that class. Indeed, Ferdinand II tightened the bond of mutual interest between king and noble estates more firmly than ever. Though many of the oldest and most illustrious families in the kingdom had died off toward the end of the sixteenth century, Rudolph and Matthias had replaced them. Whoever the great lords and knights of Bohemia were, they would still control about 80 percent of the land not held directly by the crown. Ferdinand II only improved the positions of his titled subjects during his reign. Confiscations of properties throughout the kingdom's towns and countryside supplied wherewithal for a style of loyalty-cementing patronage that far outstripped what earlier Habsburgs could afford.

Both the humble and Ferdinand's noble intimates such as Johann Ulrich von Eggenberg had good reason to thank their sovereign. The estates of Silesia were ordered in 1621 to turn over land to the late Emperor Matthias's furrier, one Peter Göbl, who had been promised the property in reward for his faithful service. With the death of the last of the Bohemian Rožmberk line in 1622, Eggenberg received their vast estates in Krumlov (Krumlau). Ferdinand would also make him duke in the area, an imperial prince, and governor of Inner Austria where the nobleman also had large holdings.[13] Karl von Liechtenstein (1569–1627) added to his already large territories in Moravia extensive holdings taken from the Žerotíns, Moravian Protestants who had been among the leaders of the anti-Habsburg faction in the Bohemian estates. That Karl oversaw the land seizures in the kingdom undoubtedly aided the fortunes of his entire family. His brothers Maximilian (1578–1643) and Gundaker (1580–1658) also stood out among the beneficiaries of Ferdinand's generosity. In Moravia alone, the number of subjects on their properties rose from 4758 to 16,156 between 1620 and 1650. More came to the family as they acquired holdings in Lower Austria and in Bohemia proper as well. Indeed, by the second half of the seventeenth century the Bohemian and Moravian nobilities held a far greater share of these lands than did the ruling house itself.[14]

The Bohemian royal estates and their individual members also continued to carry out central public functions that were closely related to their role in the landed economy. The Renewed Land Ordinances of 1627 gave them important administrative responsibilities throughout their kingdom; they also retained the right to approve and to collect taxes, a concession that would come back to haunt the dynasty in the future. Major royal offices continued to go to the high aristocracy; nobles also retained immediate legal authority over serfs who lived and worked on their demesnes. The Bohemian landlords were thus well positioned during the Thirty Years War to add to the unpaid labor (*Robot*) that peasants owed them, thereby offsetting the fiscal pressures that the Habsburgs were putting on the estates almost constantly. The foreign Catholic aristocrats brought into the kingdom to replace their émigré evangelical counterparts adjusted themselves uncritically to these privileges.

Thus, the Bohemian estates, once purged of their obstreperous Protestants and their supporters, were still an active force in the kingdom, even positioned to act as a kind of counterpoise to royal power.[15] If anything, the Habsburgs had reinforced the hold of nobles throughout this kingdom on vast stretches of productive terrain, the arrangement that had prompted the dynasty from Ferdinand I on to accommodate its interests to these families. Nobility and its privileged status continued to shape the economies of all the other Habsburg lands as well. In short, neither Ferdinand II nor his seventeenth-century successors had command control over legal or fiscal affairs in any part of the monarchy. Nor did they apparently want it, as long as erstwhile centers of rebellion such as Bohemia and Upper Austria paid their taxes promptly and in full and stayed Catholic.

It has been suggested that because his sovereignty was no longer in question, Ferdinand II was free to give himself wholeheartedly to the work of recatholicizing his lands, which he and his advisers, particularly the clergymen among them, believed was the prime mission of them all. He therefore saw no need to manage secular affairs in his holdings as tightly as did the kings of France or, closer to home, the Bavarian Wittelsbachs. It is also possible that he and those who immediately succeeded him may not yet have had an adequate pool of trained people to call upon for service as minor functionaries.[16] Whatever the reason, they continued to carry on a rather loose form of princely government in the Habsburg lands. Except for religious affairs, noble estates retained key functional responsibilities. The wellborn landlord was central in many activities of the state and even more central in the lives of those who worked for them. Peasants in areas such as Austria above the Enns were in truth becoming more productive in the seventeenth century to still the voracious fiscal appetites of the regime in Vienna. Nevertheless, it was the local noble and sometimes more well-to-do peasants to whom that laborer paid the dues that enabled territorial aristocrats to meet their commitments.[17]

This style of government helped the dynasty as well. Distributing lands throughout their domains to aristocratic supporters, regardless of where the latter were born, the Habsburgs were turning these families into a kind of pan-Austrian noble clientage. Even the most powerful of these aristocrats was virtually forced to look to the lone common element in the structure, the house of Habsburg and its resources, to defend him, his heirs, and their properties. That many of these nobles also occupied the major offices in that dynasty's government made that circle complete.[18] Thus, the overall political position of the house of Habsburg improved markedly throughout its patrimony following the Thirty Years War. So did its confessional program. Some modest concessions were made to Protestants in Silesia, but Leopold I (1640–1705) and his son Joseph I (1678–1711) all but ignored them. Nor were the Habsburgs forced to restore properties confiscated from Bohemian nobles, Protestant and Catholic alike, after 1620.[19]

The Thirty Years War, Europe, and the Habsburg Borders

The Habsburg success in reasserting its authority in Bohemia and the Austrian lands was not altogether matched in other areas that the dynasty wished to influence. Relations with its most important strategic outpost, the Holy Roman or German Empire, changed substantially. After his Bohemian victory of 1620, Ferdinand II, his Catholic clerical advisers, led by his Jesuit confessor William Lamormaini (1570–1628), and the ecclesiastical electors of Mainz, Trier, and Cologne tried to reverse the tide of the Protestant Reformation in Germany as well. A handful of military victories encouraged the emperor to issue the Edict of Restitution in 1629, which rolled back the territorial gains of Protestantism in Catholic ecclesiastical lands to the year 1522. Had the order prevailed, the influence of the reformed confessions in Germany would have drastically declined. But the measure marked the beginning of a downhill slide in Habsburg fortunes in Germany. Neighboring Protestant states, first Denmark, later Sweden, then Catholic France jumped into the conflict either directly or through surrogates to trim the power of the house of Habsburg in central Europe.

The Peace of Westphalia that closed the conflict in 1648 was actually two treaties – one arranged in Osnabrück between the emperor and

Sweden, the single mightiest Protestant realm in the conflict when it ended, the second executed in Münster between the emperor and France. The latter realm, which used the war to extend its boundaries on the Rhine eastward, was clearly the territorial winner, leaving the house of Habsburg with little choice but to accept as part of the agreement a number of institutional changes within the empire that seriously affected both the relationship of the German princes with their emperor and his military and diplomatic strategies throughout the continent. The muscular tone of the Edict of Restitution had frightened even some of Germany's Catholic princes. Political direction of the empire shifted to the imperial diet and the territorial states whose envoys spoke in it. The role of the emperor in this body was correspondingly scaled back.[20] Though the German principalities had negotiated with non-German rulers for decades, they now had the formal right to do so. Who had final responsibility for allowing foreign recruiting of German mercenaries was never fully settled. But with the German princes now formally independent players on the international stage, the Habsburgs confronted new challenges in defending their northern borders. Saxony, Prussia, Bavaria could all conceivably unite with some hostile non-German state to attack these boundaries massively or nibble away at them independently. Bohemia and Silesia were particularly exposed.

The Habsburg answer to this problem was to find ways to establish the kind of collaborative relationships with the German states that they were fashioning with estates in their own lands. The dynasty did not have to start this process from scratch. Not all of Germany's territorial rulers, especially of smaller principalities in Swabia and Franconia, dared to dispense with the protection that the house of Austria had given to them in the past.[21] The dynasty also enjoyed a few lucky breaks. Efforts of the imperial chancellor and elector of Mainz, Johann Philip Schönborn (1605–73), to give leverage to Germany's international position by steering a more pro-French course collapsed. Louis XIV (1638–1715), the Bourbon king of France, had embarked on an aggressive program of rounding out his eastern borders that led many German territorial rulers to rethink the value of French alliances. The Sun King's annexation of Strasbourg in 1679 and his ruthless bombardment of Heidelberg nine years later changed many minds. The long-dormant Ottoman government began regathering its military machine in the later decades of the seventeenth century. Only an emperor could organize defense against such enemies, and that role fell to the Habsburgs, particularly to Ferdinand II's grandson Leopold I.

The Habsburgs also worked quite expertly with what they had to promote useful and meaningful connections with Germany and its princes. Marriage alliances were a time-tested strategy, and while the dynasty did not produce large numbers of legitimate offspring during the seventeenth and early eighteenth centuries, they deployed them economically in protecting their northern and northeastern frontiers. Daughters of Ferdinand II, Leopold I, and Joseph I wed the electors of Bavaria. Two archduchesses were queens of Poland as well.[22]

The Habsburgs also retained some formal presence and powers in Germany that eased the dynasty's diplomatic problems and gave German princes and nobles reason to cultivate the government in Vienna. The emperor was still the imperial *advocatus ecclesiae* with power to enfeoff bishops with diocesan lands. Ferdinand II and his successors made sure that the recipients of these holdings were sound and known Catholics, either Habsburgs themselves or aristocrats firmly committed to the Church of Rome. In 1668 sons of the house of Thun, great landholders in Bohemia, sat as bishops in Salzburg, Passau, Regensburg, Brixen in the Tyrol, Trent, and Gurk. The dynasty was especially careful with major abbeys (*Hochstiften*) such as Konstanz, Salzburg, and Brixen which had chapters within the Habsburg Austrian hereditary lands. While many of these figures had well-defined interests of their own, their close links with the ruling dynasty forced them to consider Habsburg wishes when making policy decisions.[23]

With the help of his astute Rhenish court chancellor, Theodore Heinrich von Stratmann, Leopold I also carefully worked his way into the good graces of many members of the newly prominent imperial diet. Sitting in Regensburg after 1663, this body presided over imperial business in virtual perpetuity. Leopold's real or virtual presence and those of his successors acted as an informal check on the ambitions of any one prince or on schemes among them to form shadow governments.[24] More important still, the emperor remained the territorial suzerain of Germany and could confer lands and titles there. The Habsburgs endowed loyal nobles from their own territories with properties in the empire that often had seats in the imperial diet attached to them. Sometimes titles alone were handed out. The Liechtensteins, the Harrachs of Lower Austria, the Kaunitzes, whose demesnes were scattered throughout Bohemia and Moravia, the immensely wealthy Bohemian Lobkovic, either received lands in the empire or were named imperial knights.[25] The house of Habsburg itself added modestly to its German domains. During the latter decades of the eighteenth century, Joseph II (1741–90) as emperor would confer vacated German fiefs upon his mother, thus turning them into dynastic holdings.[26] The emperor also continued to adjudicate disputes over property. Two high courts for the empire handled such matters; one, the imperial cameral tribunal (*Reichskammergericht*), at first sat in Speyer, then in Wetzlar. The other, the aulic court, was linked to the *Hofrat* in Vienna. Both bodies heard many appeals from the imperial knights and free cities who were resisting the expansionist ambitions of Germany's larger polities.[27] The *Hofrat* had standing in religious disputes in the empire as well; Germans had been eager to be stationed near the imperial administration to provide input on these matters, even when the emperor was in Prague as was Rudolph II. Rudolph was also a bit freer than his immediate predecessors in granting titles of nobility, another reason for supplicants to stick close by the source of favor.[28]

Thus, Germany was still a key consideration in Habsburg political strategies, and the emperor's court as crucial to the careers of many German princes and nobles as it was to the aristocracy of the Habsburg patrimony itself. Privilege and opportunity hung on the will of a sovereign whose environment was so singular that he was exempt from normal legal requirements. Those who served him were therefore singular as well. Accredited members of the imperial household and other crown officers were tried by a court tribunal except in capital offenses. Courtiers were freed from local imposts, an important advantage for those living in heavily taxed Vienna. Officers routinely picked up monetary considerations for arranging access to the monarch, a practice that had become especially common during the reign of the aloof Rudolph II. Some succumbed to the lure of shady financial operations. Count George Ludwig von Sinzendorf (1616–81), the president of Leopold I's treasury for 20 years, was eventually dismissed after he had defrauded the government of over two million gulden.

Unlike other realms in seventeenth-century Europe, most notably France, the Austrian Habsburgs frowned upon selling court offices, except for chamberlains (*Kammerer*), who occasionally did pay their way into their positions.[29] Titles and the benefits attached to them were another matter. Princes and nobility throughout the Habsburg lands and Germany never seemed to have enough of these distinctions, regardless of what they cost. Membership in the exclusive Order of the Golden Fleece, controlled by the house of Austria acting as dukes of Burgundy, was very costly. Nevertheless, the position, once purchased, allowed nobles of the Habsburg lands – the Khevenhüllers and Herbersteins of

Inner Austria, the Šliks of Bohemia – to rub shoulders with sovereign princes, which they eagerly did.[30] This 'mutual interdependence of the crown and its subjects upon the flow of privilege from above downward in return for loyalty and money flowing upward' functioned beyond the circles of the noble and clerical elites.[31] In Vienna the emperor awarded privileges to the recognized guilds of the city, to Jews, and to an assortment of other particular interests in return for support.

Habsburg efforts to cultivate noble clients also affected the city as a whole. The dynasty had moved around some in the sixteenth century: Ferdinand I kept his household in Innsbruck for long stretches of time, and Rudolph, of course, shifted his administrative staff to Prague altogether where he added Moravian, Bohemian, and Silesian nobles to a government that Germans had long dominated.[32] It was only under Emperor Matthias that both imperial and dynastic establishments went back to Vienna; from that time on the Habsburgs conducted the bulk of their affairs from that city. However, the trend to use Catholic members of the Bohemian, Moravian, and Silesian nobility as high officials along with Germans continued. So did the practice of conferring properties on these people on both sides of the Austrian–Bohemian border. By the beginning of the eighteenth century, their wealth and sophisticated tastes were recasting the very streetscape of what had become the imperial capital. While many of these men continued to maintain residences on their farflung estates throughout the Habsburg lands, they had also commissioned city palaces which in both size and elegance eclipsed the imperial residence of the *Hofburg* itself.[33] Some of these vast dwellings had begun to spill even beyond the cramped confines of the Inner City around the court.

The Habsburgs were still among the poorer of Europe's monarchs in the seventeenth century. Yet, with the possible exception of the elector of Brandenburg, the imperial title and the way they had used it continued to confer upon the dynasty a majesty beyond that of the rest of Germany's provincial princes, or *Ortsfürsten*, as Leopold I's court chancellor, Theodor Altet von Strattmann, snobbishly dubbed them.[34] The Habsburg establishment in Vienna still had many attractions for German princes and nobles, even though the emperor's formal powers over them had diminished. The house of Austria had also weathered a serious religious and political challenge to its interests sparked by noble estates throughout its lands and reestablished a modus vivendi with both the clerical and secular elements in these bodies. All of these arrangements, however difficult they had been to put in place, enabled them to meet their overriding preoccupation – the control of the territorial complex they had cobbled together by accident and a kind of reactive design a century earlier.

Reconquering Hungary

One part of the house of Austria's farflung territorial sphere of influence and responsibility, however, persistently refused to coordinate its purposes and local institutions with Vienna in return for status and livelihood. This was Hungary, where a sizeable segment of the native nobility would never be drawn into the subtle vortex of the Habsburg court. Summoned there for business they came, only to return to their properties and homes in Royal Hungary, Croatia, and Transylvania. Wherever they lived, they protected their traditional rights tenaciously; the defense of Protestantism was a further vital concern for the Transylvanian estates well into the eighteenth century.[35]

Hungary was hardly a case of exceptional development within the Habsburg monarchy, especially in the seventeenth century. Around 1600 the confessional profile of the non-Ottoman areas of the kingdom was much like that in the other Habsburg lands. Evangelical creeds flourished; large numbers of Hungarians had followed Luther, even though some leading nobles feared that the new faith would advance the germanization of their homeland. Calvinism had made heavy inroads in the east. An energetic and effective Counter-Reformation was also underway, supported by the Habsburg rulers and led by Péter Pázmány (1570–1637), the archbishop of Esztergom and primate of Hungary from 1616 to 1637. A Jesuit who had studied at the University of Vienna among other places and taught at the University of Graz for a time, he brought immense wit, eloquence, and learning to his polemics, often using Protestant doctrine against itself. He was persuasive enough to return some of Hungary's major noble houses to Catholic orthodoxy, an accomplishment with a multiplier effect that gladdened the papal household in Rome. Legions of hapless serfs and peasants who worked the properties of great aristocrats had no choice but to conform to the faith of their masters. Territorial nobilities in Bohemia and the Austrian lands were equally useful in spreading Catholic discipline on their properties.[36]

The dynasty and the nobles of Habsburg Hungary were also finding ways to advance their fortunes to mutual profit. The sixteenth-century codification of Hungarian constitutional law, Stephen Werböczy's *Tripartitum*, left to the monarch the power to name nobles and to assign to them categories of lands associated with their various ranks. It was possible for a king to take someone out of serfdom and ennoble him, a status that exempted such a person from servile duties forever. Moreover, until the house of Austria acquired the crown of St. Stephen, Hungary's aristocrats could not routinely pass titles to their children. To ingratiate himself in his new realm quickly, Ferdinand I made more of such distinctions hereditary. His successors, almost always under dire fiscal pressure, continued the policy, often as the price of substantial loans from the richest of their Hungarian subjects. By the middle of the seventeenth century, all Hungarian magnates could pass their titles down in their families. The crown increased the size of their properties as well. The number of magnate families with the ranks of baron or count grew markedly, rising from around 40 in 1600 to 100 at the beginning of the eighteenth century.

Ferdinand II and Ferdinand III were also very generous in creating new noble lines, a policy which would eventually be applied in Transylvania. The Habsburgs even had propertied titles to offer landless nobles or 'sandal nobility' (*bocskoros*) who served the dynasty, especially on the military frontier, in the seventeenth and eighteenth centuries. Important offices in the kingdom and its associated lands therefore stayed in the hands of these great families. Five extraordinarily wealthy magnate houses supplied bans, or royal governors, for Croatia and Slavonia, tucked to the east between the Save and Drave rivers, between 1600 and 1800. By the beginning of the eighteenth century, every Hungarian archbishop was the offspring of the kingdom's high aristocracy.[37]

Nevertheless, for all these parallels with the other Habsburg lands, Hungary was unlike them in ways that enabled nobles great and petty to elude Vienna's network of patronage and service. The sheer size of Hungary's aristocracy taken as a single class, roughly 25,000 families or 5 percent of the total population in the seventeenth century, made a difference. During the Middle Ages Hungary's rulers had occasionally ennobled whole groups of people. In Bohemia, by way of contrast, where there were only a few hundred aristocratic houses, 51 princely lines dominated the kingdom. The number of nobles in the Austrian provinces was also relatively modest – 467 in all in Lower Austria, for example, around 1620.[38] Unlike other Habsburg lands, the kingdom of Hungary was also formally under arms, which could be turned on anyone, including the house of Austria's rulers. Menaced constantly by Ottoman skirmishers, most aristocrats themselves kept private forces whose loyalty belonged only to the man who paid them. A number of troops were also deployed along Hungary's borders. Theoretically under royal control, they too were often available to others for a price.[39]

Accidents of politics and conquest also gave Hungary's magnates and assorted lower nobilities opportunities that their counterparts elsewhere in the Habsburg lands did not have. The tripartite split of the kingdom between the Ottoman overlords in central and southern Hungary, the princes of Transylvania, and Habsburg Royal Hungary in the north and west allowed the elites of the realm to play off competing centers of interest to great profit.[40] Indeed, the apartness of Transylvania could be, at times, as problematic for Ottoman sultans as it was for Habsburg emperors. A unique construct within the Habsburg lands and within Europe itself, the principality was home to three 'historic' nations – the Hungarians, the Hungarian-speaking Széklers, and German settlers called Saxons – as well as Rumanian shepherds who had no political standing in the early modern era. All three peoples were largely self-governing within their groups, but the diet that spoke for them always elected a Hungarian prince as a territorial ruler. The latter usually came from some of the wealthiest and most powerful aristocrats of the area who consistently championed the reunification of Hungary and the primacy of the Magyar aristocracy throughout the kingdom.

Ferdinand I's conflict in the sixteenth century with John Zápolya and his son foreshadowed relations between the Habsburgs and the duchy for the next century and a half. A prince of Transylvania, Stephen Báthory (1533–86), had outfoxed Maximilian II in competition for the Polish crown. But Transylvania's potential to turn into a breeding ground for Hungarian resistance to Habsburg rule became especially clear during the troubled reign of Rudolph II. Casting about in 1603 for funds to underwrite the Fifteen Year War against the Turks, the emperor and king ordered the arrest of Stephen Illésházy, a wealthy landowner in northwest Hungary, on trumped-up charges of high treason. Up to that point Illésházy, though a Protestant, had supported the Habsburgs to great profit. Indeed, his properties came largely from lands that the dynasty had awarded him, along with a baronial title. Now insulted, he looked for help from Transylvania and its ruling prince, Stephen Bocskay. Himself pro-Habsburg – he had been raised at the court in Vienna –

Bocskay had been, as we have seen, transformed into an armed opponent of the regime by the marauding of the imperial armies in Transylvania during the Turkish conflict.

Illésházy's case was settled in 1606, his lands were restored, and two years later he became royal governor of Habsburg Hungary. But an autonomous Transylvania continued to give the Hungarian nobility a refuge where, for whatever motives, they could promote schemes that allegedly met Hungarian, rather than Habsburg–Hungarian, concerns. During the Thirty Years War Gábor Bethlen, also a ruling prince in Transylvania, withdrew from the conflict on the promise from Ferdinand II of seven counties in northeastern Hungary and a yearly tribute of 50,000 florins. Moreover, until he died in 1629 Bethlen allied himself with the anti-Habsburg states of Protestant Europe and acted as a spokesman for Hungary's territorial integrity.

The Hungarian nobility also commanded constitutional powers and privileges of unusually long standing. Hungary's nobles, no matter how poor, were free of royal and ecclesiastical taxes. They could legally take up arms against any ruler who encroached on these liberties. In contrast to practice elsewhere in the Habsburg domains, the title of magnate was specifically associated with certain properties rather than with the size of a noble's holdings. The king theoretically governed with the aid of the great officers of the crown – the palatine, treasurer, chancellor, and procurer-general – baronial magnates elected to their position by the diet.[41] Habsburg efforts to bypass this custom had never quite succeeded. The chancellor was almost always a high clergyman and was usually with the monarch either in Vienna or Prague. All magnates, whom the crown personally invited to attend the diet, and major clerical officials sat in its upper house.

The simple nobility, which ranged from a propertied gentry to families with titles but little if any land, held forth in the lower house. Here they were represented by two of their peers elected in each county, administrative subdivisions that by the sixteenth century were almost completely controlled by the local nobility. The lord-lieutenant (*főispán*) of each county was usually born to a magnate house; however, the assistant lord-lieutenant (*alispán*), nominated by the *főispán* but confirmed by the country squires, conducted the tasks connected with both offices. The county structure endured even in areas under Ottoman control where short-lived peasant counties were sometimes formed when resident noblemen failed to provide for self-defense.

In Habsburg Royal Hungary, county delegates to the central diet often held local offices too. County juries of their peers adjudicated the cases of nobles, and the local nobility served as the judges for peasants and named their village supervisors. Outside of customs personnel and other minor treasury functionaries, the monarch had no direct representative in these districts. The Hungarian small nobility was well versed in the legal texts and biblical precepts that legitimized their protests against innovations coming from Vienna. The royal or free cities were also dominated by the nobility, many of whom acquired residency rights there after fleeing Ottoman occupation of the central plain of the realm.[42]

Thus the size of the Hungarian nobility, the institutional structure of the kingdom, and entrenched political divisions exacerbated by the presence of two hostile powers in the kingdom, all combined to frustrate Habsburg efforts to coopt Hungary's aristocrats with lands and titles. The alignment of dynastic and noble interests that the Habsburgs had achieved in the Austrian lands and even more in Bohemia thanks to the victory at the White Mountain in 1620 eluded them in Hungary.[43] While a rudimentary Hungarian court party did exist, particularly among the magnates, it did not offset the influence of an indigenous petty nobility the members of which retained key rights in their home territories and had no compunctions about looking either to Transylvania or the sultan himself for moral and military support should their privileges seem threatened from Vienna.

The dynasty's most serious failing in the eyes of Hungary's nobles, however, was military. Well into the seventeenth century, the Habsburgs had not driven Ottoman rule from the kingdom, the very mission that they had been elected to perform. The disappointed among the Hungarians found it hard to distinguish between Habsburg and Ottoman regimes. Both sides, said an anonymous local gentleman in 1664, had plundered the country mercilessly.[44] The Turks were frightening, to be sure, but clearly not invincible. Though the imperial army's behavior during the Fifteen Years War had set off Bocskay's uprising at the beginning of the seventeenth century, the conflict from 1591 to 1606 had not ended badly for the house of Austria. The Peace of Zsitva-Torok in 1606 had recognized the emperor and the sultan as one another's equals. A final payment of 200,000 gold *forint* (florins) to Constantinople released the Habsburgs from the humiliating duties they had been paying since the sixteenth century. Luckily for Ferdinand II and Ferdinand III, the Ottoman armies were tied down during much of the Thirty Years War with conflict on other borders. However, during the

1650s the lust for yet another great campaign in the west stirred once again in Constantinople. Behind the move were the ambitions of the Köprülü family, an Albanian dynasty of grand viziers, the chief court officers of the sultan.

The Turks first turned on Transylvania where the *voivode*, George II Rákóczi (1621–60), technically the sultan's vassal, longed to pursue an independent foreign policy. In 1658 George had joined a coalition that invaded Poland, a realm which historically had not shuddered when the Ottomans bested imperial forces, at least on distant battlefields. The fury of the Ottoman punitive expedition brought a sharp reaction from the new Habsburg emperor, Leopold I, the men in his court circle who wanted the Habsburgs to play a heavy role in central and east central Europe, along with refugees from Transylvania, and other Hungarian nobles. By 1663 the Turks had installed their direct authority in Transylvania; they were also ready for further campaigning.

This they began during the spring of 1664, only to be overwhelmingly defeated by the imperial forces on 1 August at Saint Gotthard on the Raab river, just inside the southwestern tip of Hungary. For a moment influential Hungarians expected the reconquest of the central plain, or *Alföld*, of the kingdom, the seat of the Turkish occupation, to begin. But the naturally cautious Leopold was torn between two factions at his court, the 'easternists' and the 'westernists', who were more worried about moves that Louis XIV of France was making in the direction to his south and east. The latter won the day, persuading the emperor that he should not give way to Hungarian distractions when France threatened to diminish the dynastic patrimony in southwestern Germany and in Spain. Leopold therefore did not follow up on a major victory. Instead, in the peace of Vasvár, concluded in 1664, he agreed to return conquered territory to the government in Constantinople.

Dynastic egotism along with inexcusable lethargy in high places had trumped Hungarian interests, or so influential nobles of the kingdom thought. From then until 1711, Hungary was in an uproar, made all the more chaotic by repeated missteps on the part of the dynasty and some exceedingly poor planning and organization among the various dissidents. The first uprising, the Wesselényi Conspiracy, named after the Hungarian palatine Count Ferenc Wesselényi, brought together some of the most important magnates of the realm. Vowing to rid Hungary of Habsburg rule altogether, they sought help from Louis XIV and even the sultan. Each of these, for their own reasons, declined. Undeterred, the plotters began an insurrection in 1670 that allowed Leopold and his advisers to dust off the scenario once played to great effect in Bohemia. Accused of having breached their contract with the monarchy, several ringleaders were executed in 1671. Backed by Hungary's Catholic magnates, the Habsburg regime also set to cleansing the realm of Protestantism where it could. The rights of the estates, including the *jus resistendi*, were suspended, and Hungary was transformed into a hereditary monarchy. Dispossessed nobles fled to Transylvania, vowing to recover some of their lost status.[45]

By 1681, however, the government in Vienna was in a serious predicament abroad. Leopold faced almost certain war on two fronts. The Turks were rearming for a major offensive; France, in the west, was chipping away at Germany's borders. Even the papacy believed that Islam, and not the fractious Hungarian nobility, was Christendom's most dangerous foe. The emperor therefore yielded to pleas for restoration of the traditional Hungarian rights, in effect dropping his claim that the sedition of some nobles justified punishing the entire order. Meeting personally with the estates in Sopron in the spring of 1681, the emperor agreed to end the military occupation of Hungary, halt what the estates called unlawful taxation, and reestablish Hungary's independent judicial offices. Not all of the magnates were satisfied: even as the Turks were organizing for attack in 1682, a dissident nobleman in northeastern Hungary, Imre Thököly (1657–1705), whose seat was in Kosice, went on the offensive again with the encouragement of the *voivode* of Transylvania, Mihály Apafy (1632–90), and the sultan's military governor in Pest. Thököly captured more territory in Upper Hungary. Even more troublesome for imperial troops once the long-anticipated Ottoman offensive got underway early in 1683 were the harassing tactics of his insurrectionist (*kuruc*) troops.[46]

The crucial moment of the Turkish campaign was the siege of Vienna, which lasted from 4 July until 12 September 1683. Guided by his councilors and his own timorous character, Leopold had left a somewhat disgruntled city before the sultan's forces arrived. He was not ideally positioned to wage war. While by 1654 Ferdinand III had stripped the Austrian estates of any rights to refuse extraordinary taxes for military purposes, they could still haggle over amounts. They could also drag their feet in meeting what commitments they made. The Bohemian estates voted their king military aid, but would not allow troops from Saxony to forage on their way to the south during the siege of Vienna.[47]

The emperor enjoyed advantages, however, that earlier Habsburgs had not when faced with Ottoman offensives. Leopold I and Ferdinand III before him had done much to prepare Habsburg armies for such a show-down. Experience in the Thirty Years War had taught the house of Austria as well as other German princes that standing armies were superior to the seasonal pick-up forces that manned the armies of central Europe during the fifteenth and sixteenth centuries. In 1649, Ferdinand III commanded 19 of the 52 regiments created for the Thirty Years War to remain on duty perpetually. Further improvements initiated by Habsburg military leaders themselves, particularly Raimondo Montecuccoli (1609–80) and Eugene of Savoy (1663–1736), and clarification of lines of authority also did much to make Habsburg forces more effective. A professional officer corps had begun to take shape, and the common soldier now owed his loyalty to his sovereign rather than to the colonel who recruited him. Leopold could also draw upon experts for sieges and fortifications as well as artillery specialists. The calibre of Ottoman com-manders, on the other hand, had deteriorated, and a long-standing preference for taking cities left the sultan's forces relatively untrained for the open-field combat that eventually characterized the reconquest of Hungary once the siege of Vienna had been lifted.[48]

But above all, the dynamics of the Habsburg victory in 1683 vindicated the advice of *Princeps in compendio* that princes should stay in the good graces of other princes.[49] Leopold received heavy and unstinting financial support from the papacy. The aggressive ambitions that had dominated the sultan's court for over two decades had made many central European princes edgy. Leopold, on the other hand, had con-vinced these men that he was improving his armies not to conquer foreign lands, but to defend his borders, at least as he understood them. The force that withstood the siege of Vienna was an international coali-tion. While heavily German, it received significant support from other realms, including a Polish contingent led by its king, John Sobieski (1629–96). And, it should be noted, Leopold once again had a stroke or two of luck. The sultan's armies arrived before Vienna about a week later than planned. The prospect of having to feed their forces through a chilly fall made the invading commanders all the more eager to leave.

The Ottoman withdrawal from Vienna marked the beginning of their ejection from Hungary as well. Leopold I received a significant amount of cooperation from important Hungarian noble families once it be-came clear he was committed to the reconquest of the kingdom. His Hungarian court officers were helpful, especially a new palatine, Paul Esterházy (1635–1713), who contributed 6000 troops and raised 9000 more from the Hungarian nobility in a failed attempt to retake Buda in the summer of 1684. Catholic solidarity helped; some of the men whom Esterházy enlisted were also in the service of Hungarian Catholic magnates defending themselves from the Protestant Imre Thököly and his bands.[50] But the imperial army swiftly wiped out most of the Turkish garrisons in Habsburg or Royal Hungary, and the still-rampaging Thököly *kuruc* were brought to heel as well. On 12 January 1684, Leopold agreed to pardon all of Thököly's followers if they swore allegiance to him. Compliance was generally good; Thököly himself fled for Turkish territory in 1685.

Leopold, however, did not press his strengthened position too far. In the Pressburg Agreement of 1687, he and the combined membership of the Hungarian and Croatian estates struck a tentative balance that met major concerns of all sides. The estates retained their right to vote taxes and their virtual monopoly over local government. Leopold also guaranteed religious freedom among his Hungarian subjects, though many suspected his sincerity on this point and held out on accepting any of the compact's provisions until he yielded on this matter. For their part, the estates dropped their demands for restoration of the hallowed *jus resistendi* and elective monarchy; the emperor's eldest son, Archduke Joseph, was named heir to the Hungarian throne as part of the proceedings.[51]

Leopold and his councilors also avoided challenging the economic privileges of the Hungarian nobility. Like Habsburg rulers before and after him, he was eager to develop new sources of revenue. As early as 1657, the emperor was hearing advice that reduction of forced labor among the peasantry of his realms would encourage agricultural productivity. The government in Vienna repeatedly, but futilely, ordered Bohemian landlords to lower these requirements. The Hungarian nobility was equally impervious. Leopold's regime erred seriously in 1697 when it asked for a tax on noble demesne lands and limitation on unfree agrarian labor of three days per week, the same amount as had been suggested in Bohemia. A ferocious outcry ensued; Leopold contented himself with setting up regional royal courts where peasants could bring complaints against landlords.[52]

Nobles around Transylvania, however, led by Mihály Apaffy, held out somewhat longer. They still feared the wrath of the Turks, who were still in the neighborhood of the principality. Unable to negotiate with the *voivode*, Leopold took Transylvania by force in 1689 and annexed it to the Hungarian crown, though Vienna would govern it through a separate chancellery.[53] But even here the Habsburg ruler acted more as a conciliator than a conqueror. In 1690, Leopold acknowledged the three nations' right to self-government in return for a fixed annual contribution of 100,000 florins that could be raised to 400,000 when war was on.[54] Though the crown had to approve the choice, the estates could still elect a native governor. Leopold also confirmed a limited religious freedom in the principality that left out Eastern Orthodoxy, the faith of the Rumanian peasantry, and Armenians.[55]

Subduing the Hungarians

Toward the end of his crisis-plagued reign, Leopold I seemed near to establishing an enduring form of collaboration with the Hungarian estates. The terms were not quite as favorable to his dynasty as those prevailing throughout the other Habsburg lands, but they were an improvement over earlier arrangements. Some Hungarian noble families were cooperating consistently with the dynasty in return for substantial rewards: loyalty and service to their Habsburg kings raised the Esterházy from the poorer ranks of the Hungarian nobility to one of Europe's wealthiest aristocratic families by the beginning of the eighteenth century.[56]

Nevertheless, serious points of friction still remained. Leopold's conspicuous patronage of Hungarian Catholic foundations disturbed the many Protestants still in the kingdom, particularly in the east.[57] More bothersome still, Leopold I's advisers did not always have in mind the interests of Hungary's landed magnates when they made decisions about their kingdom. A crucial example was the resettlement policy that the government in Vienna adopted for the Hungarian central plain as the Ottomans vacated it, an accomplished fact by 1699. Austrian and Bohemian counselors, and not local officials, dominated the commission that reassigned the territorial spoils. Their decisions, or so the Hungarians thought, respected the law of conquest far more than indigenous sensibilities. Property restoration of land in Hungary, long a dream of the native nobility, took little account of their wishes; newly liberated territory often passed to non-Hungarian owners. As in Bohemia, the Habsburgs were far more comfortable with reliable 'foreigners' than they were with Hungary's stubbornly independent landed elites. Particularly favored were Serbs, who had fled the Turks for Hungary's southern borders. Hungarian nobles who did receive liberated holdings had to pay a substantial administrative charge before they took possession of them.[58]

Such grievances, along with an angry flare-up of peasant unrest over feudal burdens and generally bad economic conditions following the Ottoman withdrawal, ignited further conflict between nobility and ruler in Hungary at the beginning of the eighteenth century. This episode was led by Ferenc II Rákóczi (1676–1735), a scion of one of Hungary's oldest noble houses which had its seat in Upper Hungary around Kosice. The family had been closer to the Habsburgs than many Hungarians of their order; Ferenc II's branch had been princes of the Holy Roman Empire since 1645. Though his immediate forebears were Protestants – his widowed mother had actually married Imre Thököly – Ferenc II had been raised a Catholic by Jesuits in Prague. His subsequent falling out with the dynasty was therefore doubly challenging to the growing Habsburg hegemony. Rákóczi's mother, Ilona Zrínyi (1643–1703), was the daughter of a noble whom Leopold I had executed for his role in an earlier noble conspiracy. Ferenc had been taken from her to be educated by Austrian Jesuits in Bohemia following the collapse of the *kuruc* uprising in 1688; he later claimed that Habsburg insults to his house inspired much of his sedition.[59]

Participants in the peasant insurrection of 1697 tried to enlist dissident nobles, among them Rákóczi. His hostility to the dynasty mounted as Leopold I's government put down the rural uprising with remorseless brutality. Elected prince of Transylvania by the diet there in 1704, Rákóczi put himself at the head of a war of liberation for which he tried – and, like earlier Hungarian conspirators, failed – to get foreign support, this time from Tsar Peter the Great of Russia along with the ubiquitous Louis XIV.

Rákóczi was clearly a voice for the Hungarian nobility to whom he had very deep ties. He asked for restoration of *jus resistendi*, of the elective crown, and for an independent Transylvania ruled by himself. But in an effort to rally peasants to his cause, Rákóczi promised to exempt them from feudal dues. That proposal cost him the support of many members of the Hungarian landlord class in his ranks. By 1711, his forces were sadly spent. His chief general, Count Sándor Károlyi (1679–1743), surrendered in that year to his imperial counterpart, János Pálffy, himself a member of one of Hungary's great families.[60]

Leopold died before the Rákóczi uprising ended. It was his son, Emperor Joseph I, who in 1711 concluded the Peace of Szatmár that restored the status quo ante bellum in Hungary. The monarch offered, and Rákóczi's supporters accepted, a general amnesty. The stipulations of the Habsburg–Hungarian agreement of 1687 would thereafter define the constitutional relations of the house of Austria with Hungary. Joseph, therefore, received once again Hungarian promises to renounce elective monarchy and the right of noble insurrection.

Sealing a Hegemony

An uncommon string of military victories and diplomatic achievements were but two elements of the Habsburg *imperium* in central and east central Europe during the early modern era. From the end of the Thirty Years War until the middle of the eighteenth century, the dynasty's rulers also took virtual command control over a set of cultural assumptions and practices that impressed themselves upon the minds and hearts of many of their subjects and would remain there for decades to come.

Part of the dynasty's success lay in the uncomplicated way in which the Habsburg monarchy presented itself and its claims to rule to its peoples. The cosmology of the Baroque Catholicism that took root in the Habsburg lands posited the existence of two mysteriously interactive realms, one secular, the other spiritual. The world in which mankind performed its assigned role in an elaborately articulated hierarchy was God's theater, in place for him to watch and judge mortal behavior as well as to represent his designs and purposes. Habsburg government and the privileged elites with whom it worked used all the visual stratagems at their disposal to reaffirm with simple viewers just whom God had chosen to rule them and why his choice should be respected. Literacy was the hallmark of Protestantism and Protestantism the engine of sedition. The Habsburgs made little use of political philosophers to explain their eminence, preferring instead to make their statements about themselves visually and ceremonially. The Baroque world order was hierarchical, with God at its pinnacle and monarchs not far below him as his lieutenants. By observing the sacraments publicly, by personal service in pilgrimages and liturgical processions – during the Thirty Years War the dynasty's participation in the ceremonies surrounding the Feast of the Eucharist became a virtual act of state – and by vigorous advocacy of the veneration of the Virgin and of select saints, the territorial ruler showed himself to be an appropriately Christian ruler for a Christian people.[61]

Even less complex, and in many ways more durable, artifacts were available to dynasty and nobility alike to send the message of their authority. From 1650 to about 1720, central and east central Europe was the scene of a major building boom, fueled in part by pent-up need for renovation and new construction after years of Ottoman occupation, but also by the triumphal energies stirred up by the long-sought defeat of two formidable religious and cultural foes: Protestantism and Islam. The style of construction was Baroque, a word of uncertain origin but which had found a home in Italy and Spain, particularly in religious edifices, during the sixteenth century. Its models, which combined linear exuberance with overwhelming structural mass, were the perfect answer to the celebratory and representational needs of central Europe's elites and rulers.

With church, noble, and government edifices going up or under alteration to conform to contemporary tastes all about them, townsfolk and rustics alike found it hard to ignore who governed the empire and from whom these exalted figures drew their support. The aristocratic elites, spiritual and secular, of the early modern Habsburg empire put its place in this hierarchy on display in secular and religious settings as well. Great structures bespoke preeminence: monasteries such as Melk in Lower Austria, remodeled by the Tyrolean architect Jakob Prandtauer (1660–1726) in the first quarter of the eighteenth century, and noble residences such as Eugene of Savoy's Belvedere Palace just beyond central Vienna, designed by Johann Baptiste Fischer von Erlach (1656–1723), all informed the eye of who ruled the empire and the resources that enabled him, his family, and his supporters to do so.

Even today, a traveler in the lands of the former monarchy quickly notices the striking architectural consistency of pre-World War II government and ecclesiastical buildings, even urban residential construction.[62] An eerily dilapidated castle on the outskirts of Ustí nad Labem (Ustí on the Elbe) in the northeast Czech Republic is reminiscent of Melk, which looms above the Danube just before rural Lower Austria becomes the suburbs of Vienna. The finest realizations of Baroque interiors are as well, if not better, represented in Prague as they are in Vienna. The library ceiling of the Strahov monastery on the outskirts of the Czech capital and the inside of the church of St. Nicholas (Sv. Mikuláš) and its sumptuous organ are mandatory stop-offs for connoisseurs of the style. From Milan to Budapest to neighborhoods in

Sarajevo, L'viv (Lemberg), and Chernivtsi (Czernowitz) in Ukraine, one finds look-alike buildings and public spaces clearly modeled on counterparts in Vienna.[63]

The spiritual dynamic that gave rise to this program, and the buildings that went with it, was the renewed and reinvigorated Roman Catholicism of the seventeenth century. It traveled with the Habsburgs wherever they went. Conquests of the monarchy were conquests of the church; they encouraged both partners to dream of yet greater victories, particularly in the east. The gradual recapture of central Hungary from the Ottomans after 1683 conjured up thoughts in the Catholic hierarchy of extending its message to Russia, even to Asia. The Holy Roman Emperor, a Habsburg from the fifteenth century to the beginning of the nineteenth, had in theory some responsibility for the propagation of the faith to all humanity; the imperial court often received news about Christians throughout the world. The grisly fate that ended the lives of some martyrs in Japan was made known to the Viennese public in sermons from the very popular preacher Abraham A Sancta Clara (1644–1709).[64]

Pockets of Protestantism in Transylvania, in the so-called Partium, a strip of Royal Hungary east of the Tisza river, and in what was left to the Habsburgs of Silesia after the Seven Years War survived the ruthless recatholicization promoted in Vienna and Rome during the seventeenth century.[65] The overwhelming majority of the dynasty's subjects, however, until the end of the eighteenth century when large numbers of Eastern Orthodox Christians came under Habsburg sway, were, or became, Roman Catholic. Many had made their decision at sword's point or close to it; the eradication of evangelical groups in Upper Austria during the Thirty Years War was especially brutal.[66] Nevertheless, while authentic faith and forced conversion are all but mutually exclusive, the passage of time and life in a relentlessly orthodox but familiar setting went far to validate Catholic belief for most people except the most resolute Protestants.

The Habsburgs had become mighty indeed. Ridden with fraternal rivalries at the beginning of the seventeenth century, and challenged with noble dissidence in its core kingdoms of Bohemia and Hungary, the dynasty had recovered through internal self-discipline, force of arms where necessary, and diplomatic opportunism. Its implacable support of militant Roman Catholicism was not admired through all of central Europe – Germany's Protestant princes remained wary of their emperors' territorial ambitions – but the Habsburg role as defender of the Church of Rome justified their rule among many of their subjects who might not have cooperated so readily with the house of Austria on political grounds alone. A kind of hegemony emanating from Vienna had settled over central and east central Europe, administratively imperfect perhaps, and in need of constant oversight, but functional all the same.

Chapter 3: Creating a State

A Dynasty at Risk

Even during the Rákóczi interlude the dynasty's armies fought victoriously onward through the south and east of Europe in the first two decades of the eighteenth century. Some of their most impressive triumphs came under the imaginative leadership of Prince Eugene of Savoy, the president of Joseph I's war council and a firm believer in using military power to enhance the house of Austria's standing in the world. Temesvár, taken from the Turks in October of 1716, had been a Hungarian royal redoubt in the Middle Ages. As a crown possession, it did not represent an expansion of Habsburg borders. Belgrade, captured a year later, had no tie to the crown of St. Stephen at all. The Peace of Passarowitz (Požarevac) signed on 21 July 1718 during the reign of Emperor Charles VI (1685–1740), Joseph's brother, marked the highpoint of Habsburg penetration of the Balkans against the Ottoman empire.

Joseph also pushed the borders of his holdings more directly into Italy. Milan, historically a fief of the Holy Roman Empire, had been governed by the Spanish Habsburgs since the middle of the sixteenth century. From that time on, Spain had dominated the north Italian plain while generally exercising much influence throughout the entire peninsula. That control threatened to unravel, however, with the death at the beginning of the eighteenth century of the last male Habsburg to rule Spain, Charles II (1661–1700). The frail king, a grotesque martyr to his dynasty's preference for inbreeding, had allegedly been near expiring for years. When the moment finally came, he agreed that his crown should pass to Philip of Anjou (1683–1746), a nephew of Louis XIV. The French king had a combustible list of grievances against the house of Austria, among them the unpaid dowry of his Spanish consort, the one-time Infanta Maria Theresa of Spain. The vacancy of the Spanish crown affected complex territorial arrangements in Europe and overseas rivalries as well; the Habsburg–Bourbon War of the Spanish Succession (1701–13) drew in Europe's major powers, including Great Britain and Holland, as well as a swarm of German principalities.

Leopold I had been trying to contain French expansion into Germany for several years; he had also begun preparing to defend Habsburg Italy and the Spanish Netherlands even before Charles II expired. Indeed, these lands were more important for the emperor than any possibility of acquiring royal Spain's empire in the New World. Leopold was still alive to see some imperial successes in northern Italy in 1701. Helped by a massive international coalition, his younger son, Charles, briefly assumed the Spanish title of Charles III in 1706. The Bourbons were thereby blocked from ruling both Spain and France, the stuff of nightmares for the British and the Dutch. By 1708 Joseph I, with the help of Eugene of Savoy, had taken over Milan and an assortment of other principalities in the north of Italy. He was only, he said, reasserting imperial feudal claims in the area.

Joseph died of smallpox in 1711. His brother Charles, now Emperor Charles VI, was in control not only of Spain but of much of central and east central Europe. France resisted ceding so much influence over the continent to the house of Habsburg; the British and the Dutch disliked the idea too. Charles VI yielded; Philip of Anjou ascended the Spanish throne as Philip V, but the Habsburgs held on to the Italian lands. Still edgy with Louis XIV just across their southern border, the Dutch now felt free to allow the Spanish Netherlands to become the Austrian Netherlands. The regime in Vienna had a plan for the area. The elector of Bavaria was eager for a royal title; indeed, as the husband of one of Leopold I's daughters, he was asking for the Spanish throne as well. To pacify him and secure the northwestern border of the Habsburg lands, the government in Vienna was thinking of offering the Wittelsbachs the Low Countries in exchange for their Bavarian patrimony.[1]

Like the reconquest of southeastern Europe from the Ottomans, the expansion of the Habsburgs into Italy had the air of the dynastic land-grab about it. The various accords which ended the War of the Spanish Succession, beginning with the Peace of Utrecht in 1713, together with side agreements in Rastatt and Baden a year later, left the Austrian Habsburgs with Milan, Mantua, and the Spanish fortifications, the so-called Presidii Ports, to the southwest of Tuscany. Moreover, Habsburg policy on the peninsula during the first years of the eighteenth century was at best arbitrary and at worst rapacious. Its status as an imperial fief made Milan and its environs liable to heavy taxation to support the house of Austria's forces locally.[2] Mantua, another imperial holding, was treated the same way. Unlike major Habsburg acquisitions in earlier times, the dynasty acquired its Italian principalities through military might and treaty alone without the process of give and take with local intermediate authority that had gone on in Bohemia, even in Hungary. Italians, therefore, were not collaborators in their own fate as were the estates of the house of Austria's central European kingdoms. Italian high culture dominated the Vienna court during the first half of the eighteenth century, but not because of the political preeminence of the land that produced it.

Habsburg caution with noble estates reaped great benefits for all sides during the reign of Charles VI. An active bisexual, he had yet to sire any legitimate children when Joseph I died leaving only two daughters. The house of Austria did not exclude the possibility of female succession: betrothal agreements for daughters always specified a payout to the bride in return for her renunciation of succession rights. In Spain, where women had ruled on occasion, the claims of princesses to thrones were even stronger. Leopold I's plans to divide the Spanish and central European holdings of his house between his two sons after the death of Charles II of Spain had taken account of possible female successions. Charles VI, however, had three problems. Because Ferdinand II had confirmed the rule of primogeniture in his house, the rights of Joseph I's daughters had to be set aside should Charles himself have only female heirs. Secondly, Charles wanted those lands to be acknowledged to be a unity, at least for testamentary purposes, to discourage bilateral agreements about future successions between individual lands and the crown.

The emperor also wished to keep other rulers from activating claims to his lands should the male line of his house die out. The Habsburg Austrian patrimony was technically held in fief from the emperor, an office that no woman had ever held.[3] While Charles did not challenge that tradition directly, he feared that his successor in the empire might redistribute the Habsburg German holdings. From 1712 or so on, he applied himself to this problem at the expense of just about every other serious responsibility he had.

Fearing total incorporation into Hungary should there be no legitimate successor in the Habsburg lands, the estates of Croatia and

Slavonia had spontaneously moved in 1712 to accept a female succession; now Charles sought to formalize this arrangement throughout all of his territories. His first effort, the Pragmatic Sanction of 1713, called for the Habsburg inheritance to pass to his daughters. Only his estates, however, could guarantee this outcome. The emperor promoted his agenda very cautiously, a measure of the importance he had assigned it. As a written and notarized expression of his will, the measure circulated first among his privy councilors and other chief officers in April of 1713. Negotiations began with his various estates after this, most of whom tried to extract some concessions in return.

As usual, the Hungarians were very demanding, trying to get guarantees of support from all the Habsburg lands for the defense of the kingdom in return for their assent. Charles refused to involve himself in all the conflicts such a proposal would surely create, but discussions went on. In the meantime, legitimate children finally arrived. A son, Leopold, was born in 1716, but died within the year. Three girls followed, the first of whom was Archduchess Maria Theresa. In 1719 the diets of Austria both above and below the Enns promised that only after the house of Habsburg died out completely could a new dynasty rule them, a delicate formula which protected both the rights of the estates and the interests of the house currently governing these provinces. The following year, both they and the estates in Bohemia accepted the arrangement. Hungary and Transylvania went along with it in 1722, though the Hungarians specified that they would recognize only Roman Catholic heirs of Leopold I, Joseph I, and Charles. The Austrian Netherlands assented in 1724; in 1725 the order was proclaimed in Lombardy.[4]

Foreign acknowledgement of the succession arrangements also fell into place; Spain under Philip V was the first in 1725. Were concessions required to get the consent of a ruler, Charles was ready to make them. In return for Russian support, the emperor declared himself willing to allow its rulers to begin expanding into southeastern Europe. In Germany Charles allowed the king of Prussia to acquire Berg and its chief city, Düsseldorf, once in the hands of the elector palatine. To get the signatures of the mercantile powers of Great Britain and Holland, the emperor promised to disband his new overseas East India Company.

At Charles's death in 1740, the Habsburg holdings were home to around 17 million people.[5] Some boundaries had receded a bit; a disastrous Turkish War, which Charles had entered as an ally of Russia, ended with the emperor formally withdrawing from Belgrade. Regaining Spain was all but impossible, if only because foreign powers, whose goodwill had contributed heavily to the survival of the monarchy after 1648, were unlikely to support such a move from Vienna. Nevertheless, the house of Austria's dominion in central Europe was more secure than it had ever been. Workable relationships had been hammered out between territorial ruler and the constitutional intermediate authorities of individual lands. Raw force had wiped out the most serious religious divisions between Habsburg rulers and their subjects; noble ambition for preferment and a general relaxation of spiritual anxiety throughout central Europe after 1648 soothed these tensions even more. The Pragmatic Sanction would become a key constitutional document within the house of Habsburg itself, steering its members through succession crises until the dissolution of the monarchy in 1918. The durability of these achievements, however, still depended on the personal and intellectual mettle of the Habsburg rulers themselves. And Charles's successor, Archduchess Maria Theresa, seemed, at her father's death, as improbable a candidate for that role as his house had ever brought forth.

The Unlikely Empress

The Habsburgs, as a rule, paid close attention to the education of their heirs-apparent. Maximilian I never sat still long enough for any tutor to do much with him, but his immediate successors in central Europe valued formal learning and even enjoyed it. Ferdinand I, Maximilian II, and Rudolph II were much influenced by their classical educations. Though Ferdinand spoke German haltingly as a youth, all three men were fluent in Latin, Spanish, and, to a lesser degree, French and Italian. Maximilan and Rudolph could handle themselves in Czech as well. The schooling of Ferdinand II and Leopold I was more narrowly religious – the latter actually prepared himself for a career in the church – but Joseph I was unusually conversant with both sacred and humanistic studies.

Maria Theresa's training was of a wholly different order. Charles VI died unexpectedly in 1740. Though assiduous in protecting his daughter's succession, he had given little thought to her intellectual development. The archduchess grew up a conventional *Hofdame*, uncritically pious and more at ease with intricate needlework and light reading than matters of state. Her husband since 1736, Francis of Lorraine (1708–65), was a good-natured man and a distant cousin; the couple shared Emperor Ferdinand III as a great-grandfather and generations of Habsburg ancestors back to the fifteenth century. He brought to the marriage his title –

the formal name of the dynasty would henceforth be the house of Habsburg-Lorraine – and a knack for canny investing. Entrusted with managing the state debt, Francis consolidated it, thus scaling back interest payments from 6 percent to 5. Though far less adept in political and military affairs, he was a great favorite of Maria Theresa's father.[6] It was Francis, not his wife, who sat in Charles VI's privy council.

New Threats From Abroad

As an instrument of foreign policy, the Pragmatic Sanction, along with its side agreements, was a dismal failure. The emperor was dead not quite a week before continental rulers great and small moved to exploit Maria Theresa's inexperience and questionable title to her inheritance. Just as Charles VI feared, with no son as emperor to uphold the integrity of the Habsburg holdings, others would annex, or at least occupy, his daughter's patrimony in short order. Francis of Lorraine was Vienna's choice for the imperial office, but Elector Charles Albert of Bavaria (1697–1744), married to Joseph I's younger daughter, had never agreed to the Pragmatic Sanction. Announcing his candidacy immediately, he was elected Charles VII in 1742. Frederick II (1712–86), the aggressive Hohenzollern ruler of Prussia, supported him. Frederick had for some time coveted one of the Bohemian crown lands to his south, the economically productive duchy of Silesia; all he needed was a pretext to gather it into his own holdings. Augustus III (1696–1793), elector of Saxony, king of Poland, and the husband of Joseph I's elder daughter, longed for a bridge between his German lands and his realm to the east. He repudiated his assent to the Pragmatic Sanction and backed the Prussian offensive in Silesia. Should Frederick be successful, the Saxon king–elector would be free to take what he wanted of Moravia. Other powers on the continent, especially France and Spain, were also willing to have the sprawling Habsburg conglomerate in central and east central Europe pared down to something less imposing. The Spanish were keen on reconstituting their presence in Italy.[7] Within the Habsburg lands themselves, even some of Maria Theresa's advisers anticipated the arrival of a Bavarian territorial ruler. The estates of Austria above the Enns openly supported the move.

Among the dynasty's nobilities, the Bohemians listened most sympathetically to the grievances of Joseph I's daughters. Their allegiance to the house of Habsburg had ebbed markedly during the last years of

Charles VI's reign; his Turkish wars had increased taxes in Bohemia and shifted the dynasty's interests to Hungary and southeastern Europe. The gradual displacement of the Bohemian magnates as a group at court by the French, Spaniards, and Italians, a process that continued throughout the eighteenth century, added to their discontent.[8] At the end of 1741, as French and Bavarian forces were occupying Prague, a large number of Bohemian aristocrats gathered in the city to pledge their support to Charles Albert of Bavaria as their king. Though the group did not make up a majority of their order, some came from the kingdom's greatest families: the Kinskýs, the Kolowrats, the Černíns, Waldsteins, and Choteks. The archbishop of Prague also joined them.[9]

The most seasoned ruler would have had trouble withstanding this onslaught of crises; the future of the novice Maria Theresa and of her dynasty's empire looked suddenly bleak. Luck, grit, and a keen understanding of public relations did much to save her. The birth in 1741 of a male heir to the Habsburg lands, the future Joseph II (1741–90), dispelled fears about the viability of her line. She turned for support to Hungary, an unlikely source given previous Habsburg experiences in the kingdom, but one where the high judge (*Judex curiae*), Count Pálffy, spoke out against Frederick II as soon as Prussian forces entered Silesia. Hard bargaining between the Hungarians and their new sovereign took place: the queen agreed to the perpetual exemption of nobility from taxation and to reintegration of some lands in the south of the kingdom into Hungary's central administration. In return, the estates loudly proclaimed their loyalty to the house of Habsburg and agreed to fund a force of over 100,000. Their generosity was unprecedented, and the empress thanked them effusively and in person with the infant Joseph clutched in her arms. The practical effect of this high drama was disappointing: the substantial aid that the diet granted never completely materialized. But the initial Hungarian enthusiasm for their new ruler moved Maria Theresa's other lands to return to her side, indeed, to support her generously. It also made Frederick II more cautious.[10]

Experience with Maria Theresa's enemies also made the Habsburg lands and some imperial principalities rethink their allegiances. Many of the German territorial rulers disliked Frederick of Prussia and suspected his every move. The Habsburg princess and her husband, who was the alternative to Charles Albert of Bavaria, thus found it relatively easy to change minds in the empire.[11] Frederick II's invasion of Silesia discouraged Bohemia's nobles from introducing yet another German dynasty into the kingdom. They did not like French occupation either. Charles

Albert's abject dependence on Louis XV's forces and his obedience to all that France asked of him lessened the Wittelsbach appeal even more. The Bavarian elector's regime in Prague collapsed quickly. In 1744 he tried to return, this time with the direct support of Frederick of Prussia, but the Czech nobility was now strongly pro-Habsburg. A year later, Emperor Charles Albert died; Francis of Lorraine was elected Emperor Francis I. The house of Habsburg-Lorraine had revalidated itself with Germany's territorial rulers who were happy to have the dynasty serve as a counterweight to the slippery Hohenzollern king and his army.[12]

The Treaty of Aix-la-Chapelle (1748) confirmed Frederick II's conquest of Silesia, but Maria Theresa did not give up hope of recovering it. She contested her loss through the Seven Years War (1756–63). Now allied with France, which shifted sides as England began supporting Prussia, the imperial forces often seemed near to retaking the province, but they could never beat Frederick decisively.[13] The Prussian king's resourcefulness did much to save him, but so did disorder and tactical incompetence in the Habsburg armies.[14] The Treaty of Hubertusburg (1763) confirmed the status quo ante bellum. The king of Prussia kept Silesia, but did promise to vote for Archduke Joseph in the imperial election. Threatened by hostile princes on almost all sides at the outset of her career, Maria Theresa had done astoundingly well.

Worrisome Frontiers, 1763–80

Maria Theresa's French alliance endured, bringing new security to the Habsburg hold on the Netherlands. A marriage in 1770 between the French dauphin, the future Louis XVI (1754–93), and her daughter, Archduchess Marie Antoinette (1755–93), further solidified the relationship. Other dynastic unions between the empress's numerous progeny and rulers in Naples, Parma, and Modena reinforced the Habsburg presence in Italy. But after the Seven Years War, Habsburg attention shifted to its strategic priorities in central and eastern Europe. The Turkish threat had subsided, but Russia clearly wished to play a greater and potentially hostile role in the Balkans. Such prospects worried Count Wenzel von Kaunitz-Rietberg (1711–94), a Moravian nobleman who was the dominant Habsburg minister in the latter decades of the eighteenth century. In 1771, he concluded a treaty with the Ottoman government to shore up the Habsburg position in southeastern Europe. Concern about Russian expansion also prompted Maria

Theresa to come to the table with Russia and Prussia in 1772 to divide Poland, opening up a process that led to the total dismemberment of that venerable kingdom in 1795. The Habsburg empire would come away with Galicia, the southern part of the realm. Further east, they had also acquired Bukovina from the Turks in 1775.

The empress and Kaunitz also had to keep close watch on the king of Prussia. Control of Silesia had put Frederick II in a good position to invade Bohemia, Moravia, and, through them, the Austrian lands themselves. A Prussian–Turkish alliance was always possible. Frederick's reputation in Germany had improved as well, particularly among Lutheran and Calvinist princes put off by the Habsburg government's harsh exile in the late 1770s of several thousand covert Protestants from the Austrian provinces to Transylvania where they were permitted to exercise their evangelical creed. Frederick II would also protect Bavaria from a Habsburg takeover during the same time. Larger military and political concerns at the end of the eighteenth century, the wars of the French Revolution chief among them, did turn the Habsburgs and the Hohenzollerns into confederates. Nevertheless, relations between the two remained sufficiently tense for Vienna to want to keep its hold on the imperial crown, the instrument that legitimated the Habsburg influence in Germany.[15]

Survival Through Reform, 1740–80

The most masterful foreign policy imaginable, however, could not protect the Habsburg monarchy without a restructuring of its government, its society, its economy, indeed, of the world-view that informed them all. Some reinforcement for this program, particularly after 1750, came from the changing notions of kingship that were reshaping royal governments in western Europe and even in German principalities such as Hanover and obstreperous Prussia. The seventeenth-century Glorious Revolution in England had brought forth a contractual philosophy of government that cast monarchs as executive governors of their lands and not as agents of God-on-earth, whose chief task was to oversee an immutable social and political order.[16] The good ruler was one for whom improving their states and the well-being of their peoples were ends in themselves.

Maria Theresa stood in awe of a divine Providence that had 'singled me out for this position without move or desire of my own.' But the lackluster performance of her army and her court officials during the War of the Austrian Succession (1740–48) and afterward persuaded her that she had to do more than preside over her empire in God's name. She herself had little trouble reconciling what she took to be her Maker's will with the interests of a more effective Habsburg government. In doing so, however, she would challenge institutions of her lands so entrenched that they seemed to be part of a higher order. Sketchy formal learning along with uncommon awareness of her own deficiencies made Maria Theresa a lifelong good listener. She needed sound advice and noted its absence when it was missing. The officials in service after Charles VI's unexpected demise in 1740 were, with the exception of Johann Christoph Bartenstein (1689–1767), the secretary of her privy council (*Geheimer Hofrat*), a self-protective and quarrelsome lot. Bohemian and Austrian magnates, entrenched in their separate chancelleries, used these offices as head-quarters for their personal and provincial affairs rather than for the business of their common sovereign. Altering the positions of such men and the institutions that sheltered them added yet another dimension to the pattern of 'contest and collusion' that had characterized Habsburg relations with the elites of their lands in the previous two centuries.[17]

Habsburg armies generally had enough troops. Compensating and supplying them, however, was always difficult. Funding still depended primarily on the largesse of provincial estates whose normal modus operandi was to authorize only as much money as was needed to secure their own territories. Crown officials and advisers, who came from the same social order as the noble members of the estates, usually had the same goals. Nevertheless, immediately after the Peace of Aix-la-Chapelle in 1748, Maria Theresa and a new and very energetic minister, Count Frederick William Haugwitz (1700–65), a displaced Silesian with little more than a title to his credit, asked the estates for a regular contribution to defray the costs of a standing force of 108,000. The money was to come from direct levies on noble demesnes; beyond collecting the tax and finding troops, the estates had no further role in the process. Enforcing these measures would be a new level of provincial government officials answerable to the *Directorium in Publicis et Cameralibus*. This office, created in 1749 and based on a Prussian model, combined the Austrian and Bohemian chancelleries. Headed by Haugwitz, it was to administer these provinces as a unity. Though the *Directorium* failed to resolve the conflicts over responsibility that had plagued the regime of her father, the direction in which Maria Theresa wanted to move was clear.[18]

The nobility protested vigorously; indeed, Maria Theresa's chancellor, Count Frederick von Harrach, whose family had been richly rewarded for its uncommon loyalty to the house of Habsburg, led the charge. Defending the policy, Haugwitz pointed to the threat from Prussia, calling it worse than what the Habsburgs had faced from Constantinople and France. Maria Theresa herself stood her ground; Harrach resigned after he refused to present the government program to the estates of Lower Austria, where he was also the provincial governor.

Haugwitz's argument hit home: the estates of Lower and Upper Austria, Bohemia, and Moravia accepted the new system of military funding more or less in full.[19] These provinces now voted such taxes for ten years at a time rather than on an ad hoc basis. The government paid its troops far more regularly than before; morale and performance improved accordingly. Nevertheless, the empress was not one to press her cause among estates when she did not have to, or thought that she might very well fail. Less exposed to Prussian invasion, the Netherlands and Lombardy had generally supported their own defense; they were not touched by her controversial reforms. Nor did the reforms have the impact on Hungary and Transylvania that they had in the Austrian lands and Bohemia.[20]

Personnel policies within Maria Theresa's armies changed too. Her predecessors had always ignored political boundaries in making command appointments; class, as well as loyalty and talent, had been the dominant considerations. Among Maria Theresa's important field marshals, Leopold von Daun (1705–66) was from the Rhineland and Gideon von Laudon (1717–90) from Latvia; they were a count and a free knight respectively. Probably on Kaunitz's suggestion, she moved to create a kind of military service aristocracy whose chief allegiance was to the sovereign rather than to their ancestral houses. At the beginning of 1757, she made patents of nobility available to all officers who had irreproachable records and had been in the Habsburg forces for at least 30 years. Six months later, she established the Order of Maria Theresa, to which candidates could nominate themselves, thereby insuring that no worthy person would be overlooked because of favoritism. The heraldry of the medal, which highlighted the ruler rather than the customary religious themes, bespoke the purposes behind this policy. Following the Prussian model, she also introduced general conscription.[21]

These changes did not remove aristocrats from the center of Habsburg power, however. The nobility from the Austrian lands had been losing its preeminence in the monarchy's officer corps since the Thirty Years War.

Of the 75 field marshals named between 1700 and 1740, only nine came from the hereditary lands.[22] But their names – Auersberg and Khevenhüller, Dietrichstein and Trautson, Herberstein and Harrach, to name only a few of the most illustrious – still appeared regularly among officers of both the state and the court.[23]

To keep the Habsburg monarchy alive in the competitive state system of the eighteenth century, Maria Theresa had to do more than reorganize and fund her armies. The loss of Silesia had been costly. By the eighteenth century, the region and its flourishing textile industry were contributing 25 percent of all monies collected from the rest of the Bohemian crownlands and the Habsburg Alpine holdings taken together. Credit had paid for the Seven Years War; by 1763, state debt came to 300 million florins, the modern equivalent of roughly three-quarters of the gross national product. Interest on this sum – about 35 million florins – amounted to 50 percent of all government income. More regular tax collections rationalized fiscal projections. It would do nothing, however, to increase the productivity of an already surly peasantry whose labor the landed nobility would almost surely increase to offset the pain of Vienna's new levies.

Mercantilism, or its central European variant called cameralism, was the contemporary remedy for ailing royal treasuries. Governments were to subsidize domestic manufacturers, then to skim off directly or indirectly some of their profits realized through sales abroad. The Vienna court had been discussing such programs since the latter decades of the seventeenth century. Philip von Hörnigk's *Österreich über alles wenn es nur will* (*Austria Over Everyone If Only It Wills It*, 1684) drew upon concepts of dependence and independence developed by the French pamphleteers Jacques de Cassan and Antoine Aubery to defend Louis XIV's military and political policies. Hörnigk rolled their ideas into an extended argument for strengthening the Habsburg empire through controlled economic growth. The goal was an 'independent' monarchy, a fiscal and commercial unity that it was the emperor's obligation to 'will'.[24]

Out-of-home industry was underway in the Habsburg lands by 1672 when the first factory producing wool opened in Linz in Upper Austria. Charles VI founded the Ostend Company to promote overseas trading, but lost interest in the project when England and Holland, whom he wanted as allies, objected to the potential competition. It was Maria Theresa and her advisers who made fostering manufacture and trade their central mission. An administrative department, the General Commercial Directorate, along with subsidiary offices in the provinces, supervised such enterprises throughout the empire. Where local technology and personnel fell short of the job, or were altogether absent, the regime offered special payments and exemption from military service to lure knowledgeable foreigners to the Habsburg lands. Italians and Netherlanders were especially prized for their skills in textile, paper, and glass manufacture. Where workers and employers would not replace outmoded production techniques, the government forced change upon them. For example, penalties were handed out to papermakers in Bohemia and Moravia in 1754 and 1756 for resisting the latest methods.

Theresan cameralism also looked upon the Habsburg holdings as a kind of inner-European colonial empire, self-sufficient enough to free the government from dependence on outside suppliers. The western areas of the empire were to house the empire's industrial base for which the eastern lands would serve as a kind of agricultural hinterland. While this scheme appeared plausible, its operation was often imperfect. Some provinces continued to send goods to traditional markets rather than to sell them at home. Hungary, for all practical purposes, was outside the system. The southeastern lands, Carinthia and Carniola, still directed the bulk of their exports further south to the Mediterranean. Other lands, however, were much easier to coordinate. By 1760 Maria Theresa had turned her Bohemian and Austrian domains into a limited tariff union, with Italy, the Netherlands, and Hungary excluded. In treating Hungary as a foreign country, the empress was thinking punitively as much as she was economically. That kingdom's estates were paying much lower taxes toward support of the military than were her other holdings; import and export duties from this ever vexing realm would enable her to lessen inequity and raise revenue at the same time. The Hungarians did, unfortunately, need the textiles and iron that were no longer coming from Silesia, a lucrative market that manufacturers in Upper Austria were happy to supply.[25]

Cameralists also argued that a large and healthy population was essential for economic expansion. To shield its public from epidemics, the Habsburg administration placed a *cordon sanitaire* around its borders with the Ottoman empire in 1770. Other problems affecting the common well-being, however, were not open to such simple and direct remedies. A vigorous and efficient peasantry was the mainstay of any well-fed army whose prowess would insure the monarchy's survival. Peasant lands taken together also generated more taxes for the central government than state income from noble properties.[26] By 1770–71, however, the condition of Maria Theresa's overwhelmingly agrarian subjects had become a deep concern. Rapid population growth – a universal feature of eighteenth-century life – had set off both a subsistence crisis and a rural mutiny in the Habsburg lands. Eye-witness accounts and a mounting backlog of unpaid taxes in Bohemia made it clear to Maria Theresa and her advisers that her empire had an agricultural productivity problem that could not be offset by raising taxes once again. Burdening the common people went against the empress's Christian principles; the small middle class bore the heaviest indirect imposts, the peasantry provided the greater part of direct taxation. The rural folk were also the pool from which the new conscript army was to come. Noble demesnes, aside from those in Hungary, were already contributing more heavily to the treasury. The answer was to make the monarchy's peasantry produce more by giving them a greater stake in their output.[27]

Both the empress and Kaunitz committed themselves to modifying the system of forced labor, or *Robot*, that was common throughout central and east central Europe. Maria Theresa applied her program to herself. During the 1770s she reduced the forced labor on her crownlands; in 1775 she renounced the practice altogether in favor of cash rentals. Crown peasants were also eligible for long-term leases. Though she did not enforce the same practice on noble estates, she hoped that aristocrats would follow her example. This was not hard to do in some areas of the monarchy: in Upper Austria cash payments were fast becoming the rule. *Robot* requirements were relatively light in Lower Austria as well.

Some noble Austrian, Bohemian, and Moravian landowners also wished to make their properties money-making operations. They too thought that the well-being of their peasants was crucial to success. Throughout the eighteenth century, the more enterprising among them had been deploying their serfs in remunerative wool and linen factories on their estates. When as many as 16,000 peasants died in Bohemia during the famine of 1771–2, an already troubling labor shortage worsened. To encourage textile production on his domains, Count Johann Nepomuk Bucquoi (1741–1803), one of Bohemia's more far-seeing landowners, ended forced peasant labor on his lands. Carl Egon von Fürstenberg, among the kingdom's richest noble landholders and governor of the realm from 1771 to 1782, believed that forced labor depressed both the economy and the moral fibre of the kingdom's rural population. He too commuted peasant labor on his holdings to rental payments.[28]

Original thinking, however, was beyond most landlords, as were qualms of conscience. During the famine, some Bohemian noblemen realized respectable profits by selling their grain in Saxony and Prussia rather than sharing their stores with the hungry.[29] Where large-scale agriculture prevailed – in Bohemia, Moravia, and the scraps of Silesia still left to the Habsburgs – peasants found themselves working far harder. As the price of grain rose in the eighteenth century, landlords throughout these regions were eager to extract as much as they could from their labor force. The average number of days per week spent at *Robot* rose from two to three and on some estates to six. Seeking greater profit still, some nobles simply took control of peasant fields altogether, either through outright confiscation or through conversion of long-term into short-term leases.

The government, however, was now resolved to aid its peasant subjects more frequently. In 1775 obligatory labor in Bohemia was set at three days a week for those occupying a quarter to a full holding. Maria Theresa also attempted to force nobles to pay something to peasants whose lands they had seized. The law also barred Bohemian landlords from raising rents, though they could put a price on pasturage and firewood, which had sometimes been free of charge. On the whole, however, Maria Theresa moved with great determination on the agrarian question. The patents setting labor requirements for Bohemia in 1775 and Styria two years later were issued without the assent of the appropriate estates.[30]

Maria Theresa's campaign to increase the output of the rural work-force in the Habsburg lands predictably strained the dynasty's relations with its noble landed elites. Complaints about official peasant policy were numerous and heated. Reductions in labor requirements increased pro-duction costs, the last thing that such landlords wanted. In 1771 the con-servative Bohemian court chancellor, Count Rudolph Chotek, adamantly opposed abrogating labor service and turning peasant property into private holdings.[31] None of this resentment, however, sparked protracted or massive resistance among the Bohemian nobles or their counterparts in Moravia, where *Robot* was also eased. To some extent, local circum-stance explained Moravian behavior: a very small but wealthy nobility with long attachments to the house of Habsburg dominated the province. Moravia was firmly Catholic, and its well-organized ecclesiastical estab-lishment determined to keep the margravate that way. Maria Theresa also rewarded such loyalty generously: in 1770 she turned the Moravian diocese of Olomouc into an archbishopric.[32]

More importantly, however, Bohemia and Moravia's nobilities were still well positioned to ride out attacks on their financial privileges as long as other aspects of their legal rights went untouched. Taxes on noble demesnes remained lower than the duties on peasant households. Bohemia's aristocrats were a relatively small segment of the population: a bare 0.1 percent of the kingdom's inhabitants. They therefore had little trouble preserving estates of scale.[33] When restrictions on forced labor raised manufacturing costs on some of their holdings, the very size of their properties allowed these men to shift part of their capital enterprises to agriculture and forestry from which they also profited splendidly. In 1780, more than 100 Bohemian noble families may have had incomes of between 50,000 and 100,000 florins annually. Only one aristocratic house in Frederick II's home base of Brandenburg was so fortunate. Moreover, Bohemian landowners accomplished this feat by making their existing holdings more productive rather than by taking over more land.

Vienna, therefore, had done little to alter the status of Bohemia's magnates in their kingdom. Even after Kaunitz disbanded the *Directorium* in 1761 in favor of an even more tightly centralized council of state, the Bohemian estates continued to sanction taxes and disputed the level at which they were set. Aristocrats retained their vast domains and patriarchal control over the rural folk whom they employed.[34] They circumvented *Robot* regulations by writing forced service into peasants' contracts and specifying just what that forced labor should be – transportation, or forestry, for example. Agricultural and domestic workers had to pay a wage tax.

The Habsburg regime also shifted criminal jurisdiction from landlords' courts to state tribunals in 1765. Nevertheless, noble property holders in Bohemia as well as in Galicia, Austria above and below the Enns, Styria, and Carinthia exercised lower justice on their domains until 1848. Some 900 patrimonial magistracies functioned in Bohemia alone. The government could only ascertain the rights of each party should landlord–peasant conflict arise. Though the crown could have confiscated noble land, it did not. On the contrary, the regime continued to treat manors as private property. Indeed, throughout the 1770s Maria Theresa, Kaunitz, even the outspoken heir-apparent, Joseph II, were not eager to violate such a fundamental right in Bohemia or anywhere else in the Habsburg domains. The enormous noble estates of Galicia also remained intact.[35] Distressed though some Bohemian aristocrats may have been over their sovereign's intrusion into local labor conditions, they did not turn their backs on the government in Vienna. No regime other than the one they already knew could defend them from predators like Frederick II. Their opposition to Maria Theresa's succession never escalated to outright rejection of Habsburg rule, as the king of Prussia expected.[36]

For its part, the government still made it worthwhile for nobles to collaborate with the house of Austria. The number of crown officials in the Habsburg provinces did grow, a sign that administrative control of the empire was shifting to a preeminent center. But the fledgling bureaucracy in Vienna offered employment for the well-educated smaller nobles of the monarchy. Indeed, Maria Theresa all but built them into her service. Young men had to be at least knights to function as captains of administrative districts. To remedy deficiencies in their education and to train them in diplomacy, military science, and cameral policy, their sovereign erected several academies throughout the empire, beginning in 1749 with the eponymous Theresianum. New chairs of political science, history, and natural law installed during a series of educational reforms during the 1750s extended the study of these disciplines to the university level.[37]

Access to the highest authority remained important to noble families. Both husbands and wives of aristocratic dynasties, even from secondary lines, figured prominently on court payrolls.[38] Only an intact Habsburg empire made noble cross-territorial holdings possible, and the wealthiest aristocrats were still eager to enrich themselves through this arrangement. The chief properties of two of the richest Hungarian houses in the eighteenth century, the Illésházy and the Serényi, were in Moravia. Conversely, the Berchtholds of Moravia had sizeable holdings and important relatives in Hungary.[39]

The most enlightened of nobles made these calculations: including state chancellor Kaunitz himself. One side of him scorned the typical prejudices of his class, territorial particularism among them. Bohemia, in Kaunitz's opinion, was among the monarchy's German lands and he applauded the unification of the Austrian and Bohemian chancelleries in 1749.[40] Though on civil terms with many members of the Bohemian and Moravian estates, particularly the latter, Kaunitz had little patience with their demands that government and administration stay in local hands. In his opinion, such arrangements were only unwelcome challenges to the kind of central regime that the Habsburg empire desperately needed. Provincialism, he said in 1763, ran counter to sound reason.

Kaunitz also believed that the lot of the common man had to improve. In 1771-2, against the wishes of most of the Bohemian nobles, and even against Maria Theresa herself at that moment, he argued for the reduction of *Robot* to three days a week. Though he backed away from this step

in 1775 because he did not want to give the appearance of being in-
timidated by a peasant uprising then underway, he consistently endorsed
radical reform of agrarian labor requirements. He applied the prescrip-
tion to his own holdings in Moravia, freeing the serfs there in 1773.[41]

Nevertheless, raw personal ambition tied him as closely as it did any of
his more conventional colleagues to the Habsburgs and their interests.
Like others of his class, such as the enormously wealthy Liechtensteins,
Kaunitz wanted to be made a prince of the Holy Roman Empire with a
vote in the imperial diet. To exercise the latter privilege, however, he
had to hold land from the emperor directly. Kaunitz hoped to use some
claims that his family had in the remote province of East Frisia to support
his quest. His competitor, however, was none other than Frederick II of
Prussia. The chancellor, therefore, had every reason to do what he
could to strengthen Habsburg defenses against the Hohenzollern ruler.
When Maria Theresa's French allies had to abandon East Frisia in 1758,
Kaunitz's claims fell through. To the Moravian aristocrat's great chagrin,
Joseph II, when he became German emperor, gave him no more than
a consolation prize – a personal right to be called an imperial prince
but without voice or vote in the diet. More vexing yet in the competitive world of the court, this was the same distinction that imperial
vice-chancellor Rudolf Colloredo (1706–88), major-domo Joseph
Khevenhüller (1706–76), and field marshall Karl Batthyány (1698–1772)
also held.[42]

Even in Lombardy, which remained something of an administrative
and political anomaly within her lands, Maria Theresa challenged traditional privilege. Unlike the Austrian provinces, Bohemia, and Hungary,
where territorial rulers and estates had both historic constitutional standing and over two centuries' practice at developing a working co-existence,
the Habsburg presence in Italy was far less controlling. In Milan, a local
patriciate, acting in a senate, remained the operative political authority
in the city and its adjacent territories; the governor from Vienna, or
earlier from Madrid, acted as a kind of bridge figure between the ruler
and the machinery of municipal self-government, and vice versa. Judge-
ment guided him far more than did explicit rules and procedures.[43] The
relative informality of these arrangements did not deter Maria Theresa
from further maximizing the financial resources of the area for military
needs. While she never forced Lombardy into her customs union or to
accept the tax program imposed on the Austrian lands and the kingdom
of Bohemia, she did substantially reorganize her administration in northern Italy. Between 1743 and 1745, the governor's office was divided in

two. One handled civil functions; the second concentrated solely on military concerns that included determining what revenues were needed, then collecting them regularly.

Such changes put new constraints on the powers of Milan's senators and their counterparts in Venetia and in Parma, Modena, and Tuscany, which were governed by cadet branches of the house of Habsburg-Lorraine. Nevertheless, as in Bohemia and her Austrian provinces, the empress managed to work her will in Italy without alienating traditional local elites. Regional patriciates remained the largest property holders in areas where the Theresan program was carried out. Italian notables such as Gian Luca Pallavicini, a Genovese patrician, and Karl von Firmian (1712–82), the offspring of a house in the Trentino that had sent generations of bishops into the Habsburg western lands and the empire, served as the general representatives, or 'plenipotentiaries', of the Vienna regime in Lombardy.[44]

From a narrowly administrative standpoint, the impact of the Theresan reforms was slightest in Hungary. There, the nobility remained exempt from all general taxation and retained all of the authority it had traditionally exercised in county life. Though some division of labor took place during the eighteenth century, nobles as a class remained responsible for oversight of taxation for military purposes; upkeep of bridges, roads, and hospitals; village government; regulation of building projects, commerce and trade policy; property registration and surveying; and police and fire protection.[45]

The queen's reluctance to challenge the Hungarian nobility head on did not, however, constrain her efforts to ensnare as many of them as she could into her circle of supporters. Though a few Hungarian noble families, both husbands and wives, were part of the court by the end of the seventeenth century and thereafter, their numbers never remotely approached those of the Austrians, Bohemians, Italians, and Germans who attached themselves to the Habsburg establishment. By creating a corps of Hungarian bodyguards in 1760, Maria Theresa did attract more of Hungary's petty aristocracy to the court in Vienna. She also furthered good relations with her estates in Hungary by transferring direct control of her officials in Croatia, its port city of Rijeka (Fiume), and the recently acquired Banat to the Hungarian crown.[46]

The Theresan regime was equally circumspect in taking on the other major privileged institution of the Habsburg lands – the church. Sincerely devout, and committed to promoting Catholic orthodoxy, the empress's extensive efforts to change the institutional relationship of government, state, and church during her regime seems somewhat out of character. Nevertheless, contemporary criticism of the church, both in her own lands and in Germany more widely, echoed some of her own concerns for the well-being of her faith. In Venice, the clergyman–historian Ludovico Muratori (1672–1750) argued that a decline in the quality of general piety could be arrested only through good pastoral work and sound education rather than the gaudy pilgrimages and countless holidays that were then staples of popular devotions. Similar sentiments were also circulating around northern Italian universities and those in the Netherlands. Called Jansenism, these ideas did not have much in common with the Calvinist-tinged variant of Catholicism that once plagued the regime of Louis XIV, but stressed the need for Catholic institutional reform. Reducing the number of cloisters and curbing clerical influence in political councils were critical goals. Another strand of this thinking, Febronianism, had taken root in Germany. Named after the *nom de plume* of Nicholas von Hontheim (1701–90), an auxiliary bishop of Trier, it gave the secular state a supervisory role in religious affairs at the expense of the papacy.[47]

Such ideas along with her firm conviction that church entitlements depressed the productivity of her subjects as much as did a reactionary aristocracy or lethargic servile labor moved Maria Theresa into action. By 1751, she seems to have concluded that increasing the wealth of the church through property donations, many of which had come from her own ancestors, made little economic sense. In 1762, persuaded that many monks spent most of their time avoiding labor of any sort, she proposed reducing their numbers. The hostile reaction of the bishops in her lands was a more or less foregone conclusion. Nevertheless, with Kaunitz's advice she created a government department that allowed the state to intrude far more easily into ecclesiastical affairs. All church business, save matters of purely spiritual concern, was to be handled by secular authorities. This step was followed by a number of decrees that significantly altered the role of Catholic institutions in the Habsburg empire during the last 15 years or so of the empress's reign. Limits were set on the number of future novices and assets these houses could acquire. A young person could not take final vows before the age of 24. Some small cloisters in Lombardy, where the number of such establishments was especially large, were simply disbanded. Maria Theresa redirected the monies once dedicated to monastic institutions to more intense parish activity. Some of these funds were used to improve public and higher education, though the regime's greatest windfall of erstwhile church revenues came from Jesuit property confiscated after Pope Clement XIV (1705–74) disbanded the order in 1773. Public schools were often put up on these lands, which now belonged to the state; in some instances, Jesuit elementary schools were simply turned over to state-sponsored education.[48]

Nevertheless, Maria Theresa did not turn her back on all the interests of her church. She did not bar the clergy from the classroom altogether. When Kaunitz recommended importing Protestant scholars from Germany to improve the quality of the university faculties in the Habsburg lands, she flatly refused. She did, however, try to appoint Catholics who were more or less abreast of modern disciplines and outlooks. Most importantly, the two men who spearheaded the drive in her administration to reform public education in her administration were clergymen. Johann Ignaz von Felbiger (1724–88) was a Silesian abbot, and Gratian von Marx (1720–1810) was a Piarist, an order that was closely attuned to the science of the Enlightenment in the eighteenth century. And while Maria Theresa was eager to limit the number of church holidays that took people away from work, she also looked for ways to get more of her subjects into churches on Sundays.[49]

Thus Maria Theresa initiated fundamental, to some alarming, changes in church–state relations in the Habsburg empire; she also adjusted the parameters that would shape the religious politics of her successors both in Rome and within their own domains. Yet, along with aristocracy, Catholicism and clericalism were still at home in her lands. Faced with Enlightenment secularism and an era of lackluster papal rule, her clergy had reason to be grateful for the empress's genuine spiritual concerns. Her practice of reform without revolution, a common goal of several contemporary German territorial rulers and their advisers, did much to preserve the links of the monarchy with the elites of the Habsburg lands.[50]

Indeed the privileged generally had good reason to think that they had a meaningful stake in the dynasty's survival. A reign that began under attack from much of Europe would end in a time of some prosperity, particularly in the Bohemian and Austrian lands. Great landowners whose properties reached throughout the empire had no reason to question the notion that 'the ruler was the state – not in the sense that he [she] could always get his [her] way, but in the sense that no one else had concerns coterminous with the state.'[51] Most important of all, the Theresan fiscal reforms had met their central purpose by the empress's death. A more or less sustainable armed force of 300,000 was now in place to caution potential aggressors against invading the Habsburg lands.[52]

The Limits of Collaboration, 1780–90

If the reign of Maria Theresa was a lesson in the art of the possible, her successor, Joseph II, made his mark by ignoring political realities. That he was ambitious and arrogant was common knowledge long before he ascended the various thrones of his territorial inheritance in 1780. Many of his policies, like those of his mother, would indeed have a lasting impact on the Habsburg monarchy. What many of his measures did during his lifetime, however, was to antagonize the more powerful of his subjects so thoroughly that he had to repeal many of his innovations and reforms before his death in 1790.

Frequently indulged as a child by the ladies-in-waiting to his mother, but hyperdisciplined on other occasions, Joseph developed into a man who was at once cocky and insecure, always difficult to counsel and to aid. His schooling, unlike that of his mother, had been the topic of detailed and repeated discussion among his parents, court officials, and his instructors. He was thoroughly, in some ways quite progressively, educated under the general supervision of Maria Theresa's trusted Bartenstein. His studies included history, which was to teach the archduke the intricacies of state relations and enhance his understanding of law. Theology and philosophy, presented to him in acceptably orthodox terms, were to sharpen his moral sensibilities. He received, however, thorough schooling in rationalist thinking; he also picked up a smattering of unconventional views from the ongoing discussions about the Enlightenment in western Europe at the court in Vienna, as well as from some of his reading in political economy and theory. He had heard of the state as an instrument for promoting the common good long before he actually tried to make it so.

All of these experiences probably led him to the views of his position and its possibilities that drove him at the outset of his career: that he was responsible for the general welfare of his subjects; that reform of certain institutions, particularly of a still overly rich and self-serving church, was crucial to his goals; that the influence of anachronistic political institutions, especially in Germany, was to be tempered. While he did allow room for traditional behaviors, such considerations were not high on his list of priorities.[53] Perhaps most shocking of all, at least to his family, was his enthusiastic admiration of Frederick II of Prussia, both for the latter's military exploits and his efforts to promote a more efficient and productive regime in his lands.[54]

Reigning monarchs and their heirs-apparent were often at loggerheads, but relations between Joseph and Maria Theresa were an exemplary case of the ordinary. Holy Roman emperor and, by 1765, co-regent with his mother in the Habsburg lands, Joseph was far keener than Maria Theresa to push her reforms to radical conclusions that she almost reflexively avoided. To spare himself the frustration of dealing with her – the empress's long hours at prayer and devotions after her husband's death in 1765 particularly tried him – he absented himself from a court whose formality he found tiresome in any case. The empress, whose relationships with most of her 12 living children were more managerial than maternal, did her best to put a good face on his travels. That he was introducing himself to foreign courts without instruction worried her, but Joseph was, she said, acquainting himself with a variety of European rulers and customs. She acknowledged that both of them gained something from policies he recommended after making these trips. Nevertheless, Maria Theresa saw in his travels a criticism of herself and kept track of his itinerary anxiously.[55]

Joseph thus came to power with all of his dynasty's familiar determination to preserve its position in its lands and in European affairs. Such a mission required him, or so he believed, to restructure the customs and institutional arrangements of his realms, the quicker and the more thoroughly the better. Maria Theresa had opened up her circle of advisers to talented members of the middle class, but still preferred to work with clever and well-educated aristocrats. Joseph's closest collaborators were not his nobles – Kaunitz, who lived until 1794, had considerable influence over Joseph II's foreign policy, but had ever less to say in domestic affairs. The emperor, however, when he made use of collaborators at all, turned to intellectuals like the jurist Joseph von Sonnenfels (1733–1817), a clear-headed, if distressingly opinionated, legal reformer and cameralist. His service to the state, not his lineage, had brought him his title. Gottfried van Swieten (1733–1803), the son of one of Maria Theresa's key advisers, was particularly close to Joseph in cultural affairs. 'From industry springs every good', sing two figures in his German translation of the text for Joseph Haydn's oratorio *The Seasons*, completed 11 years after Joseph's death but expressing a view that the emperor never forsook.[56]

The sweep of the Josephinian reform program was breathtaking, both in the number of institutions it affected and the depth of its impact.

Religion was not to interfere with participation in the larger purposes of the state, chief among which was to foster productivity in every level of society. Between 1781 and 1783 he granted toleration to the major Protestant confessions – Lutheran and Calvinist – and the Eastern Orthodox Church. The step greatly pleased the reformed magnates of eastern Hungary, a group which had often regarded the Habsburgs as agents of Satan himself.[57] Many of the restrictions on Jews disappeared as well, particularly laws that held them apart from the Christian population around them. They could now live outside of specific ghettos, though the tax on Jews (*Judensteuer*), paid to the central government, endured until the second half of the nineteenth century.

With the Catholic establishment, Joseph picked up where his mother left off. Dismayed at the emperor's concessions to heretofore disadvantaged religious minorities, the church was brought into ever closer alignment with government purposes. The still huge number of cloistered establishments in the Habsburg lands was sharply reduced; their residents, whose chief preoccupation was theoretically prayer and contemplation and not teaching or hospital duties, were turned out into a secular society that was wholly unfamiliar to many of them, particularly the women. The revenues that supported these foundations went instead to parishes for educational and pastoral work among people whose labor was far more important for Joseph's state. When the majority of the bishops of the emperor's lands, particularly the archbishop of Vienna, Cardinal Christoph Anton Migazzi (1714–1803), resisted these innovations, Joseph took over supervision of clerical education. In 1784 he set up state-run general seminaries in each of his provincial capitals and put theological studies in the hands of universities and other state-run schools of higher education.

Joseph also continued with the agrarian reforms begun by his mother and Kaunitz. He himself had long supported the project and indeed pressured his mother into going further than she had wanted. In 1781 he issued an order removing most of the conditions of serfdom that still burdened the peasantry of his lands, a measure he extended to Hungary in 1785. Serfs were no longer bound to the land, though if they remained, they were still answerable to their noble masters. Unless landlords had credentialed qualifications for the position, however, they could no longer act as judges in manorial magistracies. A higher crown official had to examine fines or imprisonments handed out to a peasant if the latter lasted more than eight days.

Joseph's assault on customary privileges in the name of increased general productivity extended to the cities and towns of the monarchy as well. Guild restrictions were a serious restraint on manufacture and commerce, and Maria Theresa had done little about them. Joseph, however, chipped away at such regulations industry by industry. By the end of his reign he had made considerable progress, especially in the textile sector.[58]

Political and social corporatism was clearly at risk in the Habsburg lands, symbolically as well as concretely. Joseph not only sharply increased the number of elementary schools throughout the empire, but allowed Jews and members of other Christian confessions to sit with Catholics in their classrooms. Other public facilities were opened to groups previously excluded as well. The first Jew to hold a law degree from the University of Prague received it in 1790. Such policies further threatened the near-monopoly over learning once held by the church. Archbishop Migazzi, once sympathetic to some of the Theresan reforms, bitterly criticized the government for encouraging contact between Christian and Jew. Even the dynasty lost some of its august apartness, as Joseph opened some of his properties in Vienna, the Prater in the Jewish ghetto of the city, and the Augarten, which was not far away, for general public use.[59]

That he wanted to tie his lands as closely to their ruler as he could was utterly clear. Joseph's removal of the Hungarian crown of St. Stephen, the Bohemian crown of St. Wenceslaus, and the ducal hat of Lower Austria, stored in the monastery of Klosterneuburg outside Vienna, to Vienna itself betokened his intention to rework the structure of functional dualism that had prevailed in the Habsburg lands for decades. In the same vein, Joseph refused outright to be crowned king of Hungary. In 1784, he announced that German would be the common administrative language of his realms. The Hungarians, who had continued to use Latin for this purpose, took great offense at the order, as did the Italians. The following year, to further judicial and legal consistency in Hungary and Croatia, he abolished the Hungarian counties, the traditional seat of aristocratic influence. To replace them he created districts of approximately the same size, which royal commissioners would administer.

In 1786, Joseph tried to extend to the Netherlands his ecclesiastical reforms and a thoroughly renovated penal code. The latter, among other things, abolished capital punishment in favor of hard labor and various types of open-air disgrace. This was a region whose particularistic subjects Maria Theresa had always been reluctant to antagonize. He also sought to divide the territory up into nine administrative districts à la hongroise, each of which was supervised by an intendant. Under them were royal commissars who carried on the work of the state in the subdivisions of each unit. Joseph also enforced conscription with unaccustomed rigor in the Low Countries. Local estates, which had long played major roles in government and legal institutions, lost their legislative powers, as did municipalities with similar rights. The same policies were applied in the Habsburg Italian lands: the senate and council of state in Milan were disbanded and replaced with a governing council named by the crown. Here, too, intendants assisted by royal commissars ran the actual business of local administrative districts. Practical enforcement of Vienna's directives was in the hands of the 'plenipotentiary'. A governor, usually a cadet member of the house of Habsburg, was also empowered to deal with a carefully circumscribed range of business.[60]

Nowhere was Joseph's attack on aristocratic entitlement more forthright than in his bureaucratic reforms. Here, too, his goal was to strengthen the role of the monarch. This was a mission in which the emperor had a great deal of help. Sonnenfels shared his vision, as did Karl Anton von Martini (1726–1800), a political theorist, who was especially interested in improving education, especially in the training of civil servants. Perhaps the most enduring part of the Josephinian reforms was the view these men had of public administration: they saw it as a skilled profession with its own identity and ethos. Through such prescriptions the emperor hoped to assemble a body of officials whose loyalty was to himself and the state.[61]

Maria Theresa had concluded early in her career that a ruler's advisers were chosen to do more than to compete with the ambitions of their colleagues. Joseph's efforts in this vein were therefore not unfamiliar. But what the mother had written comparatively small, the son proclaimed in capital letters. Serving him was akin to taking clerical orders. 'He who is only interested in the perquisites or honors attached to his service, or takes serving the state as an incidental consideration, is better off saying this right away and leaving a position to which he is neither worthy nor inclined.' The larger public welfare, not the advancement of a class, was the central responsibility of government. The first duty of his officials was to meet performance standards assigned to them, not to distinguish themselves as individuals. Birth did not qualify one for a position. Education did, particularly legal studies.[62] The likeliest sources of such men were the small nobility and the middles classes of the Habsburg lands, people who were far more inclined toward uncompromising loyalty to the crown, even if they received service titles. Though the greater efficiency that he hoped to realize from these changes did not live on after him, Joseph's bureaucratic ideals remained alive in the Habsburg empire until its end.[63]

Though many of Joseph's statist convictions were clearly on a collision course with both the traditional constitutions of his lands and their aristocratic and clerical champions, his bureaucratic reforms went largely unchallenged, even in Hungary, which was otherwise unreceptive to many of his innovations. In this case, the need to add personnel to meet the expanding duties of central administration provided employment opportunities for several classes of society. The ratio of the great nobility in high administrative position to the numbers of non-noble officials who found government office decidedly favored the latter. Nevertheless, between 1781 and 1841 the number of high aristocrats in major judicial appointments and in the various government chancelleries – for Hungary, the Illyrian provinces, Transylvania, and Galicia as well as the Austro-Bohemian department – also increased modestly.[64]

But Joseph's peoples finally lost patience with most of the emperor's revolution from above, encapsulated in the 6206 decrees he issued during his nine-and-a-half-year reign. In 1787 aggrieved elites in Lombardy, the Netherlands, and Hungary exploded in protest against his administrative reforms. Even estates in the Tyrol, the only part of the Habsburg patrimony to remain steadfastly Catholic during the Reformation, rose up against his efforts to eradicate their privileges, among them the right to determine whether or not they participated in military campaigns beyond their borders.[65]

The breadth and depth of hostility throughout his lands truly shocked Joseph. Having once lifted many curbs on free speech and the press in the hope that broad public discussion of his policies would lead to general approval, he reinstituted strict police censorship to counter sedition. The uproar, however, did not keep him from cobbling together a program of tax reform that turned out to be the last straw for an enraged population, particularly in rural areas. Promulgated in the name of fairness, but designed to give the state greater access to agricultural wealth, it in effect insured that a portion of a peasant's income went directly to Vienna – about 12 percent of what he made. Around 18 percent went to the landlord, the church, and various local institutions. The peasant himself could keep roughly 70 percent of what he made.[66]

The program never went into effect, but the damage had been done. Joseph thought that peasants would support him for abolishing serfdom;

instead, they withheld taxes altogether in the hopes that further concessions would grant them portions of noble lands. Aristocratic reaction was
even angrier. Joseph's earlier emancipation orders had hinted that landlords would be compensated for loss of serf labor; the 1789 program was
simply an attack on proprietary income.[67] The Bohemians, whose hold
on court and high administrative positions had slipped even further,
organized to defend their privileges. But it was in Hungary that the
resistance was most serious. Having had their exemptions from taxation
confirmed by Maria Theresa in 1741, the nobility of the kingdom was
prepared to mount armed resistance against a government in Vienna that
threatened such liberties. By 1790, an embattled and very bitter Joseph
had given up reform for retreat, countermanding some of his orders even
as he lay dying.

Traces of the Future

Noble dissidence, even rebellion, were familiar challenges to Habsburg
governments. Past episodes, however, had ended either wholly on the
dynasty's terms, as in Bohemia after the Battle of the White Mountain,
or, more frequently, through mutual, albeit imperfect, accommodation
with the estates as in Hungary and Transylvania. At the close of the
eighteenth century, however, some discontented aristocrats seemed to be
taking a new direction in establishing a modus vivendi with their territorial sovereign. For all the non-Czech origins of many of Bohemia's great
families, they had kept alive the hallowed belief in their right to speak
for the 'Bohemian nation', of which all those who lived in the kingdom
and its crownlands were a part.[68] They were a bit fuzzy on what that
'Bohemian nation' was: themselves corporately, or a broader generality
that they alone could represent. Nevertheless, as increased taxation and
the economic inconveniences of agricultural reform pressed ever harder
on some of these men, they began enlisting scholars to reinforce their
conviction and increase the general understanding of what a nation was.

Opponents of Josephinian centralization were prominent in the
movement. There was Franz Anton Nostitz, a passionate patriot and, as
the high burgrave of Prague, the chief territorial official in the kingdom.
Tutor to his sons was Franz Martin Pelcl (1734–1801), an equally patriotic historian of his Bohemian homeland. Others eager to know something of Bohemian history in order to argue coherently against Joseph's
misuse of power had once served the government in Vienna. Franz Karl

Kressl von Qualtenburg had at one point been Bohemian and Austrian chancellor; Count Prokop von Lažanský was an erstwhile president of the unified Austrian–Bohemian chancellery. The latter, and the reform-minded Count Bucquoi, wrote the *Desiderata* of the Bohemian diet in 1790. Presented in 1791 to Joseph's successor, his brother Leopold II (1747–92), the document called the nobility, and not the monarch, the spokesmen for all the peoples of their land.[69]

An even greater departure from the status quo was the concoction of routine grievance and revolutionary politics sweeping through Hungary. From 1780 to 1790 a flourishing pamphlet and periodical literature, sometimes radically reformist, less often in defense of the *ancien régime*, had appeared among Hungarians living in Vienna, where the ideas of the French *philosophes* circulated widely, if unofficially. A key figure was György Bessenyei (1747–1811). A member of the Hungarian lesser nobil- ity and a great admirer of Voltaire, he was brought up and educated in the Habsburg capital; he joined Maria Theresa's Hungarian bodyguard in 1765. Indeed, the empress took a personal interest in Bessenyei, giving him a sinecure as her honorary court librarian. Leaving the guard in 1773 to represent Hungarian Calvinists in the Habsburg capital, he also devoted himself to a variety of literary projects. Some of these explicitly questioned the entire institution of absolute monarchy. That Joseph II did not like him, indeed withdrew the writer's pension, could have prompted or confirmed Bessenyei's views.

The Enlightenment ideals that attracted Bessenyei, even the anti-absolutist aspects of the French Revolution itself, which began in the summer of 1789, touched a live nerve in many Hungarian nobles, great and small. Anti-clericalism, a constant in *philosophe* rhetoric, was especially appealing to the Calvinists in the east. Ordinarily the most self-serving of men, these aristocrats also reworked the fashionable terminology of social contracts and rights of people to justify their historic privileges as weapons against centralized monarchy. During the summer of 1790, the organized Hungarian gentry demanded that Leopold II sanction far-reaching restraints on royal power as a way of restoring what they believed was their true constitution. This argument by itself was hardly novel. Bessenyei's critique of absolutism, however, had a singular spin. He applied the revolutionary language of the rights of man to the rights of small nations. Such ideas were very difficult to square with Habsburg rule in the kingdom. By the beginning of the nineteenth century, and now back on his properties in eastern Hungary, Bessenyei would declare 'the nation', and not the integrity of the Habsburg domains as a whole, to be the prime concern of political activity. The Habsburgs could continue to hold the crown of St. Stephen only if they respected this understanding of their constitutional duties and operated a separate court in Hungary, an arrangement finally realized in the Dual Monarchy established in 1867.[70]

But this was a future program. The task at hand for the Habsburg regime was to subdue the uproar that had engulfed it and parts of western Europe shortly before Joseph's death. The French Revolution had already put Europe's venerable dynasties on notice that the deference of their subjects might be only conditional. At the center of these troubles was Joseph's sister Marie Antoinette, the queen of France. The prospects for forceful diplomacy out of Vienna were doubtful. Toward the end of his life, Joseph had withdrawn from a disastrous war in the Balkans that he had entered into in order to burnish Habsburg prestige. Even the monarchy's borders were less secure, as Joseph had cavalierly managed to offend as many people in the Holy Roman Empire as he had in his own lands. Regarding the whole structure as an anachronism, he cancelled all payments for imperial officials in 1782, thereby alienating the men most committed to keeping German territorial states in the Habsburg orbit. A clumsy attempt to trade the Austrian Netherlands for Bavaria in 1785 brought the ageing Frederick II into a league with the electors of Saxony and Hanover and a string of lesser imperial princes to block Habsburg expansion. By 1786 Joseph had abandoned this scheme, but his reputation in the empire had suffered considerably. Prussia could now plausibly claim to be the protector of Germany's numerous polities, Protestant and Catholic alike.[71]

Maria Theresa and Joseph shared the same goal: to put the government and economy of the Habsburg monarchy on a footing that would secure its status as a major power. Both rulers were open to contemporary ideas that would help them realize this agenda. An instinct for the important and a willingness to accept a draw rather than to press on for decisive victory allowed the empress to accomplish a great deal. Joseph created a tradition of state service that lives on even today, but some of his most far-seeing and intelligently crafted policies failed ignominiously because of his inability to calculate his subjects' responses to them. An ideal ruler would have combined the better qualities of both mother and son. In 1790, with the Habsburg empire now in peril from within, no one stood in greater need of all these talents than did the dead emperor's brother and successor.

Chapter 4: Holding the Center

Rescuing the Habsburg Monarchy from Within

Grand duke of Tuscany since 1765 with his capital in Florence, Archduke Peter Leopold – the Peter was a courtesy to his Russian godmother, Tsarina Elizabeth, and common only in Italian renderings of his title – had personal failings of his own. Fits of depression and sexual compulsions assailed him throughout his life. While the latter distraction yielded an array of legitimate children, some of whose progeny continue the family of Habsburg-Lorraine and its branches even today, it also ensnared Leopold in countless illicit liaisons. But he had more attractive qualities too, some of which replicated Joseph II's better traits. The new emperor shared his elder brother's distaste for court protocol and his liking for people beneath his station, attitudes that their mother often deplored. He was, however, intellectually more versatile than Joseph and better educated too. He was uncommonly observant of other people as well as an adept and eager student with a keen interest in science and technology and a knack for languages.

Leopold went to Florence as a champion of social, fiscal, and legal reform; once there, he quickly began consulting leading figures of the north Italian Enlightenment, Pompeo Neri (1706–76) for one, who were also committed to these same goals. Their immediate challenge was to help the principality recover from protracted famine after a series of bad harvests. To encourage economic development, Leopold made the entire grand duchy a free trade enclave for grain, flour, and bread. The program won him the plaudits of Europe's Physiocrats, advocates of unrestricted circulation of basic commodities as a way of increasing general wealth. The Habsburg grand duke created a state office for commerce, skilled crafts, and trade, loosened guild regulations on manufacturing, and tightened state control over taxation and revenue disbursement. Like his mother and brother, he secularized monastic lands and put in place administrative innovations which reworked everything from the army to the police to sanitary regulations. Privately very critical of his brother's bureaucratic absolutism, Leopold even gave some thought to introducing a form of parliamentary representation in Tuscany, an idea that Joseph successfully scotched.[1] Leopold was not beyond making some exceptions to these rules for the sake of special interests, particularly his own and those of his dynasty. But what he promoted had the effect of unifying the grand duchy under one controlling legal authority – the state.

The programs that Leopold and his Italian advisers developed made Tuscany a kind of model for princely enlightened reform. That he was successful and Joseph II, who had similar goals, saw what he had done unravel, was in part the result of the differing conditions in which they worked. Florence was not the vast and multivariate Habsburg empire. Leopold's Medici predecessors had accustomed their citizenry to rule from the top, something that the Habsburgs in Vienna had yet to accomplish. Nor did he have to cope with predatory neighbors, either on the Italian peninsula or in Europe as a whole. Commerce and manufacture were time-honored pursuits in the city of Florence itself.

Leopold also imposed his measures more tactfully than did his brother, introducing them as 'academic experiments' in single regions rather than throughout his land all at once. Tuscany's traditional elites did protest at times, but Leopold sensed how far he could push these men before he had to give way. Regional bishops resisted his attacks on church landholding practices vigorously, and he gave way a bit. Even as they allegedly promoted the welfare of the less advantaged, some of his major reforms had protective loopholes for the monied. Agrarian reforms with which Leopold had hoped to soften local class distinctions – the formal orders of clergy, nobility, and towns did not exist as such in Tuscany – benefitted the wealthy too. Nothing in the law forbade them to buy up lands supposedly freed for peasants to purchase, which few of the latter could afford. A kind of long-term purchase contract, the *livello*, was available for those without ready capital, but since anyone could buy these instruments, the rich snapped up most of them as well.[2] And Leopold himself was certainly no republican, let alone a late eighteenth-century democrat. Equality under the law had his approval; comprehensive political egalitarianism was another matter altogether.[3]

Thus, even before Leopold returned to Vienna in 1790, he was accustomed to distinguishing necessity from preference, a habit that the more successful of his forebears had cultivated as well. Such an outlook certainly helped him to resolve the problems that his brother handed on to him. Domestic malcontent was hard enough to deal with; when it spilled over into foreign policy, Leopold needed great flexibility to negotiate advantageously for his house. Uprisings in Hungary and the Netherlands, for example, turned out to have ramifications for his Balkan interests and for Habsburg relations with Prussia. An Ottoman attack in 1787 on Tsarina Catherine the Great had set in motion an Austro-Russian mutual defense pact concluded six years earlier. The initial successes of the Habsburg–Russian forces persuaded Frederick William II of Prussia (1744–97) that the balance of power in eastern Europe would be best served were he to ally himself with Constantinople. Prussia, therefore, was once again an open opponent of the house of Habsburg-Lorraine.

Even before Joseph II died, dissidents in both the Netherlands and Hungary had looked to the court in Berlin for support. In the summer of 1790, a few Hungarians were even exploring the possibility of inviting Grand Duke Charles Augustus of Saxony-Weimar (1757–1828) to be their king. While Frederick William II and his adviser throughout these maneuvers, Count Ewald von Hertzberg (1725–95), his chief minister, would probably have backed away from dismembering the Habsburg monarchy outright, they did not immediately discourage these overtures either.

Such meddling with the Low Countries and in Hungary was potentially an attack on the Habsburgs from within, and Leopold had to put an end to such an intrusion as quickly as he could. In July 1790 he signed the Convention of Reichenbach in which he assured the king of Prussia that he would halt the war against Turkey and abandon any claims to whatever regions under Ottoman rule the Russian–Austrian alliance had conquered – Serbia, the Danubian Principalities, possibly even Bulgaria. The conflict ended a year later with the terms of the agreement largely observed. For its part, Prussia withheld support from the Hungarian and Belgian uprisings. But even the chance that political dissent at home might lead a foreign power to encourage territorial separatism in the monarchy triggered alarms in Vienna.[4] Clear distinctions between domestic and foreign policies were counterproductive in such situations. The complexities they almost always created would tax the conceptual and tactical cunning of the Habsburgs and their advisers throughout the next century.

Leopold, for one, answered this challenge adroitly. Once denied Prussian assistance, Belgium yielded bloodlessly to his forces, who also entered Hungary unopposed in the summer of 1790. That much accomplished, he turned to a much larger problem. *Opes regum corda subitorum* – A King's Riches Are the Hearts of his Subjects – was the new emperor's personal motto. Subduing dissidence throughout his empire was only a first step; Leopold wanted the loyalty of his peoples too. Abandoning some of Joseph's most offensive initiatives was the easy way to quiet aristocratic protest; Leopold used the tactic liberally. The Austrian and Bohemian nobilities backed off after he cancelled his brother's agrarian labor reforms and new tax code. He restored serfdom in Polish Galicia as well, though on the less onerous terms that the Theresan regime had put through rather than on the requirements long exacted in the region. As long as the practice continued in the province, however, the future of the Polish gentry and magnates was secure, guaranteed as they were with a cheap labor supply, largely drawn from Ukrainian peasants, for their substantial estates. When Leopold dissolved the general seminaries and even restored several monasteries, the Catholic establishment throughout the Habsburg lands calmed down as well. Traditionalist forces in the estates of the Austrian Netherlands were especially pleased. Ongoing social and economic differences that had often divided his brother's critics gave the new emperor added room for maneuver. The Habsburgs seemed increasingly the lesser evil to conservatives in the Low Countries whose chief worry had become the democrats among the rebels whose inspiration was coming from revolutionary Paris.[5]

Hungary was more intractable. The new king was as eager as any of his predecessors to dilute the influence of the Hungarian nobility in the kingdom. Leopold moved at least symbolically in that direction by allowing the nobles of Hungary's Serbian minority and representatives from their Orthodox clergy to sit in the diet. To the great dismay of Hungarian aristocrats, he also allowed Serbs to hold a national conference. But under pressure from Kaunitz and the minister of police, Count Johann Anton von Pergen (1725–1814), both of whom believed that without serious concessions to the rebels no calm would return to the kingdom, Leopold gave in to the aristocracy on significant matters.

As in the Netherlands, he was not dealing with a monolithic group. Though Hungary's nobles both great and small played important constitutional roles in the kingdom, their interests were not always the same. When the king called the Hungarian diet together in September of 1790, the magnates were growing very uneasy over a self-serving agenda that the more numerous gentry were pushing.[6] Though both factions had resisted Josephinism, the small nobility wanted access to high positions of state that had been traditionally in the hands of great landowners. Their talk of nationalizing the church's allodial properties dismayed high clerical authorities in the upper chamber of the diet as well. Leopold had little choice but to work with all sides; and, while he had to yield some degree of royal authority in the kingdom, he did win a significant measure of cooperation from the estates, at least temporarily.

His strategy was to put aside the most objectionable parts of the gentry's program, but to meet demands that all of the dissidents could agree upon. He reaffirmed the principles that royal power was subject to the law of the kingdom and that Hungary as a realm apart from the other Habsburg holdings was not to be governed like them. The Hungarian diet would retain its privileged status in many areas of taxation; responsibility for raising military contributions would stay in the hands of the counties. Both the magnates and the lesser nobility could, and would, bitterly oppose new or higher imposts. Though the general treasury in Vienna still had final oversight of the treasuries in both Royal Hungary and Transylvania, both the royal diet and the county estates had a decisive say over what monies left the kingdom and for what purpose.

Such policies kept more than a quarter of the total population of the Habsburg empire – around 24,500,000 by the end of the eighteenth century – legally beyond the reach of the central government unless it chose to force its will upon the kingdom.[7] For the first part of the nineteenth century, the overwhelming majority of Hungary's nobles remained free of royal taxation. Their often vast properties remained intact as well. In Royal Hungary, though not in Transylvania or Croatia, around 200 families owed roughly half of the kingdom's rural property in an economy where 90 percent of all who lived in the kingdom were engaged in agriculture. Indeed, every second Hungarian was subject to some noble, or, put plainly, at the former's mercy.[8] Even the gentry, whose most ambitious political and administrative schemes had been sidetracked, did not come away from Leopold empty-handed, especially as individuals. Favor was to be gained at court: their chief ideologue, Péter Balogh, would be a loyal supporter of the dynasty once he became a county lord-lieutenant and joined the imperial state council in 1794 at the invitation of a new Habsburg emperor, Francis II.[9]

When challenged by nobles and the privileged clergy, the Habsburgs had always been willing to compromise with these orders. The new economics of eighteenth-century life, however, and the need for resources to keep the monarchy internationally competitive had broadened the field of constituencies with which Habsburg rulers had to deal in order to protect their positions. Maria Theresa and Joseph II had deliberately cultivated the goodwill of social groups beyond the elites of property, blood, and church; Leopold continued this policy. He listened carefully, though often cynically, to the grievances of such people. Making clever use of the press and of the political aspirations of a more educated Hungarian bourgeoisie, he broke some noble resistance in Hungary by threatening to allow the middle classes of Hungary's royal cities some deliberative voice in the kingdom.[10]

Regardless of his motives, Leopold did enough to persuade bourgeois advocates of civil liberties that he understood their concerns. He continued the surveillance of public speaking and private thinking that Joseph II had hoped would throttle sedition, but modified important aspects of the program. Turning over the ministry of police to Sonnenfels – Pergen resigned when Leopold ordered him to accept legal restraints on his investigative powers – the emperor insisted that his subjects be better informed of their rights. He also endorsed Sonnenfels's revival of an earlier understanding of the term 'police' (*Polizei*) that stressed the regulation of public welfare broadly and not just illegal behaviors. Among the most widely popular innovations of Sonnenfels's office were sanitary ordinances, a growing necessity in the centers of industry beginning to take shape in the Habsburg lands.[11] Leopold also opened up several provincial estates to wider membership, particularly from the middle classes. With the permission of the crown, the towns of Styria, after a persistent and well-organized campaign, won greater representation in their region's deliberative institutions. The gains of the bourgeoisie also emboldened the local peasantry to ask for similar privileges.[12]

Thus, appeasement, compromise, and a touch here and there of deviousness brought Leopold II a general status quo ante bellum both beyond his borders and within them. Hungary, where the practical conditions of the privileged orders down to 1848 changed very little, was but a gross example of a social and economic pattern that was widespread through the Habsburg lands. But, like his mother and brother before him, Leopold acknowledged middle-class interests as well. That he would have preferred to curb traditional privileges even further is clear, but the choice was not his. He was already dead in 1792 in the midst of a great political change in Europe. The Habsburgs needed all the public support they could muster to arrest the most dangerous features of that change at their borders.

An Old Empire and a New

Revolutionary France posed a many-sided threat to the government in Vienna. The emblem of Bourbon–Habsburg cooperation was the marriage of Leopold's sister Marie Antoinette to Louis XVI, giving Leopold particular reason to worry. He urged his sister and her husband to cooperate with the National Assembly, but the ill-advised flight of the royal couple from Paris in 1791, which aroused suspicions that they were going to enlist counter-revolutionary support, ruled out that strategy. The great changes that took place in the kingdom questioned the legitimacy of monarchical rule and eventually argued for something the radical Jacobins called the 'nation' as a sovereign authority. The total overthrow of the royal government also disrupted a network of alliances that Vienna had relied upon since the middle of the eighteenth century. France could no longer be expected to aid the Habsburgs against either Prussia or Russia.[13]

Leopold tried military diplomacy. Seen from the perspective of Vienna, his compact with Frederick William II of Prussia, the Declaration of Pillnitz of 27 August 1791, was a sound move. While war was the last thing the emperor's subjects wanted – the Turkish conflict at the end of Joseph II's reign was only just over – the agreement did knit Prussia somewhat more firmly into the fabric of Habsburg interests, thereby reducing the likelihood that the Hohenzollerns would open another campaign of expansion in central and east central Europe. Nor did it commit Leopold to immediate war against the Girondist government in Paris, saying only that war to return Louis XVI to his throne was a possibility should other great powers join the cause.[14]

Were an offensive against the forces of popular revolution to come, the Habsburg monarchy was in a position to undertake it, at least by contemporary standards. Cameralist wisdom of the seventeenth and eighteenth centuries argued that a great state was a populous one; the dynasty's lands were increasingly well peopled. By 1790, the empire from east to west had only 2 to 3 million fewer inhabitants than France, which had 28 million on the eve of the *Grande Revolution*. The economic legacy of the Theresan–Josephinian era had enhanced the dynasty's claim to great-power status. Commerce, manufacture, agricultural production, and a transportation infrastructure appropriate to these activities were performing far better than when Maria Theresa assumed title to her lands in 1740. While mercantilist protection was still the rule of the empire, a number of once subsidized industries, most notably the textile sector, were now profitable enough to stand on their own. Commerce in the Mediterranean basin, with Trieste as the chief port of transit, was especially lively.[15] Lastly, the privileged sectors of the monarchy's societies that had so doggedly resisted Joseph II's expansive take on monarchic authority had even less sympathy for the egalitarian institutions and values taking hold in Paris. Indeed, such groups swiftly rejected whatever concessions Leopold had been ready to make to such principles, like ending serfdom, for example.[16]

Leopold died unexpectedly in March 1792. His successor, at first Emperor Francis II (1768–1835) in the Holy Roman Empire, was 24 years old. His father had fashioned his son more or less after himself. Francis's education had been enlightened and exhaustive, designed for a man who had to rule subjects from many social classes and cultural backgrounds. While nothing about his intellectual training could offset his utter lack of imagination, he knew an impressive amount about his lands and peoples and had undergone intensive schooling in Italian, French, Latin, and German, the last of which he would always prefer. Francis was naturally bookish and musical – he played the violin. Nevertheless, he had also done an heir-apparent's stint in the army.

The new emperor's public demeanor had a common touch that proved useful in revolutionary times as well. Like his father and his uncle Joseph, he genuinely disliked court formality. Unlike them, however, he was thoroughly at home in the bourgeois setting that he brought to his imperial residences. His middle-class subjects, particularly in Vienna, approved mightily.[17] They also admired the diligent air he brought to his duties. Though somewhat unresponsive and lackadaisical as a youth, he had internalized the work ethic enough to authenticate himself as one among many of the conscientious bureaucrats in his government. His populist tastes, however, did not make him a democrat. Alarmed at his nephew's brush with Leopold's participatory political schemes in Tuscany, Joseph II had brought Francis to Vienna in 1784 for indoctrination in the values and mechanics of sovereign monarchy. The lessons took.

None of his advantages, however, could offset the new ruler's youth and inexperience. Such qualities would have been drawbacks at any time, but they were especially critical in the crisis that confronted Francis at his father's death. Responding to his subjects' opposition to financing another war when the bills for Joseph II's Turkish escapade were still outstanding, Leopold had wriggled away from the Declaration of Pillnitz. Nevertheless, anticipating a reactionary counter-revolution, the French national assembly had declared war in April 1792 on Austria and Prussia, now joined by Russia. Conflict with France was in full swing during Francis's several coronations, which took place throughout the spring and summer of that year.

The new ruler's first approach to his daunting task was to look to his highest ministers for advice. Especially important were Count Francis Colloredo, the emperor's erstwhile chief tutor, the Bohemian Count Francis Kolowrat (1778–1861), and the Hungarian Count Fidél Pálffy (1788–1864), all men of impeccable pedigree and from families with long histories of Habsburg service. To organize the monarchy for combat not only against the French armies but the ideology that they represented, these noblemen recommended stamping out the remnants of liberalism still alive in the Habsburg empire.

Francis himself had considered pursuing some of his father's more progressive policies. The plight of agricultural labor touched him deeply, and he wanted to relieve it. He would find himself, however, under the pressures of repeated defeat in war that threatened to destroy whatever influence the house of Habsburg had on the continent. Thus, he heeded those close to him who believed that to rescue his monarchy, Francis had to reaffirm the powers of clergy and aristocracy in his lands. Slowly but steadily he abandoned whatever commitment to reform he ever had. Peasants continued to have to negotiate with individual landlords for release from servile labor, and Leopold's plans to add middle-class and even peasant representation to regional estates evaporated as well. The Catholic establishment was not forgotten either: Francis closed down the commission for ecclesiastical affairs through which the state had kept an eye on church policy and behavior.[18]

Eradicating sedition, perceived or real, was crucial, and Francis's treatment of this problem would color public perceptions of his regime until he died in 1835. The Habsburg lands were not hermetically sealed from the radical currents that were flowing from Paris to the rest of Europe. The propertied had every reason to worry about them. In Bohemia, leaflets supposedly inspired by the national convention called upon rural labor to rise up against landlords during the 1790s. In small pockets of the middle-class intelligentsia there was also some sympathy for the early revolution in France. Some of Joseph II's reforms, it was being said, were similar to changes that the French had put in place. The Habsburg emperor had disbanded monasteries, eradicated forced peasant labor, and tried to distribute the burden of taxation more fairly, all goals of the revolutionary government to the west.

More active dissidence had continued to simmer among a handful of Hungarians as well. An anti-dynastic strain of political philosophy had lived on, not only among intellectuals, but among a few nobles as well.[19] Advocates of these views – they were called Jacobins – immediately caught the attention of the police spies whom Francis reempowered in his lands. Indeed, he brought back Count Pergen to direct the program. In 1794–5 swift and sometimes brutal measures brought whatever sedition there was to an end. Suspects were arrested, among them some of the late Emperor Leopold's own secret operatives. While Francis would insist that all had the right to a trial, several of the so-called conspirators were sent to prisons where conditions were almost sure to kill them before they ever got out. Nine Austrian and Hungarian Jacobins were executed in 1795, among them Ignatius Joseph Martinovics (1755–95) who was an advocate of a kind of gentry republic, though one in which peasants continued to meet their feudal obligations. Masonic lodges, viewed as hothouses of revolution, were closed, and tight censorship governed all forms of intellectual and artistic life.[20]

The emperor was indeed in trouble. His army of some 700,000 men in 1793 had already lost important battles to France. An apparently formidable alliance of Austria, Prussia, Spain, Holland, and Great Britain, the First Coalition, which came together in 1795, could not defeat a revolutionary force cobbled together through popular conscription. The need for Austria and Prussia to maintain a substantial military presence against Russia in the east also drained the resources of the two central European powers on their western fronts.

The Habsburg position deteriorated further in 1796. A new French general, the Corsican *arriviste* Napoleon Bonaparte (1769–1821), drove the Habsburg armies from northern Italy and began to march on Vienna itself. Though he relented in the Treaty of Campo Formio (1797), allowing the Habsburgs to retain their holdings around the Adriatic and to add Venice to them, Napoleon did get control of the Austrian Netherlands, a time-honored goal of French kings. The French defeat of the Second Coalition in 1799, however, removed the Habsburgs from northern Italy as well.[21] In 1801, the Peace of Lunéville ceded what remained of Germany west of the Rhine to France, along with the imperial fortifications on the eastern banks. The claim that the Habsburg emperors were the protectors of Germany had become an empty fiction.

Under pressure from Napoleon, the German princes gathered in 1802 to dismember the venerable empire as advantageously to themselves as they could. The result, the *Reichsdeputationshauptschluss* of 1803, eradicated almost all of the ecclesiastical principalities. These lands were then absorbed by secular states who had long hoped to take them over. Several formerly free cities met the same fate. While Napoleon, now a self-declared emperor, did not abolish the imperial office in Germany, he introduced changes in the college of electors that virtually ruled out the likelihood that a Habsburg would ever hold the position again. The idea of reestablishing an Austrian emperorship in Germany or part of it lived on for some time in the minds of intellectuals and politicians throughout the Napoleonic wars. Francis himself, however, did not encourage them.[22] He did not, he said, choosing his words as disarmingly as he could, want to be sovereign over people whose trust he no longer had. His advisers, who had toyed with the idea of turning Germany into part of the Austrian patrimony, accepted the new order as gracefully as did their prince. They had no alternative. The Habsburgs had not only been defeated in Germany, but Napoleon's reconfiguration of its territories had wiped out the most loyal support that the house of Habsburg had in the empire – the ecclesiastical principalities, the free cities, and the imperial knights were no longer there.[23]

But were the Habsburgs anything more than counts, kings, and dukes in their own patrimony? Much discussion among his councilors gave birth to the proposal that Francis and his successors be called Austrian emperors. No longer Francis II of the Holy Roman Empire, the Habsburg would be Emperor Francis I of Austria. The idea was both contrived and fraught with weighty constitutional issues for those who chose to see them. From a formal perspective, however, the move had decided advantages for the dynasty. Never before had the house of Austria held a title that comprehended all of their central and east central European holdings. Furthermore, the estates throughout Francis's lands did not contest it. Even the Hungarians, normally quick to spot encroachments upon constitutional prerogatives, remained more or less silent. The execution of the French king and queen in 1793 had aroused a general wave of horror throughout the Habsburg lands, and the anti-aristocratic Terror finished the job. By the end of the eighteenth century, Hungarian nobles and their colleagues everywhere in the monarchy viewed Napoleon as the unwelcome bequest of a bourgeois revolution that they wished to keep as far from their properties as they could; they cooperated more or less willingly with the government in Vienna almost to the end of the conflict.[24]

Francis's policy of intimidating those people most prone to dissidence had also had the desired effect. His ruthless suppression of the so-called Jacobin conspiracy cautioned the boldest in Hungary and the Austrian lands, as did his systematic campaigns over the course of his reign against secret societies and other likely pockets of sedition. But where he could, he respected Hungarian institutions during the early years of his regime and even supported some changes that the royal estates wished to see in the kingdom. He renewed his father's guarantees of autonomy originally given in the so-called Law 10 of 1790 and, by and large, followed constitutional customs in the kingdom deferentially during most of the Napoleonic wars. Until 1812, he called the diet every three years to raise funds and troops to counter French armies. Demands for reconsideration of Hungary's disadvantaged commercial relations with the rest of the Habsburg lands went unattended. Francis could, however, use his position advantageously in the eyes of some members of the nobility. Though always dubious about basic aspects of Habsburg rule, the few aristocratic spokesmen for liberal reform in late eighteenth-century Hungary, most notably Gregory Berzeviczy (1763–1822), were not principled opponents of monarchy. The greatest problem of the realm, in their opinion, was a socio-economic structure that privileged so few at the expense of the common good. If he were determined to remedy this imbalance, a strengthened king would be an asset to Hungarian society as a whole. A sketch of a new Hungarian constitution that Berzeviczy drew up in 1809 was dedicated to Napoleon, no comfort to Vienna, to be sure, but a testimony to a continuing faith in monarchical systems.

Here and there Francis also gave signs that he was not programmatically hostile to Hungarian interests. In 1792 his regime allowed the secondary and higher schools of Royal Hungary to make Magyar a required subject; after 1805 some correspondence with government offices could be conducted in the language as well. Some administrative changes pleased the Hungarian nobility more generally. The separate Illyrian chancellery, which administered Croatian affairs, was abolished, thus underscoring claims in Royal Hungary that the kingdom to the south was indeed a part of the crown of St. Stephen.

Most important of all, many Hungarian nobles genuinely prospered during the Napoleonic wars. The exemption from general royal taxation continued. Hungarian contributions to the army remained lower than those from the other Habsburg lands, so that the notion of the kingdom's singularity remained unscathed. The conflict itself touched the kingdom only lightly: the French armies entered it only twice and did not stay for long. Provisioning Francis's Habsburg armies drove up grain prices for landlords most agreeably, and mercifully generous harvests gave these men plenty to sell. After 1812, financial disagreements between the Hungarian crown and its estates were both frequent and deep. By then, however, Napoleon's invincibility was also waning, so that Habsburg–Hungarian cooperation was less critical for both sides.[25]

Francis I's vow in 1806 to respect Hungary's singular political status in the Habsburg empire was no endorsement of reform, but neither was it wholly insincere.[26] He behaved well enough throughout most of the Napoleonic era to keep Hungarian royal diets from asking for new political or economic concessions from their king. The aristocracy enjoyed a measure of cultural liberty as well. Indeed, the comparative permissiveness of the intellectual environment of the kingdom made it easier for revolutionary works from France and Germany to get into Hungary than into other Habsburg lands.[27]

The magnates who dominated the Bohemian estates were no more partial to democratic revolution than their counterparts in Hungary. They were quick to read *Reflections on the Revolution in France*, Edmund Burke's impassioned critique of egalitarian rule, and to find ways of keeping egalitarian thoughts from the minds of the peasants who worked their demesnes. Compromised though it was, Joseph II's record of agrarian reform turned out to be useful counter-propaganda. A serious pamphlet literature circulated in the kingdom, arguing that the kingdom's rural folk were far better off than their French colleagues and that inequality was a fixed part of the human condition. The nobility of the Habsburg Austrian lands received Joseph's manorial regulations more calmly than their Bohemian and Hungarian colleagues. Nevertheless, all three aristocracies deplored the abolition of all seigniorial rights that took place during the initial phase of the French Revolution. Napoleon, therefore, did nothing to shake their opinion and loyalty to their sovereign.[28]

As with his father before him, however, Francis and his advisers, and even other members of the imperial dynasty, believed that relentless policing and attention to the mutual interests of crown and estates alone would deliver to them the support needed to crush popular revolution and the remarkable Corsican who embodied for many its most appealing promises. Though they were urged to accept the world as they knew it, the masses of the Habsburg lands continued to believe that their lives required improvement. Wartime conditions sensitized an already resentful agricultural workforce to the inequities of its condition. Except for military officers, all nobles as well as the clergy, bureaucrats, officials on noble domains, physicians, and citizens of royal cities were exempt from conscription. Peasants were therefore the chief source of troops for the government in Vienna, but by the beginning of the nineteenth century many men were hiding out in forests or foregoing fixed residences to avoid being called up. Even during the Napoleonic wars, terms of service for draftees had to be lightened. What was once virtual impressment for a lifetime became 10 years of duty in the infantry, 12 years for the cavalry, and 14 in the artillery. Other peasant demands, however, the complete abolition of servile labor chief among them, were put off indefinitely as too experimental to be taken during a life-and-death conflict. It was always possible, therefore, for another wave of armed discontent to break out somewhere in a rural population whose cooperation was crucial to the defense of the Habsburg monarchy.[29]

One Dynasty, One People

Countering these sentiments while stiffening the popular will to fight on were especially difficult tasks when the French regularly defeated the Habsburgs and their allies. Some strategy was called for to convince the generality of Habsburg subjects that they shared the dynasty's stake in the conflict. What began therefore in Vienna as a struggle to preserve the dynasty's territories therefore turned into an effort to create, or at least recreate, a vision of a state that was something more than an expression of dynastic self-interest and its modifications at the hands of small numbers of people entitled to curb overly-ambitious rulers.

Fortunately for Francis I, the war had made his Austrian court a magnet that drew people who were eager to contribute both ideas and their time to such a project. Napoleon's rationalization of German territorial government, especially his Confederation of the Rhine, and Francis's assumption of his new imperial title after 1806 had encouraged several leading intellectuals from the old empire, such as Frederick Schlegel (1772–1829), to move to the Habsburg capital. They detested French mobocracy and Napoleon's casual disregard for traditional political institutions, all of which they traced back to the ideals of the Enlightenment.

In league with government officials and like-minded Austrian writers and thinkers, they embarked on a campaign to reconfigure the Habsburgs as the spearhead of a Germany rededicated to past values. Unqualified fidelity to the emperor and piety, preferably of the Catholic sort, were central to the program. Despite the vaporous quality of some of their thinking, these people received some encouragement from contemporary events. Royalist and clerical factions had played some role in the anti-Jacobin Vendée uprising in 1793. A German, Count Philip von Stadion (1763–1824), Francis's chief minister, and Joseph Frederick von Hormayr (1781–1848), a Tyrolean historian and publicist who fervently believed that the dynasty needed a unified people behind it, were central to the project. They hoped that a closer identification of the dynasty with its subjects and the other way around would turn the Habsburg empire into a counter-revolutionary force. Hormayr dedicated his considerable talents and energies to arguing that loyalty to a single house and church made Habsburg subjects one people.[30]

Maintaining the morale of the army was a crucial task; once again, French models suggested how to proceed. The *levée en masse*, first used by the Jacobin committee of public safety, then by Napoleon, suggested a way to assemble a more committed fighting force than the sullen troops who had heretofore shown up in Habsburg ranks. To guide this project, Francis I did not have to look beyond his dynasty. Archduke Johann (1782–1859), the tenth of Leopold II's 12 legitimate children, believed firmly – more firmly than his brother as it turned out – that arming the masses was the monarchy's only hope of repelling Napoleon's drive through central Europe. Gifted, often insightful, but unpredictable, Johann had been schooled in the principles of the Enlightenment as well as in military engineering. Two of his tutors had been Swiss, Armand, Count Mottet, and the historian Johann von Müller (1715–1809); their descriptions of the fighting spirit of cantonal militias when defending their homelands and the general sense of communal solidarity that spurred them on impressed their student deeply. The archduke would bring all of this background to bear on the problem at hand. Could this structure be transferred to the Habsburg lands, the dynasty and its subject masses would be defending one another even as they defended themselves.

Having explored the writing of Frederick Gentz (1764–1832), Edmund Burke's translator into German and after 1810 closely associated with the Habsburg regime, Archduke Johann also concluded that Austria and Prussia had a shared duty to rescue the German-speaking world from foreign, in this case French, domination. For him, as for Gentz, Napoleon's Confederation of the Rhine embodied this threat. German liberty, in Johann's opinion, had first emerged among its mountain peoples, and it was among them that he looked first as he tried to make 'the business of the state the business of the nation', as he put it.[31]

Turning his back happily on the artificialities of court life, the unorthodox archduke left for the Tyrol to apply these principles. Alpine topography was only one reason why he should start there: local Catholic sentiment was running high against the anti-clerical measures of Bavarian occupiers, who had taken over the area as allies of Napoleon in 1800–01. For a time Johann patronized an innkeeper, Andreas Hofer (1767–1810), who was apparently committed to fomenting insurrection against the invaders. In 1805, however, though he had markedly improved the organization of the Tyrolean defense, Johann had to vacate the area to the Wittelsbachs without a fight. Hofer finally began his uprising in 1809, only to be captured and executed by Napoleon. Johann himself had gone on to Inner Austria, particularly Styria, to give his program another try there.

Attempts to develop public solidarity against Napoleon through regional militia had significant support for a time in the government. By 1808, faced with the fall of Bourbon Spain to Napoleon and another possible French strike at central Europe, Francis was willing to try almost any scheme to save himself and his dynasty's position. Johann's ideas for mobilizing local patriotism in the defense of the Habsburg holdings intrigued Count Stadion as well. Indeed, the minister's take on this strategy was more radically comprehensive than the archduke's. Reversing both the spirit and the letter of Habsburg administrative and political reforms that had begun with Maximilian I and had peaked during the reigns of Maria Theresa and Joseph II, Stadion called for a revival of the position of local nobilities and provincial estates who were charged with the actual conscription process. Such measures, he thought, might possibly inspire aristocrats to shed their suspicions of central power in defense of the commonweal against French expansionism. He was remarkably successful. Though not subject to conscription, Bohemian magnate families – the Lobkovic, the Kinskýs, the Clarys – shouldered the burden of leading the realm's militia; their counterparts in other provinces also cooperated. The estates of Lower Austria produced 300,000 florins to support their contingent. To further commitment to local defense measures, militia songs were translated into Czech, Polish, and other local languages.[32] Hungary also answered this appeal, though less satisfactorily. The kingdom had not responded kindly to requests for men and money in 1807, but by 1808 the royal estates had begun to form their militia too. Ineffective though it was, the step represented a real victory for the Vienna government which thought it very important to present a united face to Napoleon.[33]

The return of leading noblemen to serving the house of Habsburg-Lorraine by serving their provincial fatherlands did not stop with military campaigns. Government-backed periodicals such as the *Vaterländische Blättern für den österreichischen Kaiserstaat* also recommended cultural programs and institutions as ways of heightening local pride and enhancing public welfare. Such undertakings would also, it was hoped, stimulate popular support for the ruling house. The connection was easy enough to make – opening the Hungarian diet in 1808, the emperor vowed to support the cultural interests of his non-German peoples. The foundations that these activities required for support, however, were likely to be most effective when local figures set them up. Only nobilities had the time, the money, the background, and often the collections to sponsor such programs; the more progressive and civic-minded of them responded with noteworthy enthusiasm. When provincial and national museums in Graz, Prague, and Budapest were founded during the Napoleonic era or shortly thereafter, it was under the leadership of Archduke Johann, Count Kaspar Šternberk, and Count Ferenc Széchényi (1754–1820) respectively. In Bohemia these ideas had been aired in noble salons even before the French Revolution; aristocrats were therefore ready to put them to use to benefit their class as a whole. Near total ignorance of their kingdom's history and their role in it often compromised their effectiveness in the estates; cultural programs that improved their understanding of the institutions that shaped their land as they knew it were therefore highly desirable. František Palacký (1798–1876), the greatest historian of the nineteenth-century Czech revival, appeared before the estates of the land in 1843 to instruct them on their privileges. Language studies never played as large a role in noble cultural policy as historical issues. Nevertheless, a few aristocrats also gave generously of themselves and their money to scholars and intellectuals who had begun movements to revive the study of the Czech language that a century of German dominance had turned into the idiom of peasants and humble urban households. Such activities positioned nobilities of the Habsburg lands roughly from 1815 to the middle of the nineteenth century to play preeminent roles not only in their local economies, but in their cultural affairs as well.[34] As long as it was made clear that the right of the house of Habsburg to rule was not in question, Vienna allowed these programs to continue.

The Dynasty Reasserts Itself

Habsburg tolerance of regional cultural interests was not new. Germanophile though he was, Sonnenfels, for example, also believed that the monarchy's subjects should cultivate indigenous customs and languages. Indeed, he thought that such diversity would encourage valuable exchanges of ideas and views among peoples who recognized one another's differences but tolerated them. 'Individuality' as he understood the term, however, was an anthropological and aesthetic concept only. In administrative and political settings it was unacceptable.[35]

Francis I, however, was not one to plague himself with such distinctions. Though he accepted the argument that he needed popular support, it was a tactic for him, not an intellectual conviction. Temperamentally and through experience he was more comfortable with the absolutist thrust of his Josephinian heritage than its liberal impulses. Micromanagement of his regime was all but instinctive. In 1808, against the advice of Stadion and his brothers, who believed that he wasted far too much time on details, the emperor made it clear that he intended to supervise all aspects of his government closely.

Initiatives that escaped his oversight were suspect to him, even when they were sponsored by his own family. Archduke Johann never did produce the military victory against Napoleon he had promised. When the archduke clandestinely supported Andreas Hofer's failed popular uprising in 1809, Francis found the move not only diplomatically inopportune, but subversive. Johann was forced to renew his fealty to the head of his house; he then left for Styria where he preoccupied himself with scientific, educational, and charitable good works to the end of his life. Stadion himself, who was a freemason, also lost the emperor's trust. He would become the minister of finance, a responsible office in a government that stared down bankruptcy three times during the Napoleonic era, but not one that was central to political policy. Francis and his circle of advisers, particularly Count Zinzendorf, who headed a consultative council of state, saw little value in broadening the influence of regional elites throughout the empire simply to cultivate their goodwill; if Francis's regime yielded to changes in provincial constitutions and relations of subjects with the central government, it was only because no alternative was at hand.[36] The moral rearmament of the Habsburg peoples against Bonapartism therefore came to a halt. Controlling his subjects was far more congenial to Francis than inspiring participation in a noble effort in which all of his people, nobles and peasants alike, shared the dynasty's interest. Napoleon, who became Francis's son-in-law in 1810, would be defeated, but by more traditional means than the ones that the populist ideologues of the Habsburg monarchy had advocated. Canny diplomacy and effective military alliances, the timeless cornerstones of Habsburg power in Europe, once again rescued the dynasty's edifice.

The chief architect of these policies was the antithesis of populism and participatory politics. Born in Koblenz, Klemens Wenzel Nepomuk Lothar Prince Metternich (1773–1859) was, like Stadion, descended from a house of imperial free knights, who had long served the Habsburgs in military and administrative positions and by keeping ecclesiastical states where they had some influence on pro-Austrian paths.[37] Metternich had been performing diplomatic chores around Europe for the Habsburgs throughout the Napoleonic wars. After 1806 he was the imperial ambassador to France. If he had any political principle at all – his tactical bobbing and weaving was sometimes so intricate that he acted at cross-purposes with himself – it was that 'events which cannot be prevented must be led'. His greatest talent was his ability to identify issues central to all the parties at negotiating tables and to turn his mastery to Austrian advantage.[38] An unreconstructed aristocrat, he believed that his class would endure only if monarchy were preserved. While he was not opposed to cultural programs and research that furthered the position of the house of Habsburg in its lands, he did not think that these activities won wars. In 1813, he squelched Stadion's program of translating propaganda into the various languages of the empire.[39]

Metternich's strategy was directed toward preserving the Habsburg empire; defeating Napoleon would further this goal, but was not an end in itself. At its core was opportunistic diplomacy, so flexible at times that it puzzled, even angered, Habsburg loyalists. There was, for example, an alliance with France in 1812, signed to give the empire time to catch its breath and regroup militarily. Bonaparte asked that the militias be broken up, and Metternich complied. He also played a major part in convincing Francis to allow the marriage of his eldest daughter, Marie Louise (1791–1847), to Napoleon, an arrangement both she and her father detested and that turned the archduchess into a lifelong enemy of the minister–diplomat.[40]

The Habsburg empire had long protected its holdings and the titles attached to them through alliances and coalitions: the defense of Vienna in 1683 and of Germany against Louis XIV were conspicuous examples. Leopold II had quickly marked the French Revolution as a threat to the status of the Habsburg empire as a great power, as well as more specifically to the Austrian Netherlands; to German security; to dynastic prestige; and to monarchy everywhere. He had also been eager to keep Prussia and Russia from going at one another in Poland, where the Habsburg empire also had a presence that it wished to maintain. A core alliance of Russia, Austria, and Prussia, he had thought, which eventually brought in Britain, Holland, and additional states, would restore Europe to the peace and stability his position in his own lands required.[41]

This machinery had been in motion throughout the Napoleonic wars, but, unlike similar Habsburg arrangements in times past, it never did function particularly well. Three coalitions, in which the house of Austria, Russia, Prussia, and Great Britain were the central partners, fizzled, in part because of conflicts among the supposed allies over territorial compensation and indemnities. The beginning of the end for the French emperor came as a result not so much of his opponents' collective efforts, but of his ill-advised invasion of Russia in 1812 and subsequent retreat. Indeed, among the French commander's forces was an Austrian contingent, required under the terms of Metternich's Austro-French alliance.

Even the fourth and final coalition of 1813–14 against France was a shaky affair, in part because of Habsburg interests. Metternich was as fearful of Russia's growing presence on the continent as he was of Napoleon, with whom almost to the end the minister thought he could strike some deal. The powerful but erratic Tsar Alexander I, at home an autocrat but a liberal idealist of sorts abroad, was determined to force unconditional surrender on Bonaparte, then march on Paris where he would allow popular mandate to decide who would rule France. Metternich brought Alexander around with threats to withdraw the Austrian army, the largest, though ill-equipped, contingent, from the alliance.

Metternich used diplomacy to the Habsburgs' best advantage at the congress in Vienna that began in 1814 as Napoleon seemed finally broken. The Habsburg minister's goals and those of Francis I were to create a stable, lasting international settlement that would allow Austria to retreat safely within its own boundaries to reassemble itself. To do this, the dynasty would nevertheless have to maintain a determining presence in Germany and Italy; it would also have to win the assurances of Great Britain that it would discourage Prussia and Russia from challenging Habsburg interests. Metternich's trump negotiating card, or so he thought, was Austria's poor military performance during the Napoleonic wars. If smaller states believed that the Habsburg empire posed no threat to them and would be a benevolent though active partner in blocking expansion of a newly vigorous Russia and a revived France, they could safely support the continuation of the monarchy in Vienna.[42]

The Congress of Vienna, which lasted until the early summer of the following year, more or less met the purposes of the emperor and his chief minister. The modesty and unimaginativeness of their agenda disappointed many. An array of lobbyists whose causes ranged from ending the slave trade to opening up more civil rights for Jews in Hamburg and Bremen converged on Vienna to press their cases, in vain as it turned out. There was also a squadron of erstwhile aristocrats and rulers of minor German principalities, Metternich's father among them, who came to plead for restoration to their estates. Beyond receiving some rights to a voice in local assemblies in the middle-sized German territories that had absorbed their former holdings, they came away with very little.[43] The assemblage of small states (*Kleinstaaterei*) of the Holy Roman Empire was now a matter of history.

In the case of states of scale, however, the Vienna settlement generally respected the doctrine of legitimacy. Traditional rulers were to be restored to their lands with boundaries more or less what they had been before the revolutionary era. This was a position congenial to Habsburg interests; the rulers of Germany's middle-sized states wanted to keep their thrones, and no one argued seriously against this, especially Metternich who saw them as useful allies. He was particularly bent on preserving what he could of Saxony as a buffer against both Prussian and Russian expansion and was willing to modify significantly his goals in eastern Europe to get his way. In return for giving back at least half of Saxony to its legitimate ruler, in this case King Frederick Augustus III (1750–1827), who had supported France during the Napoleonic wars, he allowed Prussia to absorb approximately half of the kingdom. He also submitted to a Russian scheme in Poland, the so-called Congress Kingdom that Alexander had declared might be his beachhead for the reunification of that realm under Russian sponsorship.[44] It was another way for Metternich to show that he could be helpful to Germany's dynasties.

Where Francis and Metternich did sacrifice holdings of long standing in the German southwest and the Austrian Netherlands, they did so with a purpose. Italians and Hungarians had always disliked being ruled by a dynasty with west European interests. Yielding territory in Germany was yet another way for Metternich and Francis to win the trust of the territorial rulers who remained there. Beyond the region of Salzburg, which disappeared as a prince-bishopric in 1803, the dynasty left others to carry off what they wanted from the wreckage of the old empire. The Habsburg courtship of the German princes indeed paid off in the Vienna Final Act of 10 June 1815. Though Prussia, through its Saxon annexations, was bigger than Metternich had wanted, the powers had agreed to allow the establishment of what would be the German Confederation – a defensive union of independent states and free cities that once belonged to a Holy Roman Empire. Prussia would have strong influence in northern Germany, but Austria would preside over the organization as a whole.

If nothing else, the Vienna settlement confirmed the Danube as the Habsburg base of power, a development that had been underway since the Peace of Westphalia in 1648.[45] Such a heavy eastward focus, however, compelled Metternich to shore up the Habsburg lands against Russia not only to the north and east, but even in the south. With the collapse of the Bonapartist regime in Italy in 1814, Sardinia–Piedmont, the papacy, and other regional principalities had already appealed to St. Petersburg for protection against Austrian domination. Not everyone, however, objected to an Austrian presence on the peninsula: there was an 'Austrian Party' that the Habsburg regime was able to exploit in cooperation with local elites until taxes, economic distress, and resentment of military occupation on the ground and government from afar eroded these advantages.[46] The Vienna settlement did confirm Habsburg possession of Venetia, which the dynasty's forces had taken in 1813, as compensation for loss of the Netherlands. Neither the allies nor many Italians protested seriously. Nor did the great powers at the congress challenge the Habsburg take-over of Lombardy, where Francis hoped to keep France away from his southern borders; neighboring Piedmont itself was also interested in having some protection against France. The emperor wished to be strategically positioned to keep an eye on revolutionary movements which allegedly abounded in Milan and elsewhere in the region. Local leaders thinking that an Austrian regime would be helpful in countering Piedmontese expansion were once again cooperative.

Such harmony of purpose did not last long. Various Italian regimes, including those in Parma, Modena, and Tuscany, where Habsburg offspring or cadet branches were either restored or installed as local rulers, wanted Austria to defend them but were also jealous of their sovereignty. They refused to take steps to reform their administrations, participate in confederations actively, or contribute much to their own defense. They were, therefore, unlikely prospects for long-term collaboration with Vienna. But in the short run, the Habsburg government in Vienna had achieved the position in northern and northeastern Italy that it wanted.

Metternich also found a way of reining in Alexander I and Russia. Though he had to accept the incorporation of more of Poland into the Tsarist empire than he would have liked, Austria, Prussia, and Russia signed a so-called Holy Alliance in September 1815 which bound its signatories to observe Christian principles in dealing with one another and with their peoples. Metternich himself was uncomfortable with the somewhat starry-eyed quality of the terms of the compact; he managed to have it amended to emphasize the brotherhood of legitimate monarchs and the duties of their subjects to take comfort in religion rather than political activism. Nevertheless, its consultative character gave Austria a way of restraining Russia. Metternich called it a paternal alliance of monarchs over their subjects, which is just about how he and Francis saw government all along.[47]

Thus the Habsburg empire successfully survived the Age of Revolution and Napoleonic imperialism. Its financial situation remained disastrous: bankruptcy was first declared in 1811 and by the end of the conflict its currency was still all but worthless. The Austrian empire was also far from the unity the title implied. Technically the dynasty's sway was over the something called 'the imperial-royal Austrian states' (*die kaiserlich-königlichen österreichischen Staaten*), but this solidarity did not apply to foreign commitments. While Hungary and Bohemia and the German-speaking Austrian provinces technically belonged to the Germanic Confederation, Galicia, Dalmatia, and Lombardy–Venetia did not.[48] But Habsburg claims to their holdings were still valid and their subjects still loyal – in part because that loyalty had been solicited, in part because it had been coerced, and in part because most people in the Habsburg empire had their own reasons for rejecting French hegemony.

Most important of all, however, the Habsburgs had managed once again to align themselves with the winning side, a position that enabled them to dictate crucial parts of the territorial settlement that followed the Napoleonic wars. How long states such as Russia and Prussia would routinely respect the house of Habsburg-Lorraine's interests rather than disregard them in the rush to satisfy their own ambitions was an open question. Both governments were clearly capable of pursuing foreign policies that were hostile to Vienna. But, for the moment, the Habsburg empire had awkwardly but effectively clawed its way out of a worst-case scenario that often recalled the monarchy's grimmest hours in the seventeenth century. Supreme realists that they were, Francis and Metternich could both take comfort in their handiwork.

Chapter 5: Revolution: Text and Subtext

Some Steps Toward Recovery

Napoleon died in his second exile on the bleak island of St. Helena in 1821, but his many-sided legacy fired the imaginations of Europeans for generations to come. His commitment to administrative efficiency and legal egalitarianism inspired many; others loathed such policies and the dictatorial militarism through which he had imposed them. Most widespread, however, was the longing for international peace, all the more desirable because of economic problems that almost 20 years of credit-funded warfare had created. The Habsburg empire was among the most fiscally challenged states of Europe. Inflation had become ominously routine; in 1810, rumors that the government was ready to tolerate the condition in order to pay off long-standing debt in cheaper money frightened creditors into demanding immediate return of their principal.[1] Experiments with paper currency added to the uncertainty.

On the positive side of its ledger, the empire had the means to remedy at least some of its financial difficulties and to lay the foundations of material growth and prosperity for years to come. Its population expanded rapidly following the Napoleonic wars, topping off at a little over 36 million by 1850. While agriculture remained the single largest sector of the economy in the Habsburg lands, the percentage of the population that drew its chief livelihood from agriculture dropped steadily.[2] Land use itself was more extensively rationalized. Joseph II had opened the way for non-nobles in many regions to purchase debt-ridden holdings that aristocrats by law had once had to pass on within their social class. By 1848 nearly one-third of noble property in Lower Austria would be in the

hands of people from bourgeois backgrounds who cultivated it for production of scale.

The groundwork that Maria Theresa and Joseph had laid for the industrialization of some areas in the Habsburg empire was not only largely
intact but expanding. Many internal tariff barriers had fallen, a far-flung
transportation network had begun, and domestic manufacture, sheltered
by protective tariffs, had prospered. The Continental System, Bonaparte's
strategic trade policy to keep British exports out of Europe, had unin-
tentionally freed Austrian industry from serious competition. Production
of textiles and ironwares increased especially fast during the Napoleonic
wars. Government decrees ordering traditional craftsmen either to adopt
modern technologies or lose their licenses had somewhat eased the hold
of craft guilds over methods of production. The Josephinian bureaucracy
itself had turned the administration of these policies and other inter-
ventions in the economy into a kind of calling. Their continuing effort
to break down regional and provincial barriers to trade and manufacture
were a way of advancing the welfare of all. The monopoly of the nobility
over bureaucratic positions began to slip too, as increased numbers of
middle-class officers, who were generally more dedicated to these programs, appeared in the imperial administration. Though aristocrats
continued to hold the highest offices, the educated bourgeoisie of the
Habsburg empire now had a stake in government employment as well.[3]

By supporting these policies, Maria Theresa and Joseph II were tacitly
confessing their need for both the energies of an entrepreneurial middle
class and the revenues its activities generated. Francis I and Metternich
continued the program for the very same reasons. They, too, realized
that education was the engine of middle-class productivity; the post-
Napoleonic government in Vienna deliberately cultivated and expanded
institutions and curricula that furthered industrial development in the
empire. State engineering schools had been operating in Prague and
Vienna since 1717. Though initially founded for military purposes, they
eventually taught more broadly practical, mathematical, and scientific
subjects. Of utmost importance were new technological Hochschulen,
modelled on the French École polytechnique, in Prague (1807) and
Vienna (1815). Important lecturers in both pure and applied science
came to these establishments at the invitation of the government as well
as to engineering faculties at the universities in Prague, Vienna, Graz,
and Innsbruck.

The introduction and modification of patent law to cover new inven-
tions and processes fostered innovation. One measure in 1810 awarded

inventors sole rights for ten years to profits generated by their creations. Revision of this stipulation in 1820 and 1832 updated the code to protect new techniques and devices in agriculture and chemical enterprises. The improvement of the monarchy's transportation infrastructure continued. From the end of the Napoleonic era to 1848, the government constructed 2240 km of roads. Local and private sources contributed even more – 46,400 km. Most significant among these thoroughfares were the stretches between Vienna and Trieste and between the Tyrol and Lombardy.[4]

To ensure that its monied middle classes would continue to be reliable sources of credit, Francis I's regime kept taxes very low on the incomes of wealthier merchants and bankers. Far heavier levies fell on real property and consumption, areas of particular concern to modest folk as well as to people who sustained themselves from the land generally. The government was also ready to fulfill middle-class aspirations for titles that legitimized their hopes for the lifestyles and privileges of born aristocrats. Vienna's entrepreneurs overtly prided themselves on their thrift and hard work, a sharp contrast, as they saw it, to aristocratic fecklessness. But social status meant something to them as well: noble residences, tastes, mannerisms, and honorifics were the familiar tokens of distinction. Rich bankers elevated to the service nobility were already becoming the center of a so-called second society, exclusive, though denied informal access to the court. Had the government been able to persuade the traditional nobility to accept the aspirations of these newcomers more graciously, middle-class critics of aristocracy might never have found the audience that they did.[5]

The bourgeoisie, where it was strong, in Bohemia and the Austrian lands, therefore had strong reasons to support Habsburg rule, even when the government's practical effectiveness was confined to the German provinces and Bohemia plus Galicia and the military border to the southeast. Such a regime, as members of these middle classes saw it, was their only guarantor of legal equality and active citizenship, perhaps the most enduring ideals of the French Revolution. It was the revised *Allgemeines Bürgerliches Gesetzbuch* of the Austrian empire, issued in 1811, that had first established the principle that those who lived under Habsburg rule were no longer subjects but *Staatsbürger*. It was government employment and Josephinian commitment to public education and freedom of expression that enabled significant numbers of bureaucrats and teachers to join the propertied middle classes traditionally connected with the European bourgeoisie.[6]

Accumulating Grievances, 1815–48

Nevertheless, though the economic priorities of Francis I's government and that of his clinically simple-minded successor, Ferdinand I (1793–1875), often complemented those of the commercial middle classes in Vienna and Prague, the two sides were often seriously at odds. The construction of the railroads exemplified the problem. Inspired by French and English models, independent entrepreneurs in the Habsburg lands started laying down track in the 1830s. Private banking houses, chiefly those of Salomon Rothschild (1803–74) and Simon Georg von Sina (1783–1856), financed them. After 1841, however, as the state came to appreciate the military and political significance of these projects, Ferdinand I decreed that any of these lines could be nationalized. The government itself began subsidizing rail networks; by 1848 it had laid about a quarter of all the track in the empire. These facilities were, however, largely for military purposes; what was a strategic outpost for the army was not always convenient to centers of trade and manufacture. Such a gross dissonance has persuaded at least some scholars that, in sharp contrast to other European countries, government-built rail links contributed little to the early industrialization of the Habsburg empire.[7] Metternich worked at persuading his sovereign and other ministers to pay more attention to the empire's economic affairs, particularly as he saw Prussia trying to gather north Germany into some sort of tariff union. He was, however, far from an ally of middle-class interests as they had taken shape in the Habsburg monarchy. The prince was eager, for example, to use free trade either as a weapon or as an enticement when negotiating foreign policy, a part of the liberal canon for which few manufacturers in the Austrian empire had any great enthusiasm.

Most importantly, both Francis I and his state chancellor (a title which the emperor conferred upon the Rhenish prince in 1821) had deep reservations about the non-economic by-products of middle-class entrepreneurship and capital accumulation. While both men recognized that cultural conditioning had its uses in shoring up Habsburg control of their lands, they were implacably opposed to the free-wheeling intelligentsia that was emerging all over Europe from an increasingly self-confident bourgeoisie. Revolutionary uprisings in Paris and elsewhere from 1830 to 1831 made Francis more edgy about reform than ever.[8] 'Pretention' was Metternich's term for middle-class aspirations to greater participation in the affairs of state; he was loath to back any activity that encouraged it, some industrial undertakings included.

Thus, even as the urban middle classes of the Habsburg empire looked to the Habsburg court and bureaucracy for their protection and their livelihoods, they also experienced it as an obstacle to economic, social, and political changes that they not only wanted but thought they deserved. Metternich and Francis programmatically opposed any changes that would upset the domestic peace they were diligently nurturing. When government moved at all, it moved languidly and in fractional increments, especially after Francis I's death in 1835.[9]

The disproportionality between the economic importance of the middle classes and their influence on government policy only widened between 1815 and 1848. The emperor had long since discarded Leopold II's thoughts about making regional estates more representative of all his peoples. Nevertheless, changing patterns of property holding, especially in the Austrian lands, suggested that such measures were in order. The members of the service nobility who had snapped up the regalian holdings that Joseph II had put on the market were now entitled to seats in the estates. State bankruptcy and currency fluctuations during the Napoleonic wars had only added to the attractiveness, and therefore the value, of their assets. In Upper Austria between 1780 and 1848, more than 40 sales of such land went to people who traced their ancestry largely to the commercial and manufacturing class. Equally significant, some well-to-do peasants and one prosperous chimney sweep were also among the purchasers. In regions of the monarchy that Napoleon had occupied in the south and southeast, he had abolished feudal restrictions on land holding altogether. Yet, for all that this new wealth was an important source of revenue for the regime in Vienna, the only two powers held by the Austrian provincial estates were to withhold fealty from a new territorial ruler and to hear, though not to discuss, the regime's requests for taxes.

Restraints on civil liberties also provoked steady and widespread complaint. Censorship, which even applied to art exhibitions, was especially odious.[10] The Franciscan regime had nothing against newspapers and journals in principle; indeed, it made expert use of them for its own propaganda. A flood of officially sponsored literature crafted to burnish the image of the dynasty came on the market – historical, geographic, verse – appearing in such publications as Joseph von Hormayr's *Archiv für Geographie, Historie, Staats- und Kriegskunst* (1810–37). Periodicals that subscribed to policies that the regime could not tolerate were not closed down but restaffed with more reliable people. The *Österreichische Jahrbücher*, established to demonstrate the government's commitment to sound scholarship, was turned over to a series of editors in the hope of finding one with a talent for presenting non-controversial themes so as not to upset the delicate status quo that the regime sought to preserve in all aspects of life throughout its lands.[11] Wholly uncensored revolutionary literature did creep into the Habsburg lands through clandestine routes that stretched as far as the New World. But spies lurked everywhere, even in the households of officials. Authors within the empire had the opportunity to change offending passages in their works, and often did. The system as a whole, however, was an insult to those who had internalized the ideals of free thought and expression.[12]

The relentless intrusion into public and private life of Francis I's government gradually made many members of the new bourgeoisie as split-minded about statist rule as they were about the customs and privileges of the aristocracy. Even as they passively acknowledged their respect for traditional authority, they increasingly celebrated themselves as elements apart from the government or any other segment of society. The settings for these activities were middle-class voluntary clubs, occupational, charitable, or social. The government was as ambivalent about these groups as the latter were toward those who ruled them. Francis's regime all but criminalized such organizations during the French Revolution, and Metternich always found them suspect.

In the early years of the post-Napoleonic era, however, official disapproval waned as the clubs took on some of the responsibilities for public welfare that the state could not afford. Such groups as the Vienna Legal-Political Reading Association, established in 1841, bowed to the regime's authority in return. When stocking its library, the group generally chose materials that would not attract the attention of state censors. Should the Reading Association made public statements, it did so with disciplined blandness. But its activities had a subversive side as well: the membership smuggled in some of its literature from Europe's more liberal outposts. Sister organizations in Graz and Innsbruck followed the same practices.[13]

The middle classes also pressed their particular socio-economic agenda more aggressively when the government seemed reluctant to espouse it. Such proposals often came out of so-called industrial associations, which first sprang up in Prague, then in Graz (the Inner Austrian Industrial Association) in 1837, and in Vienna in 1838–9 as the Lower Austrian Industrial Association. Old-fashioned bourgeois corporate loyalties did not figure large in their thinking. Bankers and industrialists joined, but so did artisans. These organizations were also dedicated advocates of public education. The Graz Association offered both affordable credit and news of recent technology to its members, said to be around 2391 in 1847.[14]

Fearing revolution from below, middle-class spokesmen in the more developed regions of the monarchy also urged the state to address deplorable living conditions among common workers. The populations of major urban centers, chiefly Vienna and its immediate suburbs and Prague, grew at a startling pace following the Napoleonic wars. Between 1820 and 1840 the capital had around 260,000 inhabitants; this number had grown to 357,000 by 1840. Prague grew from roughly 65,000 in 1815 to 115,000 in 1848.[15] Several factors encouraged this growth, among them the opportunity for service employment in noble houses and the personnel requirements of the government bureaucracy, but of crucial significance was the opportunity for jobs in industrial enterprises that ringed both cities. Whole families sometimes found work in these establishments. By the early 1840s, however, workers were feeling seriously pinched. The overproduction that bedeviled contemporary industry throughout Europe reduced their hours and therefore their pay. Manufacturers, especially in Vienna, had found the city a very costly place in which to do business, because shipping the raw materials for their enterprises was comparatively expensive. New machinery also displaced many workers, especially ones that printed patterns on fabrics, thus throwing out of work people who had done this task by hand. Wages stagnated, and as early as 1844 workers mutinied against these conditions in Prague. Industrialists therefore had reason to worry about their labor forces, as did the government itself.[16]

The general purpose of the industrial associations, however, was to focus the imperial regime on the needs of businesses. Reform of banking and credit practices ranked high among their priorities. Customs regulations were another pressing concern, though here middle-class opinion divided. Large industrialists wanted protective imposts scaled back, as did Metternich's supporters in the councils of state, though the motives of the latter were diplomatic and not economic. Artisans and light manufacturers generally argued against such measures. Where most of these constituencies agreed was on the importance of reworking local ordinances to encourage entrepreneurs and, above all, the free movement of labor. They were united as well in their wish for more formal input into the government that created such laws.

Not only the urban middle classes and the recently ennobled had reason to criticize their government's misguided and inconsistent ways. Traditional elites, including the Catholic establishment, also had their complaints. The nobility of birth in the estates of the Austrian lands resented any regime that overlooked distinctions between themselves and the service nobility, at least when membership in provincial deliberative bodies was at issue. Many territorial aristocrats also chafed against a tax system that tilted heavily in favor of capital formation and possession at the expense of landlords and consumers.[17]

But nowhere in the monarchy did noble discontent have a more complex and far-reaching impact than in Hungary. Here discontent with Habsburg rule always smoldered below the surface of public life, awaiting some cause to enflame it. This time it was distress over the Vienna regime's ill-fated experiment with paper currency in 1811. Hungary's magnates, lesser nobles, even its fledgling middle class all protested against the central government and those ministers whom they held responsible for such policies. The remedy proposed was even more obnoxious. Paper yet circulating was to be devalued by a fifth, then covered by silver raised through public levies five times above current levels. Hungary was asked to contribute slightly less than half of the funding for the program. The royal diet dug in its heels, not only because of the size of this request but because of the arbitrary way it was imposed and the fiscally ruinous consequences it could have on many in the kingdom.[18]

Francis, therefore, did not summon the estates again until 1825; to raise money in the kingdom he resorted to direct decree. Such high-handedness not only stoked the wrath of the royal diet, but also stirred up the rural gentry, many of whom rarely left their properties. Nobles large and small demanded, as they had always done, that their king respect their constitutional prerogatives. Far less routine, however, was their proposal to canvass public opinion throughout the kingdom on the monarch's policies. Implicit in such a tactic was a vision of political responsibility that went far beyond traditional constitutional privilege. The Hungarian nobility had long claimed that they and they alone embodied 'the nation' and had the sole right to speak for it. Their wish to hear the opinion of those beyond their own circle, however, was both new and important; it had serious consequences as well. Political awareness throughout the kingdom rose sharply, particularly within liberal groups that would become a major force in Hungarian public life after 1830.[19]

Francis finally called the royal diet together in 1825, apologized for his heavyhandedness, and vowed to do better.[20] But this controversy and the inward-looking Hungarian response was only part of a larger redefinition of the roles of aristocracy and king taking place in the lands of the crown of St. Stephen. Regardless of their constitutional authority, Hungarian nobles, like their counterparts in Bohemia, the Austrian lands, and Polish Galicia, were as much a product of the monarchical system as was the monarchy itself. Kings created nobles and legitimized noble status by acknowledging it. Should their sovereign trespass upon that power, the nobility opposed him; should that challenge come from below, it was kings who defended them. In either case the nobles recognized the monarch alone as the source of their prerogatives.

Sovereigns, however, could act in the name of the generality of their subjects without necessarily breaking the special bonds they had with their privileged aristocracies. Maria Theresa had offered several lessons in the technique. Should nobilities do the same thing, they would be seriously altering their constitutional functions at the expense of their kings.[21]

The terminology of this development had already been used in discussions between Bohemia's nobility and the regime of Leopold II at the end of the eighteenth century. 'Representatives of the people and the nation', they called themselves, empowered to advise the monarch on wrongs that required correction. They did, however, still assign their king the role of presiding over the general welfare.[22] The roots of this transformation were more solidly grounded in Hungary, even before the royal estates decided, however modestly, to use the country in the campaign against arbitrary Habsburg rule. The Bohemian nobility lost interest in the revival of the Czech language rather quickly. But in promoting the official use of their national language for educational and administrative purposes during the early years of Francis's reign, Hungary's noble reformers had embraced a cause that made them advocates for the generality of all Hungarians, within whom they located themselves. The Magyar tongue, said Mihály Csokonai (1773–1805) in 1804, an ardent champion of its use and a man well acquainted with many levels of his society, defined Hungarians more clearly than any other criterion. With it 'our parents and good teachers gently acquainted us with moral principles for the first time. How sweet sound the stories, the descriptions of nations and lands in that language in which we heard our first tales from nursemaids and others around us.'[23] Those nobles who promoted a specifically Hungarian national language and culture had become spokesmen for a shared Hungarian experience, rather than for their unique privileges in a quasi-feudal relationship with their sovereign. While not ready to renounce their noble titles, their identification with a fundamental popular cause made these men, as well as the monarch, advocates for the common welfare of the kingdom. When coupled with progressive economic ideas, this augmented understanding of nobility was even more plausible.

Count Stephen Széchenyi (1791–1860) epitomized these developments. His father, Count Ferenc Széchényi – his son dropped the second diacritical in the family name – had already made plain his commitment to the study of Hungarian history, language, and culture through patronage of the Hungarian National Museum, as well as the National Library founded in 1802. Unlike virtually all his class, the elder Széchényi also supported many of Joseph II's political and social programs. Stephen endorsed the liberal thrust of these measures as well; extended travel and observations in western Europe following the Napoleonic wars further reinforced these views.

Upon his return to Hungary, he dedicated himself to the modernization of his native kingdom's society, economy, and intellectual life along French and English models. His belief in his cause was total: in 1825 he astounded the members of the royal diet by promising to turn over that year's earnings from his estates toward setting up a national academy for the study and advancement of the Magyar tongue.[24] The first group he had to win to his agenda, however, was his own class of society whose complacent provincialism and lack of public spirit he openly deplored. He was not beyond a bit of pandering to get his way. Among Széchenyi's first efforts to improve the Hungarian economy was a program for horse breeding, a favorite noble preoccupation. Indeed, he introduced competitive horse racing on the English model to his countrymen.

For Széchenyi to enlist his aristocratic colleagues in his cause, however, he had to do far more than cater to their equestrian pursuits. He was a thorough economic liberal as the term was understood in nineteenth-century Europe. He believed that capitalism and modern banking practices, including credit financing, were the cornerstones of a productive and prosperous economy. He promoted the development of the Danube for commercial transportation; he also pushed Hungarian cultivation of new crops and manufactures such as silk and innovations in viticulture. Feudalism and its institutional underpinnings, especially serfdom, had to end. Széchenyi also wished his land to have a more representative, though far from democratic, form of government.

Such suggestions, however, both challenged and disregarded several basic tenets of Hungarian aristocratic life. To borrow more heavily from banks, nobles would have to give their lands in collateral. This step was impossible, however, when properties were inalienable, as noble holdings often were. Széchenyi's ideas for expanding Hungary's transportation and communications networks appealed to many of his colleagues, who would then be able to sell their products more conveniently. They might also, however, have to pay for these improvements through higher taxes, and this prospect did not attract them in the least.

Social and political revolution broke out in western Europe in 1830, and peasant unrest erupted in Hungary a year later, in part the result of a savage cholera epidemic. All but the most narrow-visioned among the Hungarian nobility began to worry about their future in the kingdom. Recognizing that changes had to take place if their preeminence was to endure, they gave Széchenyi a more considered hearing. But though the count's program had excited much attention in his country, he would never get the wholehearted and crucial support of his own class whose welfare was also central to his thinking. He himself finally admitted that his country was not really ready for his visions. What endured of his reform program, including the restructuring of the legal relationship of the house of Habsburg to the Hungarian crown, was put in place in the second half of the nineteenth century by Ferenc Deák (1803–76), a landowner and uncommonly skillful lawyer though no magnate, who was one of the architects of the Dual Compromise of 1867.

Széchenyi's program was no more appealing in Vienna than it had been among Hungary's nobles. When called to do battle against some of his ministerial rivals, Metternich tried to use some of the count's ideas as leverage, but the chancellor took little interest in them for their own value. The government of Ferdinand V by 1836 was in any case growing less tolerant of nationally oriented programs in the kingdom, whatever their source and purpose. Moreover, Count Kolowrat, the imperial finance minister from Bohemia, was openly hostile to Hungarian nationalism on ethnic grounds. The lone concern of Archduke Ludwig (1784–1864), the third member of the triad that was standing in for the unreliable emperor, was to perpetuate the structure of government as it stood.

Where money was needed for military purposes, in 1840 for example, Vienna could be more conciliatory toward its Hungarian subjects, but feelings of discontent in Hungary were too strong to appease. Széchenyi's passion for the general improvement of his homeland, while largely lost on his own class, had taken hold of political groups who were far more hostile to Habsburg rule than the count himself was. For all his commitment to Hungary, Széchenyi remained, like his father, a firm supporter of Habsburg rule. His most radical proposals concerning the dynasty called for reorganizing the empire along lines that assigned a central political role to Hungary. When rebellion erupted in the kingdom in 1848, Széchenyi joined the revolutionary government of Count Lajos Batthyány after Ferdinand I (V) had accepted the arrangement.[25] Younger liberals in the kingdom, on the other hand, were beginning to think that if anti-Hungarian officials in Vienna were a problem, the solution was to have ministers responsible to a separate Hungarian government in Budapest.[26]

Much of the inspiration behind such thinking came from Louis Kossuth (1802–94), one of the several charismatic figures that the pre-March revolutionary era (*Vormärz*) produced. Equally eloquent on paper and as a speaker in the diet, Kossuth was born into the Hungarian rural squirearchy whose interests and position he would always support. At the same time, his understanding of the ideals of self-government in Great Britain, revolutionary France, and the United States had already made a lasting impression on him. The political inclusiveness of the American republican experiment excited him to learn English. He would eventually call for abolition of Hungarian noble privilege and for full national sovereignty. In general, his views up to 1848 did not enjoy much support among Hungarian conservatives and even moderate liberals. Nevertheless, he and other members of the Hungarian political classes were at least broaching the possibility that the dynasty that had ruled them for over 300 years could not act in their realm's best interests. More important still, these dissidents, thanks to Széchenyi, had a concrete idea of what these interests were and were ideologically equipped to push it forward. Monarchs, as revolutionary France had already shown, were not the only defenders of the common interest.

Important constituencies among the empire's Italian peoples were also beginning to doubt the value of rule from Vienna. To disguise the aura of occupation that had always clung to the dynasty's presence, Ferdinand I was crowned king of Lombardy in 1838. The title was fictitious, but the Habsburg government wanted to give the region a status equivalent to Bohemia and Hungary. The regime also continued to award the deserving with the honorific Order of the Iron Cross, created by Napoleon in 1805, to reinforce local identification with the new kingdom. But Lombardy lacked the institution that had negotiated the dynasty's rule in the eastern kingdoms – an established body of estates – and there was no way of masking that uncomfortable piece of reality. The nearest official contender, the 'Central Congregation', acted as an advisory panel only. Finally, Ferdinand himself, good-natured though he was, inspired no one. Even street urchins made fun of a do-nothing king.[27]

Hoping after 1815 to retain its strategic position on the peninsula as well as to harvest the fiscal benefits of a comparatively developed economy, the Austrian administration tried to ingratiate itself with its Italian provinces in several ways. They were accorded considerable leeway in enforcing measures dispatched from the Habsburg capital. Communication of any kind with the Habsburg cadet lines in Parma, Modena, and Tuscany was minimal, even though the Austrian imperial forces were obligated to defend them. The confusion of responsibility that this regimen encouraged would eventually cause serious problems for the central government. It was not, however, onerous from the standpoint of people who lived in these principalities. In Lombardy–Venetia, where control from Vienna was more direct, education and social services were exemplary for the time. Law and order prevailed for the first time, according to some.

But Habsburg rule in Italy was also fomenting an array of grievances, particularly among the middle classes and traditional local authorities who felt the impact of government behavior most directly. All but the most trivial initiatives had to be referred to a distant desk in Vienna where decisions taken were often no decision at all. Official communications with Lombardy–Venetia went to both the viceroy's office, which had real, but very few, powers, and to the Italian deputation, where the day-by-day business of government took place. With Bonaparte no longer preempting the regional labor market for his armies, unemployment and underemployment was high, even among the educated middle classes. Taxes, however, were heavy.

Ever greater numbers of officials came from Vienna rather than closer to home to execute policies handed down from above. By 1848, professional bureaucrats all but exclusively manned major administrative offices in Lombardy–Venetia: only one of nine so-called delegates in Lombardy was a propertied aristocrat, the rest had bourgeois backgrounds. In Venetia, nobles occupied some of these positions, but they were largely of foreign origin. Regardless of the quality of their families, most of these men looked to the central regime for their livings and not the regional economy. Worse yet, indoctrinated in Josephinian ideals of the common welfare at universities in Graz, Vienna, and Innsbruck, they now viewed all provincial interests as suspect. The state was an instrument of the general, not the particular, good.

Both sides, Italian aristocracy and middle classes alike, and the government from Vienna, were coming to dislike one another intensely.[28] Italian notables – local mayors and other customary municipal and regional officials – who acquiesced to Habsburg rule as long as the going social order went undisturbed keenly resented being shoved aside. Other political entities on the peninsula, especially papal Rome, thought that Austria was not done with its expansion southward. Metternich's project for an Italian League never got very far, but remained a permanent threat to governments that had their own hegemonic ambitions in Italy.

Worse yet, Vienna seemed more and more ready to achieve its purposes through coercion rather than cooperation. However public-spirited many of its policies in Italy were, the Habsburg monarchy was a police state whose Italian mission was to quarantine residents from French Jacobinism and Bonapartism. Metternich was especially committed to this policy.[29] In the name of international stability, he was also ready to send troops to Italy to protect the crowns of legitimate, if sometimes execrably bad, rulers. Between 1820 and 1848, five governments would call upon Vienna to put down local sedition.[30] The first was the Bourbon king of Naples, Ferdinand (1810–59), driven from his throne in 1820 by discontented army officers and representatives of the Carbonari. The latter was an avowedly revolutionary group dedicated to establishing a national and parliamentary government in a unified Italy.

Metternich deplored the upheaval on principle. Nevertheless, he concluded that Austria had far more to gain from persuading the Italian rulers to accept revolutionary demands that were not inconsistent with a monarchical order rather than to alienate the dissidents with a summary rejection of their programs. The chancellor suggested reintroducing the Bourbon as a constitutional monarch in his kingdom, reforming fiscal policies and rooting out corruption there generally. These reforms could then be extended to other Italian states where needed. Such a strategy, he thought, could win the Habsburgs much goodwill on the peninsula.

His schemes found little support, however, even in the chancellor's own government. The bureaucracy opposed any weakening of centralized power, native Austrian colleagues resented Metternich and other non-Austrians who enjoyed high position under Francis, and Metternich's espousal of economic liberalism to ratchet up economic growth in Lombardy as well as in other parts of the empire worried those whose livelihoods such policies disturbed.[31]

Metternich's miscalculation of the Italian reaction to his ideas was even graver. Ferdinand had little respect for the procedures and values that

Metternich was recommending; the Bourbon ruler also feared that people who preferred to leave things just as they were would kill him. Metternich, therefore, had little choice but to send Austrian troops to put the king back on his throne. The step annoyed both local revolutionaries and the French, a coupling of interests that would seriously trouble European state relations when the unification of Italy began in earnest a decade later. Austria also gave significant help to King Charles Albert (1798–1849) in Piedmont where dissidents also demanded constitutional government. The refugees these movements created regrouped in Switzerland and continued to conspire in the name of liberal revolution.[32]

Unrest in the Papal States in 1831 and in Modena and Parma further underscored the difficulties that the Habsburgs were having in finding significant local collaborators in Italy, even among fellow rulers. Even when voices of criticism became very shrill, the princes in the Habsburg Italian line, especially the grand duke of Tuscany, did not overly concern themselves with politics, but plugged away at improving the fragile economies of their lands.[33] For Gregory XVI (1765–1846), a new but reactionary pope, Metternich once again recommended constructive conservatism: shoring up papal rule through improving administrative, judicial, and fiscal practices.[34] Conservatives in Rome, however, wanted no part of intervention from abroad. Once again the chancellor in Vienna faced the unpleasant choice of either abandoning parts of Italy to revolutionaries or intervening militarily. In March 1831, Habsburg forces began an occupation of the Papal States and Modena. Though little, if any, bloodshed took place, the Austrian government received little support from either its natural allies, who were clearly interested in preserving the status quo, or from the better-educated elements of the Italian population for whom reform had come to mean genuine freedom from absolutism and foreign rule and not cooperation with it.

Following an international conference to resolve the diplomatic issues created by the disorder in the papal lands, the Habsburg armies withdrew from Rome in July of 1831. By the end of the year, however, they were back as Gregory failed to control the unrest in his territories. That taxes on the local citizenry paid for these occupations, and that the economic development of neighboring Piedmont could threaten commerce and manufacture in Austrian Lombardy, did not help Habsburg relations with their Italian peoples either.[35] In short, Metternich's efforts to win Italian support by improving the operation of local governments while at the same time keeping Austria in a position of strategic advantage on the peninsula simply failed. At best it made Italians of many classes and interests less enthusiastic about remaining under Vienna's tutelage; at worst it inspired the more progressive factions among them to want uncompromised parliamentary government.[36]

Revolutions and Counter-Revolution

By 1848 the Habsburg government was at loggerheads, directly or indirectly, with a spectrum of its peoples that cut across boundaries of class, occupation, and nationality. All had come to play some role in the survival of the monarchy in an industrializing and increasingly democratizing world. The domestic opposition that the dynasty had encountered in previous centuries had come from constitutionally entrenched noble and clerical elites who, while always ready to resist encroachment on their prerogatives, had also depended on monarchical regimes to validate their privileges, status, and authority. Many in this group were now espousing cultural, economic, even political positions that reinforced their local preeminence, regardless of policies that emanated from Vienna. Hungary's noble reformers were reconfiguring their time-honored role as the spokesmen for their 'nation' as a whole and espousing programs that made them, and not the monarch, the defenders of the kingdom's general welfare. While the grievances of the Bohemian nobility were less well articulated, they, too, were developing serious reservations about the value of a regime that taxed the land excessively, as they saw it, yet gave very little in return. During the 1830s and 1840s, the estates called again and again for startlingly far-reaching economic change. The manorial system was to go and what remained of forced labor requirements along with it. More representatives of the middle-class members were to have seats in the body which also wanted a role in formulating tax policy. In 1845 the estates of Bohemia and Moravia flatly asked for the right to approve government budgets; two years later they rejected outright a request for new imposts. A general economic depression that afflicted both urban industry and agricultural production alike added to the intensity of their demands.[37] The downturn also harnessed the interests of the landed aristocracy and the middle classes into a potentially dynamic alliance.

The diet in Lower Austria had become equally restive. In 1845–6 members petitioned for an end of official censorship, the establishment of an agricultural credit bank, and an income tax, the last to be coupled with the lowering of indirect consumption duties. Like their colleagues in Bohemia, they also wanted the powers to sanction government budgets and to approve new revenue levies. They continued to draw attention to the plight of peasants and workers and to the threat of revolutionary violence.[38]

The Habsburg Italian lands had even less reason to maintain the political status quo with Vienna, even though up to 1848 Austrian-ruled Tuscany and Lombardy were arguably the freest areas on the peninsula. Metternich's decision to prop up local princes, corrupt and despotic though he knew them to be, was stiffening the resolve of an Italian national opposition even beyond those lands that the Habsburgs and their distant relatives ruled. But Francis I's governments had offended Italian elites in Lombardy–Venetia gravely, especially when they downgraded their historically cloudy titles following the Napoleonic wars, requiring greater numbers of quarterings in their escutcheons to gain access to the court in Vienna.[39] Especially noteworthy were the aristocratic voices of men such as Silvio Pellico (1789–1854), whose autobiographical descriptions of his incarceration in a Moravian political prison broadcast the dark side of Habsburg rule both to his countrymen and to influential figures; Alessandro Manzoni (1785–1873), the author of the signature novel of Italian unification, *I promessi sposi*; and the philosopher–cleric Vincenzo Gioberti (1801–52), who argued for the unification of Italy in *On the Moral and Civil Primacy of the Italians*, published in 1843. Perhaps the only favorable sign for the Habsburgs amidst this gathering discontent was that neither France nor England, each for its own reasons, refrained from taking strategic and diplomatic advantage of the monarchy's internal weaknesses.

As was true elsewhere in Europe, material conditions in the Austrian empire deteriorated sharply in the mid-years of the 1840s. Crop failures, including a general potato blight that reached from Ireland to the central continent by 1847, hit people living at the margins of the economy especially hard. The event that apparently converted this dense pile-up of grievances into violent revolution in the Habsburg lands was the February 1848 uprising against the Orleanist regime of King Louis Philippe (1773–1850) in France. The next month liberals went to the barricades in Vienna. Predominantly middle-class and young – student participation was strong – their goals were generally more moderate than the economic and social agendas of their counterparts in Paris. Nevertheless, they had substantive demands, central among them a parliamentary regime that had some control over the financing and budgetary priorities of the government. They also asked for an array of civil liberties, particularly the ending of censorship. Encouraging the economic development of the empire was another concern; they echoed the long-standing call to lift both the regulatory powers of traditional trade and craft guilds and the restrictions on the free movement of labor. To the latter end, the rebels asked for the abolition of serfdom finally and completely, a part of their program that the peasantry throughout the entire empire heartily endorsed.

The lone source of support for the government in Vienna was itself, but initial efforts to quell the upheaval outside their windows bode ill for the future of the house of Habsburg-Lorraine. Hoping to appease the demonstrators in the street, influential figures around the hapless Ferdinand I recommended the dismissal of ministers who were closely associated with the most oppressive features of the regime. Prince Metternich was the chief sacrifice; he quickly left Vienna for a brief exile in England, and went from there to Brussels. Though he returned to the city of his greatest triumphs in 1851, he would never hold another official appointment.

The government got rid of censorship too. On 25 April it also issued a constitution that created a bicameral legislature, but one chosen by a very limited electorate. The revolutionaries found this arrangement unsatisfactory and rejected it; the regime then proposed a unicameral body to be voted upon popularly everywhere in the empire except Hungary and Italy. Deputies were actually chosen in June and July; they then set to work. Their greatest accomplishment was the total abolition of serfdom, though several years went by before the process was completed.

The dynasty felt so insecure that it withdrew to Innsbruck for safety shortly after formally making its second constitutional proposal. Vienna grew somewhat quieter, but revolution now racked urban centers throughout the empire. Violent uprisings in Italy had actually begun during January 1848 in Sicily. When Austria refused to rescue King Ferdinand once again, he issued the constitution that the dissidents were demanding. Now realizing that the Habsburgs were a flimsy shield against the forces of political change, King Charles Albert followed suit in Piedmont, as did the lethargic grand duke of Tuscany. Archduke Rainer (1783–1853), the viceroy in Lombardy–Venetia, was not empowered to put down seditious street violence in Milan; revolution against Habsburg rule spread from there into Parma and Modena.

In March of 1848, constitutional government was set up in the Habsburg cadet principalities; and Lombardy–Venetia erupted into full rebellion against Austrian rule as well. Here, Charles Albert's ambitions contributed directly to the flow of events. Heir to a venerable princely house that had coveted lands adjacent to its borders in northwestern Italy for centuries, his family had much resented Austria's return to neighboring Lombardy after the Napoleonic wars. Though a Habsburg ally in 1831, Charles Albert was quick to take the initiative and attack the dynasty in Lombardy and Venetia with the support of Tuscany and Naples. By the summer of 1848 he had engineered a consolidation of Piedmont, Lombardy, Venetia, Modena, and Parma.[40] Venice was a new republic. The forces that the government in Vienna had sent to the peninsula had withdrawn within garrisons in northern Italy, a strategically advantageous but as yet unexploited position. The constitution Charles Albert had sanctioned in Piedmont was a relatively liberal one; Italian revolutionaries in Lombardy and Venetia were now looking to him for leadership against foreign – by which they meant Austrian – rule.

In Bohemia, the noble estates demanded in March that a diet be called. The meeting never took place, but many members of the aristocracy did support the demands of the middle classes for a greater role in government on the condition that these people were educationally qualified to handle the role. Such a concession, as the nobles saw it, would help them to survive new political realities.[41] That they had good reason to worry was driven home to them by the events of the next couple of months. Middle-class intellectuals, some of whom not only wanted an expanded franchise in the kingdom but were also very sympathetic to the plight of the working classes, quickly took the leading role in the revolutionary activities. A growing sense of identity among the Habsburg Slavic peoples, Poles, Ukrainians from Galicia and the Transcarpathian Ukraine, Croatians, Serbs, and Slovaks, brought their spokesmen to Prague in June of 1848 to discuss their future in the monarchy. Adding urgency to their meeting were discussions at the Frankfurt parliament in Germany about the role of the Habsburg lands in a united German state, a prospect that made many Slavs very uneasy. Nevertheless, though the Czechs dominated the assembly in the Bohemian capital, the so-called Pan Slavic Congress did not challenge Habsburg rule as a general principle. What they wished the regime to do, however, was to grant autonomy to the constituent lands of the Habsburg monarchy. Such a policy would have effectively federalized the empire, though more along historical–

political frontiers than ethnic ones, an arrangement that would have vio-
lated all sense of order among the traditionalist nobility. Bohemia, which
was to be reunited with its traditional crownlands of Bohemia, Moravia,
and the Lusatias, was to have a kind of representative parliament. The
country would thus have a status that Hungary had long enjoyed and that
the recent revolution in Vienna had brought to the Austrian German
population as well.[42]

Most serious, however, for the integrity of the monarchy was the situation unfolding in Hungary. The Vienna regime had made some last-
minute and fruitless attempts during the 1840s to recruit allies among
the nobility in the estates, a few of whom had always aligned themselves
with the dynasty in moments of crisis. Metternich had almost always used
indigenous aristocrats as crown officials in the kingdom. Among the
Hungarian magnates there was a more youthful group, calling themselves
'Progressive Conservatives', who believed that political, social, and economic reform of their land was not only required but positively desirable.
They disliked extremism of any sort, however, and were willing to yield
some points to the government if it adopted some of their important
goals.[43] The group was not altogether unwilling to submit to royal taxation, an attitude that made discussions between the sides somewhat more
cordial. Led by Count George Apponyi (1808–99), the Progressives did
reach an understanding with Metternich on several matters important to
their livelihoods and status. The government promised to enlist Vienna's
banks in the drive to raise funds for major public construction and engineering projects in the kingdom. The most notable of these, the regulation of the Tisza river, did indeed move forward under Count Széchenyi's
direction. Other items on the Progressive Conservative wish list were less
altruistic. County lord-lieutenants (*főispán*), customarily great nobles like
many of the Hungarian aristocrats negotiating with Vienna in 1847, had
not functioned as the military leaders of the Hungarian counties since
the sixteenth century. Now performing that role was the vice-lord-
lieutenant, who was confirmed in his office by the petty nobility and
served as their spokesman too. Progressive Conservatives wanted to revert
to the earlier arrangement. For their part, they would do their best to
keep Kossuth's radical followers, many of whom were those same small
country nobles, out of the lower house of the Hungarian diet. The Progressive Conservatives also promised to accept a customs union with
Austria, a concession much to the great landowners' advantage since the
growing population in the monarchy's lands outside of Hungary had
stepped up demand for the kingdom's agricultural products.

In June of 1847, however, a more liberal political camp that included a few members of the great nobility but also significant numbers of the county gentry issued a Declaration of Opposition that argued for Hungarian interests far more aggressively. Written largely by the jurist–country gentleman Ferenc Deák, the document declared the present Habsburg regime unconstitutional, at least under the terms of Leopold II's Law 10 of 1790. The sole legitimate Hungarian government was a purely national one. Its ministry was to be national and responsible to an equally national parliament that had extensive controls over the finances of the kingdom and generally aspired to a more equitable society and economy. When the royal diet came together in the fall of 1847, it was apparent that the Habsburgs had cultivated the Progressive Conservatives in vain. They and the Opposition came to the gathering in almost equal numbers. In response, the regime in Vienna refused outright to compromise central control of the empire.[44]

Talks between the sides did, however, go on in Vienna until the March revolution broke out there. The feeble government offered only token resistance to demands for Hungarian autonomy. Revolutionary forces in Budapest quickly set up a functional Hungarian state in which the strident voice of Louis Kossuth was becoming ever more prominent. A new gloss on the Hungarian constitution, called the April Laws, cut all connections to Habsburg rule save for the person of the monarch himself, shared with the dynasty's other domains. The dynasty was now governing Hungary as a constitutional monarchy in which all royal decrees required ministerial counter-signatures. Though these new arrangements made the Hungarian nobility subject to general taxation and abolished serfdom, aristocrats large and small had reduced their sovereign to very small proportions indeed, especially in the domestic affairs of the kingdom. The nobility, in a word, had won a very substantial victory, one that promised to continue through the franchise provisions of the new constitution. The vote was given to members of the middle and peasant classes who could meet educational and property qualifications; all nobles would continue to enjoy this privilege, regardless of their wealth or schooling.[45]

Nevertheless, grim though its prospects were from the spring of 1848 on, the Habsburg monarchy survived. In Italy the constellation of foreign affairs remained favorable. Though France and England would have gladly seen Austria removed from the peninsula, each decided not to intervene. Even as he committed his own army to the revolutionary cause in March 1848, Charles Albert of Piedmont rejected advice that he appeal to France for help. There was little point, as he saw it, in evicting the Habsburgs only to have the French take their place. Great Britain was equally reluctant to see French influence grow in the Mediterranean. Moreover, the British prime minister, Lord Palmerston (1784–1865), continued to think that some form of the Habsburg empire was needed to curb Russian ambitions in the Balkans and other regions of east central Europe. His Foreign Office urged Metternich's temporary successor as prime minister, Count Karl Ficquelmont (1777–1857) to make concessions to the revolutionaries and surrender Lombardy and Venetia to Charles Albert, but took no further action. Finally, France's own revolution in 1848 made foreign adventures far less attractive to its political leaders.[46]

Concerns about preserving Austria's role in foreign affairs preoccupied even some revolutionaries. One of the leading spokesmen for the Czech national standpoint, the historian František Palacký, also stressed the need to maintain some form of the Habsburg monarchy in central Europe. Asked by German revolutionaries meeting in Frankfurt for his opinion of their proposal to incorporate the Habsburg holdings into a unified Germany, he rejected the idea politely but firmly in the name of the Czech nation. While he was an advocate of federating the dynasty's empire, an act that would have required some redrawing of its traditional internal boundaries, the smaller peoples of east central Europe still needed the protection that the large government of Vienna had long offered. Should Germany unify, the matter which the groups in Frankfurt were attempting to engineer, Czechs and many other ethnic groups could be threatened by this very new power. The ambitions of Tsarist Russia could also be very dangerous to them. Stephen Széchenyi had long said similar things from a Hungarian perspective. He too believed that Hungary could not stand by itself in Europe without Vienna to defend it. Furthermore, should the kingdom choose outright independence, as Kossuth's radicals would eventually propose, the Magyars as a people would not survive the opposition of the various minority ethnic groups in the kingdom. The Slavic Croatian nobility, who had a token presence in the Hungarian royal diet, already took a dim view of Magyar linguistic nationalism. Indeed, the very intransigence of the Magyar nobility on this point turned some of their Croatian counterparts into supporters of the government in Vienna.[47]

In the Austrian lands, some of the fervor had gone out of the revolutionary cause as peasants, now assured that serfdom was indeed a thing of the past, deserted the ranks. The propertied middle classes and aristocrats here and in Bohemia had also developed serious concerns about the doctrines of social revolution they were hearing and were becoming more protective of their own economic welfare.[48] An especially alarming situation confronted the Polish gentry and nobility in Galicia. Having organized a cross-class front asking for autonomy from Vienna in the early weeks of the revolution, the aristocracy found that they had stirred up forces of Ukrainian national sentiment that threatened both their economic and their political positions. The Habsburg government had even encouraged the peasantry as a way of curbing potential Polish separatism.[49]

Military might and capital punishment met the needs of all opponents of radical revolution. The Habsburg regime, inept and compromised though it was, had never lost complete control of its army. In June 1848, Field Marshal Albert von Windischgrätz (1787–1862) subdued insurrection in Prague that had taken on strident social overtones.[50] The outbreak in Vienna of another wave of violence in October, this time led by industrial workers, brought him into the capital. He subdued the movement by the end of the month, summarily executing several liberal and radical spokesmen for Vienna's laborers.

In Italy a long-time servant of the Habsburg regime, Field Marshal Joseph Radetzky (1766–1858), won two convincing victories against the Sardinian forces upon whom hung the survival of revolutionary governments in the northern part of the peninsula. The first triumph, at Custozza on 24 July, allowed Austria to retake Milan and to start negotiations for an armistice with Charles Albert. On the urging of liberals within his own kingdom, Charles Albert resumed war in March of 1849, only to be defeated again at Novara. He was not, in any case, the ideal leader for national revolution, either temperamentally or intellectually. By preference he would have only nobles in his government, and his undisguised dynastic focus put off many. He insisted, for example, that anyone who enlisted in his army from outside his kingdom pledge their allegiance to the house of Savoy, not to a regime that represented other Italians, however distant that possibility might be.[51]

In Hungary an increasingly radicalized group of national leaders held out much longer, even though the government did its best to make use of aggrieved minorities within the kingdom. Infuriated by Magyar language policies in the 1840s, Croatians had already begun to demand separation from Hungarian rule. A joint attack by a Croatian force led by the kingdom's governor, Joseph Jelačič (1801–59), and imperial troops put the Hungarian government in flight to Debreczen in 1849.

There, in April, Kossuth severed the connection with Austria altogether by declaring Hungary to be a republic. He also turned to France and England, as well as other foreign governments, for support, but only the precariously situated republic in Venice responded positively.

A new monarch, Francis, or Francis Joseph (1830–1916) – he added the second name to mollify the Josephinists in the bureaucracy he inherited – combined what cards his dynasty still held in foreign affairs with its military superiority to save Hungary for the monarchy. Tsar Nicholas I (1796–1855) in Russia had been anxiously watching the revolutions immediately to his west. Not only was he a principled opponent of sedition against legitimate sovereigns; he also worried that around 10,000 Polish volunteers in the revolutionary Hungarian army would return to their homeland with the same mission.[52] Like Palmerston he deemed imperial Austria an indispensable linchpin in the post-Napoleonic balance of power, though for different reasons. An independent Hungary did not fit into this vision.

The end of Kossuth's regime came at Vilagos on 13 August 1849. Combined Russian and Croatian forces defeated the Hungarians decisively; Kossuth fled abroad to a long-lived exile in which he achieved iconic status for significant groups among some segments of Hungarian nationalists. The new Austrian regime in the kingdom was as brutal as the one Windischgrätz established in Vienna, if not more so. Revolutionary leaders connected with Hungarian governments since March 1848, even moderates like Count Lajos Batthyány (1806–49), who headed the first Hungarian revolutionary diet, were executed. An army of occupation under General Julius von Haynau (1786–1853) settled into the land. A pathologically vicious man whose name, as Hungarians quickly noted, was almost indistinguishable from that of a loud but notoriously stupid beast, he and his forces did more to unite Hungarians as a people than any revolutionary had been able to do.[53]

Revolution in 1848 and all that went with it had ripped into the very core of the Habsburg monarchy. Hungary's radicals had made plain that proprietary dynasticism, the principle upon which the empire had developed and stood for over 300 years, was altogether inconsistent with national understandings of legitimate sovereignty. The demands made by classes hitherto absent from politics, or only marginally active, could be fully met only by a ruthless reorganization of government and reorientation of outlook that the Habsburgs had never undertaken, even in the era of the Theresan–Josephinian reforms.[54] The German–Viennese bourgeoisie was the only new sociopolitical faction to emerge from the upheaval more or less persuaded that continued Habsburg rule was in their interest. The nearest approximation to a written constitution that the Habsburg empire had – the *Allgemeines Bürgerliches Gesetzbuch* – was in their language, after all, and had already transformed middle-class subjects into citizens. Regardless of the drop-off of government positions in the *Vormärz*, the Habsburg regime was drawing ever more consistently upon this class for its bureaucratic functionaries. With careers in mind, erstwhile revolutionaries with property and education had every reason to oppose turning the monarchy into a federation that would disperse both government, and presumably the jobs that went with it, to regional centers. Autonomy, the goal of many Hungarian political leaders, would be even worse. Closer to Vienna and at home with the aesthetic and social ideals, if not the political features, of aristocracy, these same middle classes had little reason to cooperate for long with folk who resented wealth rather than made it.[55] Galicia's Polish nobility had also discovered that Ukrainian nationalism and aspirations for Polish control either of a province or a reunified Polish state were incompatible, and would quickly become more cooperative with the regime in Vienna.[56]

But other key Habsburg lands – Bohemia, Hungary, and Italy – had been largely compelled, not persuaded, to acknowledge Habsburg rule once again. In the latter two lands aristocrats of all ranks had played key roles at one moment or another in the run-up to 1848, and in the revolutions themselves. It was Hungary's gentry who had largely rewritten their kingdom's constitution to suit themselves, and they continued to chafe against the Habsburg presence.[57] The Bohemian aristocracy returned to the dynasty's camp more docilely, but Field Marshal Windischgrätz's brutal suppression of radical students and workers in Prague only underscored their dependency on their sovereign rather than their political significance in their kingdom. Their encouragement of national sentiments had produced quite unwelcome results, and they would not play a central role in the Czech national movement again. Both the monarch and the class that had long collaborated with his dynasty had eventually been challenged by a conception of political interest altogether different from concerns of the traditional establishment. Whether the monarchy could develop that same relationship with its middle classes, not the product of monarchy as such but of entrepreneurial activity generally, had yet to be fully proven.

Troubling, too, were the serious doubts that aristocrats and other traditional elites in the dynasty's lands had developed about many aspects of their long relationship with the dynasty. While the terminology in which they had recast their roles in the homelands may have been suppressed by the imperial armies, it was never forgotten, particularly in such perpetual flash points as Hungary. Should these aristocrats continue to ally themselves with other elements of their local populations, they were opening themselves up for the game of divide and conquer through which more than one monarch had preserved his or her crown, the Habsburgs included. But if some elites had fewer sociological reservations about joining with the commoners of their lands, as was the case in Italy, more uprisings were likely to occur. Would the monarchy be willing, or even able, to rescue its long-time collaborators indefinitely? 'In your camp lies Austria', wrote the contemporary dramatist and poet Franz Grillparzer (1791–1872) in saluting Field Marshal Radetzky in 1848.[58] For how long he did not say.

Chapter 6: From One to Many

Hints of Former Connections

First-time travelers in the parts of east central and southeastern Europe that once belonged to the Habsburg empire often shake their heads at the bewildering mix of languages they encounter. Each border crossing turns up yet another: one of the various Slavic tongues and their subtle dialects, possibly Magyar, or Latin-based Rumanian, or Italian, even fragments of German here and there. How was it possible, many people ask, to govern so diverse an array of speech communities collectively? To know that mutual self-interest promoted close cooperation between Habsburg rulers and the elites in their various territories for almost three centuries explains something of the hold that the dynasty had over its lands, but not completely. How did it hold together all of its peoples, including the vast body of ordinary humankind who challenged the dynasty and its sociopolitical foundations only under extreme provocation, and openly defied it almost never?

Longer acquaintance with the region suggests some answers. One hears at all levels of society expressions that say the same thing, though in different tongues. The Austrian's 'küss die Hand', the Hungarian's 'kezét csókolom', the Czech's 'ruku libám' all say 'I kiss your hand'. They are but transplants to society at large of the court culture that once prevailed in Vienna and at smaller establishments throughout the empire. Even household servants, particularly cooks, who came from various parts of the Habsburg lands to work for more exalted folk, contributed to this matrix of commonality. The Italian's *gnocchi*, the Czech's *noky*, the Austrian's *Nockerl*, were, and are, bite-sized pieces of boiled dough,

central Europe's tool of choice for consolidating the estuaries of gravy often sprawled across one's dinner plate.

A Culture Accessible to All

Language in itself, however, was not the defining feature of cultural behavior in the early centuries of the Habsburg empire. It was religion that served that purpose, one that for all its hostility to confessional pluralism and the stern demands it placed upon believers had some usefully inclusive properties.

The God of Baroque Catholicism was a fearsome force, ready to punish even those who had innocently wandered astray. Péter Pázmány, the spearhead of Hungary's Counter-Reformation, attributed the miseries of his compatriots in the seventeenth century to divine retribution for allowing Calvinism to spread in the land.[1] Salvation was open to everyone, but not without exacting uncommon heroism of character and faith from mere mortals. Though grace could rescue anyone, humankind went through a disheartening amount of backsliding before redemption came. Many people would continue forever along the path of sin on which their weakness had set them. To serve on earth was to live in torment; individuals struggled constantly with conflicting emotions such as love and hate or moral choices in which sin could be as attractive as sanctity. God granted salvation both on the basis of how well a person met these tests and out of his infinite wisdom.[2]

The Church of Rome did not have a monopoly on this outlook, nor on the literary instruments that publicized it. In Anglican England, Lady Booby, contemplating her troubling attraction to the amoral footman Joseph Andrews in Henry Fielding's eponymous novel (1742), also found that:

Love became his advocate, and whispered many things in his favor. Honor likewise endeavored to vindicate his crime, and Pity to mitigate his punishment. On the other side, Pride and Revenge spoke as loudly against him; and thus the poor lady was tortured with perplexity, opposite passions distracting and tearing her mind different ways.[3]

In the Habsburg lands, however, confessionally driven Roman Catholic regimes enforced a dominant religious culture far more vigorously than

did the governments of Georgian Britain. By 1700, the Englishman's amusement was the Austrian or Czech's article of faith.

Catholic tactics, moreover, had some remarkably inclusive features; no one, therefore, was without the resources to see him or her through this fearsome struggle. The literate and illiterate alike could grasp great parts of the church's message and its promise of eternal reward through their senses. What people could not read they could feel and see. Pictorial, even tactile, affective techniques to provoke 'great feeling' and the virtues that these inspired were central to the teaching and missionary strategies of the Jesuits, the pedagogical spearhead of Habsburg imperial Catholicism.[4] Preparing a novice for the first Spiritual Exercise, Ignatius Loyola advised:

> *The first prelude* is a mental image of the place. . . . When the meditation or contemplation is on a visible object, for example, contemplating Christ our Lord during His life on earth, the image will consist of seeing with the mind's eye the physical place where the object that we wish to contemplate is present. By the physical place I mean, for instance, a temple, or mountain where Jesus or the Blessed Virgin is, depending on the subject of the contemplation. In meditations on subject matter that is not visible, as here in meditation on sins, the mental image will consist of imagining, and considering my soul imprisoned in its corruptible body, and my entire being in this vale of tears as an exile among brute beasts.[5]

'Don't read here: behold', read marginal instructions in the manuscript of the 1588 Jesuit play *Paterfamilias.*[6] Performed before Leopold I and his family in 1698, another of the order's presentations, *Mulier fortis,* celebrated the very inner virtue of Christian fortitude in the face of martyrdom. But even so grave a subject was classified as a *spectaculum,* something to be seen as well as heard.[7]

Language itself could be as pictorial as it was verbal. Surging from the pens and tongues of Baroque wordsmiths such as the Discalced Augustinian Abraham A Sancta Clara (1644–1709), Leopold I's court preacher after 1677, sermons and other forms of literature had the emotional vividness and communicative immediacy of painting and sculpture. A master of jest and satire with dazzling gifts for pun, word play, and resonant alliteration, Abraham experienced Vienna's defining crises in the late seventeenth century, a devastating plague epidemic in 1679 and the Ottoman siege of 1683. The first of these calamities prompted his homily

'Mercks Wien' ('Mark Ye, Vienna'), the second 'Auf, auf ihr Christen' ('Arise, Christians, Arise'). A sharp critic of the city's morals, Abraham detected God's chastising hand behind both misfortunes. Nevertheless, these tracts and others like them were immensely popular. The surface brilliance of his linguistic acrobatics dumbfounded and captivated his audiences at the same time; what he had to say was almost incidental to the way he said it. Above all, his words depicted events in the very streets where they lived. In the matter of the plague:

> The Lane of the Nobles [*Herrengasse*] is ruled by Death. In the Street of the Clever [*Klugerstraße*] Death is not clever but profligate. Death has shot off in the Street of the Bow-makers [*Bognerstraße*]. In the Street of the Singers [*Singerstraße*], Death has sung requiems for many. . . . Death has sharpened its arrows in the Lane of the Nailmakers [*Naglergasse*]. In the Lane of the Gate to Heaven [*Himmelpfortgasse*], Death has sent many to Heaven or someplace close by. . . . At High Market Square [*Hoher Markt*], Death has lowered many.[8]

Unlike the Jesuits, for whom the use of feeling was only one among several strategies, Abraham had little use for learning, a principle calculated to put the illiterate or semi-literate in his audiences at ease. Clergymen were exhorted to cultivate faith at the expense of reason; the personal experience of suffering, he argued, made good physicians, not medical knowledge. Some of his most perfervid language reinforced popular prejudice as well, another source of his appeal. Protestants, Jews, Turks, and women were chief among his targets.

Nor were hyper-vivid rhetoric and the opinionated passion that generated it peculiar to Viennese preachers or to the Austrians among the Habsburg peoples. Seventeenth-century Hungarians let their linguistic imaginations run away with them too, for example the poet–military leader Miklós Zrínyi (1620–64) in his *The Real Remedy for Turkish Opium* (*Az török Áfium ellen való orvosság*). Ruminating sometime between 1660 and 1661 about possible allies in the war to drive Ottoman rule from his land, he rejected the Russians out of hand:

> Any discussion about them can take place only in a dreamworld rather than a real one. . . . The country [Russia] is too big, the people too uncivilized, their military strategy worthless, their courage laughable, their politics silly, the entire empire tyrannical; who needs such help![9]

Habsburg government and the privileged elites with whom it worked also used all the visual resources at their command to show simple viewers just whom God had selected to rule them and why his choice should be respected. Literacy was the hallmark of Protestantism and Protestantism the engine of sedition. The Habsburgs made little use of political philosophers to explain their eminence, preferring instead to make their statements about themselves visually and ceremonially. The Baroque world order was hierarchical, with God at its pinnacle and monarchs not far below him as his lieutenants. By observing the sacraments publicly, by personal service in pilgrimages and liturgical processions – during the Thirty Years War the dynasty's participation in the ceremonies surrounding the Feast of the Eucharist became a virtual act of state – and by vigorous advocacy of the veneration of the Virgin and of select saints the territorial ruler showed himself to be an appropriately Christian ruler for a Christian people.[10]

The aristocratic elites, spiritual and secular, of the early modern Habsburg empire put its place in this hierarchy on display in secular and religious settings as well. Great structures bespoke preeminence: monasteries such as Melk, remodeled by the Tyrolean architect Jakob Prandtauer (1660–1726) in the first quarter of the eighteenth century, and noble residences such as Eugene of Savoy's Belvedere Palace just beyond central Vienna designed by Johann Baptiste Fischer von Erlach (1656–1723), all commanded the attention of the eye, often for long periods of time, in order to organize the ever-moving and often disturbing asymmetries of Baroque design.

The school and university dramas of the major teaching orders – the Jesuits and Benedictines and, later in the eighteenth century, the Piarists – gave both verbal and visual lessons in the dangers of the human condition. The underlying strategy of these works was to terrorize audiences to a point where anxiety about one's relationship to higher powers eradicated all inclinations toward self-indulgence. The texts were usually in a stripped-down and straightforward Latin, but broadly reinforced by spectacular visual and aural effects.

School theaters had central roles in the educational programs of the Jesuits as well as other Catholic orders well beyond the German lands of the Habsburg empire. Catholic nobles in Hungary went to Jesuit and, somewhat later, Piarist auditoriums, to see reworkings of the Roman comic playwright Plautus.[11] Jesuit establishments in Prague, Brno, and Olomouc before and after the Battle of the White Mountain regularly put their moral and theological programs on display in theatrical performances.[12] Explicit costumes, impressive stage mechanics, along with pyrotechnics and other forms of optical wizardry, figured prominently in their dramatic strategies. They awed, sometimes terrified, audiences, but amused them as well, the credulous and the sophisticated alike. Should viewers miss the message, sheer numbers of players drove it home. A play about the prophet Elias put on in 1610 crammed 67 performers into the courtyard of the Jesuit college in Prague. A cast of 112 enacted the life of St. Vitus in Brno in 1609. The entirety of the biblical hierarchy of being, along with important figures in historical Christianity, were often written into these works, certainly one reason for the size of many casts. *Christ the Judge,* by an Olomouc Jesuit, Štepán Tuce, presented God the Father, God the Son, along with a complex assortment of angels, the antichrist, the Old Testament patriarchs, Adam and Eve, and the fathers of the church. Sheer numbers of performers also distinguished the productions of Hungary's Jesuits from those of other orders and the Protestant confessions. And the order readily performed for all who would listen. The Jesuit college of Sárospotok in the east played in the local castle, in the town square, and on the steps into their own cloister.[13]

Only the truly stupid or recklessly self-confident could miss the meaning of what they saw and heard. Identified by some feature of their appropriately menacing costumes, the Seven Deadly Sins – Pride, Hate, Lust, Gluttony, Avarice, Sloth, Envy – battled with Virtue for control of some hapless human soul. *Young Tobias,* a play performed in 1616 at a wedding between members of the Bohemian house of Lobkovic and the Moravian house of Dietrichstein, culminates in a struggle over the soul of the protagonist between the archangel Raphael and the Old Testament prince of darkness, Asmode, who summons evil's assistants and hell's overlord himself in his cause.[14] 'The heart, not reason or understanding . . . kindled feelings of fear of God and love of God.'[15] The action was often trilocal, set in heaven and hell and on earth, so that several platforms were required along with complicated stage machinery to move the cast from one realm to the next. But such technology too was designed to make plain that what took place in this world was connected to the one beyond: the natural and the supernatural were readily in contact.

While no person was exempt from the implications of this message, certain aspects of these plays underscored the social distinctions that determined hierarchies on earth. Young men of high birth could not play tradespersons or peasants or the other way around lest audiences, which routinely came from a cross-section of the public, entertain critical thoughts about the nature of society and those who controlled it. Distinguished names such as Erdödy and Zinzendorf, therefore, headed all-male lists of performers, even in female roles, as long as these were heroic. At Hungary's Jesuit college in Nagyszombat in 1650, the 15-year-old Paul Esterházy appeared, knife in hand, as Judith, the apochryphal slayer of the Assyrian general Holofernes.

These plays also gave young gentlemen an opportunity to demonstrate their mastery of fencing and dancing, requirements in their curriculum, and to drill themselves in the arts of graceful entrances and exits and making a good physical impression. All these were skills the aristocrat might have to call upon in future appearances at court. So important to their training were these functions that in at least one province of the seventeenth-century Habsburg empire, Carinthia, aristocratic families underwrote the production costs for these performances.[16]

Within the learned communities of seventeenth-century Catholics in the Habsburg lands, or simply among Catholics with intellectual pretensions, a great deal of nuanced debate about philosophical issues also took place. Aristotelians, Platonists everywhere, even rare libertines in the household of Eugene of Savoy, had their say, at least among one another.[17] But the Church of Rome in the Habsburg empire, universal in its Christianity and versatile in its pedagogy, ready to teach through the senses and the psyche as well as through the mind, could plausibly claim that it transcended the boundaries of class, education, and language. Connected to the overwhelming majority of the empire's peoples, it promoted a 'popular' culture in the broadest modern understanding of that term. It drew together ideas from the rarefied realms of high art, literature, and philosophy, took account of the lifestyles and behavior patterns of a complex variety of peoples, and inserted itself visually into elaborate palaces, village squares, or along rural thoroughfares. Even today, woodcarvings of the crucifixion or the assumption of the Virgin and even small chapels dot the country roadsides of Catholic central and east central Europe. That the public rituals associated with these artifacts were substantially the same wherever they were carried out did much to solidify a social order otherwise shot through with the stresses of gross disparities in wealth, social position, and political influence and privilege. Distinctions between high culture and popular culture were more contingent than essential.[18] The dynasty's unwavering allegiance to the entire system legitimized it even further.

Nor was Roman Catholic Christianity the only source of shared belief in the Habsburg empire. Lodged in the minds of most of its peoples – monarchs, nobles, physicians, and intellectuals, along with the untitled and the unschooled – was a complex set of ideas, part pseudoscience, part outright superstition. Rooted in astrology, alchemy, and magical processes, these notions routinely assisted people in explaining to themselves and others the world and its events. The court of the beleaguered Emperor Rudolph II in Prague was a gathering point of astronomers, astrologers, and other practitioners of the hermetic arts at the beginning of the seventeenth century. Clergymen themselves, though more covertly, took cues from the stars and superterrestrial omens in foretelling the outcome of human affairs. Depending upon their degree of learning, different people had quite different takes on the relationship between the natural and the supernatural. The committed scholar or the speculative nobleman, on the watch for opportunities to reconcile Christian and pre-Christian cosmologies, was thinking on a different intellectual level from the peasant in awe of necromancy and demonology. Somewhere in the Habsburg empire, however, each of them found someone who understood what they did and thought. Within the high aristocracy of the seventeenth century, a German Liechtenstein, a Hungarian Esterházy, a Czech Lobkovic poured over texts and experiments, chemical and alchemical alike.[19] Some of these beliefs were common enough to occasionally bring both the sophisticated and the credulous of the dynasty's subjects into a common cause. The church, the state, and inhabitants from all classes of rural society waged a brutal campaign against witchcraft in the eighteenth century in the Austrian lands, Bohemia and even Hungary.[20]

Respect for supernatural influences on terrestrial events generally was not restricted to the Habsburg peoples in early modern Europe. The presence of such convictions, however, which responded to thoughts and feelings that church teaching discouraged among the laity but could not eradicate, added significantly to the monarchy's cultural coherence. The result was an interlocking network of art, learning, belief, and folk practice that linked the various social orders of the Habsburg empire on earth more or less along the lines of God's world theater itself. Even more rational philosophical systems fitted into this outlook. Invited by Prince Eugene of Savoy, the Saxon polymath Gottfried Wilhelm von Leibniz (1646–1716) lived in Vienna from 1712 to 1714. It was there that he wrote his *Monadology* in which he posited, and argued for, a divinely designed universe of entities – the monads – linked in a pre-established harmony. God, by definition perfect, willed only things consistent with Divine Reason. Man, therefore, could justifiably rejoice in this creation, reassured that he and all things around him, including the social and political order, were not cosmic accidents but parts of a plan. Neither the prince nor his emperor, Charles VI, had any reason to disagree.[21] While the ability of the dynasty to control and defend its territories was often in doubt in the sixteenth and seventeenth centuries, its cultural hold on its subjects was remarkably secure.

Accommodation to Diversity: Education, Language, and Dynastic Interest

Any modifications in this world-view that encouraged differences among the Habsburg peoples was a potential challenge to both Catholic universalism and the dynasty that had exploited it to such profit. Nevertheless, by the middle of the eighteenth century it was clear that the purposes of Habsburg government were no longer being well served by this outlook. Maria Theresa, Joseph II, and their advisers were among Europe's active critics of the church on moral and economic grounds. They were equally, if not more, concerned about the impact of church control over education. In the monarchy's drive to create a more productive population, the backwardness of elementary schooling was a grave failing, and official pressure for changing the system was intense.

By 1750, the Catholic establishment itself was making its adaptations to the rational and empirical currents of thought that were the foundations of the European Enlightenment. Clergymen themselves were recommending classical pagan philosophers such as Seneca to novices when scripture was not up to answering thorny moral questions. Even among the eastern Orthodox clergy of Transylvania, the vocabulary of the Rights of Man would prove useful in 1790 as Serbs and Rumanians pleaded for religious freedoms.[22] The church, therefore, was not unreceptive to government demands for educational changes, especially when these might help to reverse a troubling decline in popular piety. To many thoughtful clergymen, religion among the laity seemed closer to superstition than to true faith. They believed that illiteracy fostered ignorance of Christian precept that, in turn, might even encourage unpleasant social tensions. Emmanuel Count Waldstajn, an eighteenth-century bishop of Litoměřice, blamed a local peasant uprising on poor understanding of their religion, a condition that only learning to read could cure.[23] And teaching the young to read fluently did not mean that the church had to abandon spectacle as a didactic technique. Eighteenth-century Moravian rose festivals, in which local clergymen rewarded exceptionally conscientious, studious, and upright young ladies with flowered diadems, combined traditional and colorful village celebrations with academic and spiritual virtues.[24]

Advocates of educational reform saw that large numbers of people learned and read more quickly in their everyday tongue. The long-standing hostility of the Catholic establishment to popular print culture was now pedagogically irrelevant, as was the centrality of Latin in class-room learning. The German language in Catholic Austria, along with other tongues in the monarchy such as Czech, Hungarian, and Italian, had long lagged behind French and English as both literary and, to a lesser extent, learned languages. Where used, they were in homiletic tracts and calendars for the common folk, who were often unlettered in any case. Not much more was available for their betters, for whom French, by the eighteenth century, was the idiom of the cultured. The conversation at the Habsburg court itself was conducted in a mixture of tongues: Latin, French, Spanish, and Italian vied with German and with one another in an artless macaronic that has left its mark on speech in Austria to this day.[25] It was, however, in the interests of the dynasty and its subjects to develop educational programs in the vernacular. Joseph II's official orders often came out with broadsides in many of the languages of his peoples to explain the reasons for his measures to the general public. Indeed, numerous printers seized the opportunity to open shops in Vienna that specialized in serving one or another of the empire's several speech communities during the latter decades of the eighteenth century.[26]

The move toward education in the vernacular throughout the empire left no level of training untouched. To better prepare the bureaucrats and military commanders of the future, the government allowed some teaching after 1752 in Czech at the Habsburg military academy in Wiener Neustadt, outside Vienna, and at the Polytechnical Academy in the capital after 1754. The philosophical and even the theological faculties of universities were also affected. The most influential of Maria Theresa's pedagogical reformers, Johann Ignaz Felbiger, deplored the neglect of German in the Jesuit education he received at the University of Breslau. German- and Czech-language chairs in pastoral theology at the University of Vienna were established during the 1770s. A corresponding position was set up at the university in Olomouc that same year. Leopold II, who made use of Czech in his coronation rites, sponsored a chair in Czech language and literature at the Charles University in Prague in 1792, whose first occupant was the patriotic historian and philologian

František Pelcl. After 1777, when a Hungarian educational reform came into effect, doctoral dissertations could be submitted in all the vernaculars of that kingdom, and not just Latin.[27]

Joseph II and his advisers, especially Sonnenfels, hoped that the cultivation of German would improve the moral as well as the intellectual fibre of his subjects. For this program they looked to their brothers in language to the north where a new theory of the drama, espoused particularly by Johann Christoph Gottsched (1700–66), was promoting fundamental changes in contemporary aesthetic and intellectual values. A critic of Baroque rhetorical excesses, he also attacked courts that diverted residents and the public with superficial antics the reformers associated with the French and Italian stage. Replacing them were to be plays that embodied naturalness, transparency, and goodness, along with a humanistic version of religion, often personified by figures from classical antiquity. Such notions had hovered over the study of Greek and Latin in Europe since the Renaissance in the fifteenth and sixteenth centuries; now, however, their advocates wanted them written in German and not some foreign tongue, classical though the latter might be.[28]

By the middle of the eighteenth century, these ideas were under serious discussion in Vienna; Sonnenfels himself belonged to a so-called German Society that was dedicated to spreading them. Michael Denis (1729–1800), a Jesuit poet and the director of the Imperial Court Library, actually introduced the movement's new German poets, most notably Frederick Gottlieb Klopstock (1724–1803), to the German-speaking audiences of the Habsburg empire. Unlike Protestant states to the north, the Habsburg government did not drive music from the theater. Nevertheless, for them the good play was one that at the least observed the linguistic norms that Joseph was setting for his bureaucrats, and at best inspired civic virtues: thrift, a sense of public duty, and zeal for hard work. In 1776, Joseph reorganized the Court Theater as the German Court and National Theater to present such works.[29]

From Vernacular to Particular: The Austrian Example

The primacy that the Gottschedian reforms gave to text over spectacle, and what an author said over its staging, was very congenial to the censors working for Joseph II toward the end of his reign. Since they checked in theaters to ascertain that what they had read was actually played, a full written manuscript gave them a richer preview of its contents and how individual passages were to be rewritten or excised.[30] Such plays, however, were a sharp break from the visual theatrical experience to which the Habsburg lands were accustomed, particularly in Vienna itself. Nor did audiences especially enjoy the experience. Even as Joseph II was bringing literary reform from the northerly reaches of the Holy Roman Empire to his German-speaking lands, local authors such as Johann Pezzl (1756–1823) had begun differentiating writing that was generally German but specifically Austrian ('österreichisch') from work that was both generally and specifically German and therefore not Austrian ('unösterreichisch').

The tearful excesses of the eighteenth-century cult of sensibility that reoriented contemporary German literature as a whole were often caricatured by Austrian writers. Even the movement's fictional masterpiece, Goethe's *The Sorrows of Young Werther*, while it had admirers in the Habsburg realms, was cruelly parodied as well. Indeed, the outlook that generated such spoofs – realism about humankind, a tendency to approach problems lightly, and tolerance of the absurd, sometimes grotesque, side of one's social milieu – was a by-product of the big-city environment that Viennese authors shared and that set them apart from their colleagues both in Germany and elsewhere in the Habsburg lands.[31] Dismissing the minor effects of sentimentalism on the people of the dynasty's capital, Pezzl observed:

> This paroxysm is also behind us as well. It [the cult of sensibility] really never did take root in Vienna, as is generally true in any large city where one knows the way of the world and how to live.[32]

Joseph II's efforts to make German the administrative language of his lands would continue to have much support in the German-speaking bureaucracy that administered the Habsburg lands. It would also be the cause of divisive future controversies. The debate over whether or not Austrians were part of German literature wavered over both sides of the question into the twentieth century. By the beginning of the nineteenth century, however, writers in the Austrian lands were on their way to creating an eclectic vernacular theater of their own that combined some of the themes and the moral content of the Baroque Catholic stage with secular topics in ways that were peculiarly and non-transferably Austrian.[33] From its outset, the Baroque theater incorporated elements that entertained rather than preached. Some drifted in from entertainments at the court; increased use of dance sequences and musical interludes paralleled the growing enthusiasm for the opera and ballet in seventeenth-century Vienna and other Habsburg administrative centers. Most popular, however, were comic scenes, often in local dialect; they were especially prominent in the influential Benedictine theater of Salzburg. A humorous figure – a soldier, a drunk, a braggart or a peasant whose language quickly identified him along with his local costume – was an obligatory character in the cast.

The Benedictine abbey of Seitenstetten in Lower Austria has left an especially instructive example of the interaction of these elements and their cultural ramifications. Plays with explicitly Catholic programs were still put on in the monastery theater. The heavily musical oratorio, however, was becoming the setting of choice for the full-strength Christian message and its lengthy discourses on sin and redemption. The stage, for its part, was increasingly given over to German-language offerings by authors for whom human behavior alone was the center of interest. Just as reformed Catholic clergy consulted Seneca for moral instruction, more worldly clerics in Seitenstetten such as Pater Maurus Lindemayr looked to the comedies of the great French playwright Molière for models. That such subjects were more amusing than exemplary strengthened their appeal.

Vernacular speech underscored the specificity, not the timelessness, of places and societies within the Christian cosmos. For Molière it was Paris and its richly diverse social stereotypes, for Lindemayr and others like him it was rural Austria. The peasant Herr Riepel, the comic vulgarian Hans Wurst (literally, Jack Sausage), or the couple Hansl and Greschl commanded the stage while moral archetypes of the Catholic Baroque theater – Pietas (Piety), Clementia (Magnanimity), and Spes (Hope) – were no longer visible protagonists. Latin, Catholicism's international language of learning and liturgy, became ridiculous when used, or abused, locally. Lindemayr's play *Mr. Storax Taken by All to be an Imbecile* (*Der von allen Seiten für einen Narren gehaltene Herr von Storax*) has roles for a countrified patient whose speech baffles a physician who, in turn, confounds the bumpkin with Latin-laced German. Audiences for these entertainments came from beyond the monastery. The size of a new abbey theater built around the middle of the eighteenth century – 950 seats – suggests that there was a public to fill them. A popular playhouse in Vienna, the Theater at the Carinthian Gate (*Theater am Kärntnertor*), held only about half as many people.[34]

The *Kärntnertor* house was, however, central to the development of an idiomatic Austrian theater. It was the site of a regionally defined comedy altogether apart from the monastery. Critically important in this setting was Josef Anton Stranitzky (1676–1726). An actor, writer, producer, and director, who also never abandoned his licensed profession of tooth extraction, he wove together topics and the characters associated with them into immensely popular German-language entertainments, particularly among Vienna's middle classes.

The *Hanswurst*, an unmistakably German variant of the Arlequino who was one of the staple figures of the contemporary Italian *commedia dell'arte*, became a central figure for Stranitzky, both as a performer and as a writer. Viennese authors who succeeded him, while they distanced themselves from Italianate models, retained, indeed embellished, the character. Outfitted as a Salzburg peasant, he was at home in all the German-language theaters of Europe. Hectic, often vulgar, stage business generally displaced and sometimes parodied the stately monologues and moral lessons of high Baroque drama. Plays took on social undertones as they explored, though did not challenge, the often tense relations between upper and lower ranks of humankind. Aristocrats were mocked, often in the earthiest language and gestures, to gratify the prurient tastes of an appreciative public. The *Hanswurst* himself sometimes donned noble costume, thereby contradicting the presumed harmony of appearance and reality that validated Catholic allegory.[35]

The *Kärntnertor* theater also allowed Stranitzky's troupe to perform regularly, though they had to struggle to do so. The Habsburg court preferred the many Italian theatrical groups then in the city and liked neither the language nor the tone of the actor–playwright's programs. Municipal authorities twice evicted his company from their auditoriums on charges of general rowdiness and fire hazards. In 1711, however, he and his players moved permanently into the *Kärntnertor* arena, to great public rejoicing. A strong native vernacular institution had taken hold, which, in the works of the next generation of such writers as Philip Hafner (1735–64), focussed on recognizably Viennese characters – confectioners with aristocratic affectations or untutored but cunning servants.

The ascent of the vernacular popular comedy in the German-speaking Austrian lands reversed the traditional priorities that had dominated the official local stage. While the moral structure of Baroque Catholicism still framed the outer edges of comedy and tragedy alike, the focus of these works was increasingly character and social interaction. That clerical theaters also followed this pattern made the change all the easier. Audiences came to be amused by the regionally familiar, and not to be uplifted

through beholding cosmic archetypes. Boding ill for the cultural cohe-
sion of the Habsburg monarchy were quarrels over the language of entertainment that broke out now and again, even in the eighteenth century.
These rapidly passed beyond confrontations between a living language
and a dead one. Though the artifices and themes of the *commedia dell'arte*
influenced actors and playwrights throughout the Habsburg empire for
some time, Italian became very unpopular among the common people
of Vienna. Even though by the latter third of the eighteenth century
Czech and German were squaring off against one another on linguistic
grounds in Prague, when supporting the music of Wolfgang Amadeus
Mozart, a German, they joined against the Italian-dominated stage in
the city.[36]

The ruling house and its courtiers in Vienna looked upon this turn of
affairs with a mixture of benevolence and hostility. The Habsburgs themselves had reason to encourage occasional popular attendance at plays;
Maria Theresa often made public announcements at the theater in the
Hofburg and liked commoners to hear at first hand what she had to say.
But the Viennese comic theater and its contrivances, performed in a vernacular though they were, ran quite contrary to Joseph II's linguistic and
educational programs. He and his councilors deplored the dialect used
in the *Volkskomödie* that baffled many in the German-speaking world at
large and, according to Sonnenfels, only made plain the poverty of an
author's linguistic resources. Crude language encouraged the irreverent,
often tasteless, asides that titillated humankind's most primitive instincts.
The frequent intrusion of superterrestrial spirits and effects only reinforced the beliefs of an already superstitious population. Joseph's language programs, however, were contested throughout the empire, and
while the cultivation of a standard German remained a goal of the Habsburg educational and cultural establishment following the Napoleonic
wars, the scope and purpose of this agenda was considerably reduced.

Some aspects of Viennese culture between 1815 and 1848 retained a
universal flavor. The work of Mozart's Italian rival–admirer Antonio
Salieri (1750–1825) appeared consistently in the programs of the imperial chapel and elsewhere in the city until well past the middle of the
nineteenth century. The generally humanitarian ideology of the city's
most admired composer during the period, Ludwig van Beethoven
(1770–1827), transcended particular linguistic settings; a great deal of his
creative output had no programmatic reference at all. One cannot
understand Franz Schubert (1797–1828) without consideration of his
Viennese environment; he was, unlike Beethoven, born to it. He enjoyed

the patronage of the city's contemporary audiences, both aristocratic and middle-class, and even suffered at least one terrifying brush with the Franciscan police state. Nevertheless, the psychological depths to which his finest music reaches belonged to human nature as a whole, not just its Austrian variant.[37]

Literature, however, especially the theater, followed its particularizing course. Austrian authors continued to favor parody, satire, persiflage, the journalistic essay, and travesty for voicing their thoughts, setting themselves off sharply from their more earnest colleagues in the other German-speaking states.[38] Popular audiences, from the nobility down, had little use for plays that instructed rather than entertained. With the collapse of Josephinian authority in 1790, the *Volkskomödie* rebounded to what became classical status in the hands of Ferdinand Raimund (1790–1836) and Johann Nestroy (1801–62). Baroque reminiscences such as frequent musical interludes, supernatural agents, and linguistic extravagance remained central to their work. Raimund wove spirits both good and evil into many of his scenarios, and the deus ex machina frequently moved even his greatest plays along. Behind all the hocus-pocus there was still a Christian sensibility, half-comic, half-melancholic, that underscored the superficiality of earthly distinctions. As the humble carpenter Valentin sings in *Der Verschwender*, a play about the rise and fall of a very wealthy but feckless person:

> One man is all too poor,
> Another far too rich,
> After Fate has shaved them down,
> You can't tell which is which.[39]

Nestroy outstripped even the gifted Abraham A Sancta Clara in verbal athleticism and linguistic vividness. The image-packed lines of his characters often all but take off, driven, it would seem, by the momentum of speech itself. Analyzing the history of his emotional life in *Das Mädl aus der Vorstadt* (*The Suburban Girl*), a cripplingly shy but love-smitten character called Schnoferl – he has no given name – puts it this way:

For me love was no gaily-colored oil-painting, splendid in its bright hues, but rather a lithograph gone awry in the print shop of fate: grey on grey, black on black, dark on dirty. A factual history of my heart breaks down into three chapters: purposeless dreams, aborted attempts, worthless triumphs.[40]

Absent from this Baroque theatrical legacy of conflicted souls and verbal extravagance, however, was an explicit Christian eschatology, a reflection of the increasingly mundane nature of post-Enlightenment culture in the Habsburg capital.[41] The popular comedy, with its whole-hearted commitment to entertainment and its fascination with human foibles, therefore operated under even fewer religious constraints. Though the battle between good and evil for control of humankind raged on, the protagonists were now aspects of the human psyche rather than divine or demonic external forces. Raimund's characters in particular struggled not only with acknowledged deadly sins such as greed, lust, and avarice, but with new torments such as exaggerated suspicion of others. When there was a happy ending – and there always was one – it was on earth with the discovery of one's true and better self and the good side of one's fellow man.

This transformation also had a distinct location, in both place and time. The trajectory through which these embattled souls wobbled there-fore touched more people than themselves. Raimund, but also Nestroy and other Viennese comic playwrights of the early nineteenth century, took correspondingly great care in constructing the social setting of their comedies. Eager for large audiences, they turned to familiar local stereotypes who were almost certain to generate the laughter that their public sought in theaters. Their characters, therefore, were unmistakably Viennese or people who had been Viennafied through contact with the institutions and customs of the city. Casts list one servant after another, a testimonial to the legions of these people who came to the Inner City between 1815 and 1848 to work in the households of nobles or the newly wealthy middle class.[42] While the shape of these figures' emotional exper-iences were within the human generality to which the Baroque stage spoke, their dialect-ridden speech regionalized their action distinctively, even in the German-speaking world. Virtually dedicated to the people of the Austrian lands where it has unassailable classical standing, the popular comedy of Raimund, Nestroy, and their colleagues has never been widely programmed outside of the region.

Even at the level of high literature, Austrian writing of the *Vormärz* cel-ebrated locality, sometimes to powerful effect. Goethe's classicism and the major writers of the entire European tradition heavily influenced Franz Grillparzer (1791–1872), one of the great dramatic poets of the German-language theater. Several of Grillparzer's most important plays, however, deal with the course of Habsburg history and celebrate the Austrian lands, sometimes with deep passion. Speaking of Lower Austria in *König Ottokars Gluck und Ende* (*King Ottokar's Fortune and End*) (1825), which dramatizes Rudolph of Habsburg's defeat of the thirteenth-century Bohemian king who had taken over much of the Danube, the knight Ottokar von Hornek calls it 'a good land':

> well-suited to a prince who makes it his own.
> Where else have you ever seen such beauty?
> Look around you, wherever you can see,
> It laughs like a bridegroom face to face with his bride!
> With glittering green meadows and seeds of gold,
> Embroidered in linen-blue and saffron-yellow,
> Flavored with sweet flowers and noble herbs,
> It stretches out in broad valleys –
> A complete bouquet of flowers, wherever it extends,
> Contained by the Danube's silver ribbon!
> It rises to wine-laden hills,
> Up and up hung with golden grapes,
> Swelling ripely in God's sun, gleaming-bright;
> All crowned by dark forests filled for hunters' delight.[43]

Its pseudo-Homeric idiom aside, Grillparzer's inspiration was the Austria of his birth and an Austrian dynasty to which the writer had a love–hate relationship all his own.

The cultivation of the German tongue in the Austrian German-speaking lands, therefore, did far more than foster Joseph II's vision of a standard idiom suitable for the administration of an entire empire. Reworked in local patois, the language produced writing that was unambiguously associated with regional customs and social settings. Even Grillparzer's more standardized German was used in dramas that often had a very specific focus on the house of Habsburg. The Austrian classical theater, both high and low, never wholly severed its thematic links to the Baroque stage – mankind was always affected by agents not altogether in its direct control. Traditional conceptions of superior and subordinate classes also went largely unchallenged in these plays. Although Nestroy's disaffection with his political environment was becoming more open by the middle of the nineteenth century, he was not on the barricades in 1848. *Freiheit in Krähwinkel* (*Freedom in Nowheresville*), his look at revolutionary dynamics in a mythic hamlet near Vienna that had already been the butt of countless parodies, made fun not only of official heavy-handedness but of the disorderly idealism of starry-eyed dissidents.[44] Either in subject or in speech, however, and often in both, these works were identifiably Austro-German and did not encourage associations with all peoples in the empire.[45]

Local contemporary references abound in Austrian painting between 1815 and 1848 as well. While a complex aesthetic and moral program lay behind these works, the subjects that they idealized had recognizably Austrian traits or settings.[46] Leopold Kupelwieser (1796–1862), Ferdinand Georg Waldmüller (1793–1865), even Johann Peter Krafft (1780–1856), whose work owed much to the statuesque grandeur of French classicism patronized by Bonaparte, preferred everyday settings and situations from urban and suburban Vienna or Lower Austria to classical and Christian archetypes that embodied degrees of virtue to which few mortals, Austrians included, could aspire. The layout of even domestic interiors bespoke quotidian homeyness rather than pretensions of grandeur. Middle-class Vienna preferred furniture with simple, though rounded lines to the Napoleonic Empire style that had unpleasant associations with France and aristocracy.[47]

Thus, though they never rejected fundamental elements of the Baroque cultural capital with which their Habsburg rulers had put together their empire, Austrian writers and painters of the *Vormärz* decidedly stretched traditional norms. As an Austrian phenomenon, this development did not necessarily undermine the dynasty's political position. The territorial ruler of the Austrian lands and their inhabitants were largely of the same linguistic background, a point which the dynasty, particularly Francis I, who was genuinely comfortable with bourgeois pleasures and the family life that went with them, conspicuously reinforced. Intellectuals and artistic circles in Vienna also found ways of accommodating themselves even to censors. While the latter often asked for amendments to popular comedies, they had little reason to forbid their performance once such revisions had been made. That such plays were staged in what at the time were suburban theaters made them less threatening to the reigning political order than had they been put on near the *Hofburg* or aristocratic palaces in the central city. Perhaps most important of all, the development of national literary movements in other corners of the empire made the German-speaking Austrians very uneasy. Such interests, which raised the question of the relationship between vernacular and culture, but in a non-German environment, only underscored the fragility of the Habsburg monarchy. Applied to the non-German peoples of the Habsburg empire, the coupling of political legitimacy with the use of a specific vernacular posed serious problems for the dynasty. Many artists and intellectuals in the Austrian lands were therefore less hostile to the unpleasant features of the regime than were their colleagues in other areas of central and southern Europe, particularly the Italians.[48]

From National Language to National Culture: Italy

Unbroken Catholic allegiance and papal co-sponsorship of the Counter-Reformation placed seventeenth-century Italy far closer to Vienna philosophically and culturally than were the Habsburg lands in east central Europe. Between 1660 and 1773 the Jesuit colleges of Parma, Modena, and Bologna enrolled 9500 residential students. Ten percent of this number came from the hereditary Austrian lands, Bohemia, Moravia, and Croatia. Another 20 percent came from mainland Venice. They lived together, studied identical curricula, observed the same religious rituals and took identical training in fencing, dance, and the performing arts. The great Austrian Baroque architects Fischer von Erlach (1656–1723) and Johann Lukas von Hildebrandt (1668–1745) polished their skills there as well. Nor, before 1848, had the Habsburg holdings in Lombardy–Venetia much experience with the brute force that the dynasty had occasionally exercised in Bohemia, Hungary, and even its German-speaking lands. Should Italians themselves redefine or altogether reject their own Baroque Catholic heritage, it was highly likely that similar movements would take hold among the other peoples of the monarchy as well.

Nevertheless, as early as 1752 a high school teacher of rhetoric in the south Tyrol, Francesco Frisinghelli, declared that:

> Nations are distinguished principally by Genius, Customs, and Language. Italian alone is the Genius of our Land, Italian the thought, the dress, the manners and every other custom, and finally Italian is the language, although German is also spoken by many.[49]

The comment, which turned speakers of Italian into potential opponents of any foreign language and its culture, came in the context of a vigorous debate that preoccupied many Italian intellectuals of the day. The initial object of their concern was not German but French, the preferred language of Italy's aristocrats. Even Latin, widely used in scholarly and legal affairs, came in for heavy criticism. Antonio Genovese, a student of the idiosyncratic Neapolitan philosopher Gianbattista Vico (1668–1744), bore down especially hard in this vein. When taught in Latin, he said, most local university students would be unfit for productive life in the modern world. Worse yet, people whose laws, literature, and scholarly works were in a foreign language had no claim to a culture of their own.[50]

To familiarize their public with advances in the arts and learning, leading Italian thinkers urged the systematic study of Italian and the development of a standardized idiom. Among them was the historian and educational reformer Lodovico Muratori, for whom linguistic reform was also the beginning of a much larger program. Among other causes he championed was the restoration of Italy and its people to what he called their rightful place among the leading nations of Europe. Native sloth and indifference to their own language and history, he said, encouraged foreign occupation. Muratori did not identify the problem specifically with Vienna; France and Spain had warped the Italians' understanding of national identity too. But his general message was that Italy's rebirth would come only when Italians had a usable language and a culture appropriate to its character. Any foreign presence in Italy was an obstacle to this development.[51]

Just what that language would look and sound like was a matter of dispute and would remain so. The Italian vernacular was, like German, heavily regionalized; in many places it was no more than a patois, adequate to handle daily affairs, but without terms appropriate to the conceptual challenges of the new science, politics, and philosophy.[52] The muscular Italian of Galileo's tracts on physics and astronomy was not emulated by others, fearful that the church would associate them with the contentious scientist's prohibited ideas. Various factions struggled to uncover historical exemplars of their tongue from which they could construct a standard language. What they more or less agreed upon was that such figures had to reflect the values and behavior of contemporary Italy in ways that made them recognizably Italian to large numbers of people on the peninsula. Dante attracted many, but as a very Italianate, rather than medieval Christian, Dante. The vices which the poet ascribed to himself under the pinpricks of Catholic conscience – luxury, sloth, avarice – were read by the eighteenth-century Italian writer Gaspare Gozzi (1713–86) as Italian, not as human, failings.[53] When the master Italian comic playwrights of the eighteenth century, Carlo Goldoni (1707–93) and Carlo Gozzi (1720–1806), set themselves to rescuing

Italian comedy from the mindless vulgarity that had become its stock-in-trade, they abandoned universal classicizing themes for plots and characters closer to home. Not unlike Nestroy and Raimund who followed him a generation later, Goldoni specialized in plays based on local stereotypes and problematic situations in Italian society; Gozzi drew heavily on regional, as well as world, folklore.

The radical political conclusions to be derived from notions of linguistic particularity emerged quickly as well. Some ardent spokesmen for Italian literature and language, Silvio Pellico and Alessandro Manzoni among them, stopped short of demonizing all foreigners in Italy.[54] Others not only accepted the hostile divide between themselves and speakers of other languages but made a further link between cultural particularity and political freedom. Vittorio Alfieri (1749–1803) compelled himself to write in Italian to break his ties to French culture. Authors, he said, did their best work when immersed in their own language community. He urged Italians to hate the outside other as much and as consistently as they could in order to keep alive the sense of national particularity that would insure their liberty. Indeed, such hatred was a positive duty. Though directed toward the French, such advice could be applied to relations with other language groups as well.[55] The thinking of Joseph Mazzini (1805–72), the driving spirit behind the Carbonari, incorporated all of these motifs – political liberalism, support of vernacular language, and hostility to the classical culture of both church and throne. All European literatures, he said, had suffered from the imposition of classical models, and would only flourish when they were written in the native tongue of the author. Only when Italians spoke Italian rather than regional dialects would they develop the political identity he believed they should assume.[56]

Almost by default, an advocate of vernacular Italian, even a very learned one, became a principled opponent of rule from abroad. Muratori, too, was thinking in terms of the 'we' and the 'other', a crucial step in developing concepts of communal exclusiveness. By the end of the eighteenth century, and certainly from 1815 to 1848 when Habsburg government grew noticeably more oppressive, whatever sense of connectedness Italians had with the regime to their north faded as their intellectuals waged an impassioned campaign to fashion a language that would give Italy both a distinctive character and the national polity that would foster civil liberties. Indeed, in no other Habsburg land was the assault on overarching cultural values in the name of linguistic and national renewal more intense or more fraught with challenges to the integrity of the empire itself.

From National Language to National Culture: Hungary

An ethnocentric thread had long run through the fabric of Hungarian political life and in its church establishment as well. By the end of the eighteenth century, the Hungarian playwright and country gentleman Sándor Kisfaludy (1772–1844) had visions of Hungary disappearing amidst a sea of surrounding Slavs, Germans, and Rumanians. The only defense his countrymen had was to cultivate their language more earnestly.[57] Many nobles both great and small were therefore predisposed to read the German philosopher Johann Gottfried Herder (1744–1803) with both sympathy and alarm. Herder argued that linguistic diversity and unique cultures were aspects of a divine plan. Nevertheless, some languages and the customs and thought patterns connected with them had too few representatives to withstand absorption into the larger linguistic communities around them. Hungarian, unique in central Europe and adjacent to overwhelming numbers of Germans and Slavs, was one of them. Its extinction, therefore, was just a matter of time. Among the most frightened by this prospect, which Joseph II's German language decrees made seem all the more imminent, was the very well educated Count Stephen Széchenyi; indeed, such a prospect goaded him into thinking long and hard about the reform of his land. Intense cultivation of Hungarian and a Hungarian literature became for Széchenyi and many like him a way of developing the sense of ethnic singularity required for national survival.[58]

Hungarian, like seventeenth-century German, was far from wholly suppressed: it was used for everyday communication in the kingdom even among the polyglot high nobility. A lively Hungarian vernacular comedy existed as well; like its Viennese counterpart it specialized in social lampoons that drew a responsive audience from the nobility who much enjoyed laughing at the imperfections of the lower classes. Ardent defenders of their native tongue were to be found in the Hungarian bodyguard that Maria Theresa established to encourage noble loyalty to the dynasty; by 1790 the Hungarian diet would ask for Hungarian-speaking regiments to be posted on Hungarian soil. A move to establish a national theater to improve Hungarian moral fiber and to create a specifically

Hungarian culture was also underway. The support that the rural gentry gave to the program brought it into the country as a whole.[59]

An attack on Latin was also part of the Hungarian program. Though its usefulness had been under fire throughout most of the eighteenth century, careers in the higher vocations or politics of the kingdom were closed to those who had not mastered the tongue passably. 'To this day', complained a major partisan of the Magyar vernacular, Mihály Csokonai, in 1804, 'we stutter in the tongue of the dead.'[60] Both practical as well as moral considerations, he said, called for use of the Magyar tongue at all levels of Hungarian life, from the mundane to the spiritual. People who did not express themselves in their native language were breaking the laws of nature. If the mastery of a culture's vernacular was absent, access to that culture was denied. The otherwise quite cosmopolitan Csokonai himself confessed to having 'Magyarized' an image drawn from Voltaire in one of his works so that his readers could understand it.[61]

Latin endured in Hungary as the deliberative language of the royal diet to 1844, an indicator of the intense hostility that Joseph II's German language decrees had aroused in the kingdom. But the point had been made. To study one's language was to enter the inmost regions of one's culture. Understanding the experience of that culture, however, came only through the study of its history. Foundational origins were very important: by the second decade of the nineteenth century Hungarian intellectuals were analyzing native folksong and verse that they thought embodied the purest expression of the nation's spirit. It was the duty of literature, language's aesthetic by-product, to rework that history in ways that heightened the cultural awareness of a particular community. Writing in the Hungary of the decades before the revolutions of 1848 became a patriotic obligation, even for the minimally gifted.[62]

Like the Habsburg Austrian lands, Hungary developed its first modern classical literature between 1815 and 1848, but its leading writers brought to their work a quite different commitment. The wry anthropology of Nestroy and the quiet humanism of Raimund had little place in the work of poets such as Mihály Vörösmarty (1800–55) and Sándor Petőfi (1823–49). A prototype of the scholar/writer/activist, Vörösmarty was the author of *Zalán's Flight* (*Zalán futása*), a gory epic of the Magyar European land-taking in the ninth century. While perhaps praised more than read, it persuaded both aristocratic and bourgeois elements of Hungarian society that their national survival was at risk. Its publication in 1825, the year that Francis I convoked the kingdom's diet after a lapse of 11 years, added to its impact.

Like Raimund and Nestroy, Petőfi was a skillful conjuror of local character and place. Like Grillparzer, he soared to impressive lyrical heights when extolling the beauties of his native land. But for him as well as for Vörösmarty, writing in their language was tantamount to resisting a foreign cultural, and through it political, hegemony that had to be altered substantially or rejected altogether. Vörösmarty was the more temperate of the two: he did not like the idea of armed revolution in 1848. Yet he sketched the National Proclamation of 1848 and eventually fought for Kossuth, though he tried to tone him down. Petőfi had few, if any, reservations about going to war to secure Hungarian freedom. Indeed, he gave his life for it, dying in all likelihood during combat in 1849 against Russian forces supporting the Habsburg cause in Transylvania.[63]

The centrality of language to this outlook could, and did, lead to the politically counter-productive conclusion that speaking Magyar made one a Hungarian. Hungary's political class had always been concerned to preserve the territorial integrity of the kingdom; by the end of the eighteenth century, Magyarization programs were underway among the Slovak, Rumanian, and Serb populations of the kingdom. Such efforts predictably heightened feelings of uniqueness among these communities even before 1848 and would provoke discord among all these peoples until the collapse of the Habsburg empire in 1918. Croatian unwillingness to accept Magyar as the administrative language of Hungary prolonged the use of the more neutral Latin as well.[64] In 1842, Count Széchenyi roundly criticized this crude association of speech act with political identity; such thinking, he said, did not take account of the role of moral virtue in the makeup of his ideal good Hungarian. He did not, however, categorically deny that language and national identity were closely related.[65]

From National Language to National Culture: Bohemia

Nowhere in the Habsburg monarchy, however, was vernacular language more systematically deployed in constructing a cultural identity than in the kingdom of Bohemia. As in the case of all the vernacular tongues of the Habsburg empire, Czech was widely used in peasant households and in village churches even after the collapse of the estates' resistance to Ferdinand II at the outset of the Thirty Years War. Popular devotional literature in Czech appeared throughout the seventeenth century. By 1700, however, it was thoroughly marginalized as a literary language.[66]

Language choice defined class even more than it did ethnic distinction. Bohemian aristocratic families, Slavic and non-Slavic alike, used German so routinely that fictionalized exchanges in Czech between a great nobleman and a local peasant were hard to imagine, let alone write. In urban centers such as Prague, a sizeable and economically influential German-speaking element had historically dominated a large but, in the eighteenth century, fast-growing Slavic-speaking population. The cultural life of the kingdom was lively, but the Czech language had little, if any, bearing on its structure and content.[67]

The nobility of Bohemia and Moravia initially furthered study and wider use of the Czech language for the same reasons that Maria Theresa and Joseph II did – to raise the productivity of their lands. Learned societies to support this cause existed in the kingdom even before the Napoleonic era, and others were yet to come. A private circle of scientific amateurs established in 1774 by Count Franz Kinský and a gentleman–geologist, Ignác von Born (1742–91), was transformed into the Royal Society of Bohemia ten years later. To promote technology and manufacture a Patriotic–Economic Society of the kingdom was founded in 1788. In 1816, following lengthy discussions, a group of nobles in Moravia asked the Habsburg patriot, publicist and historian Joseph von Hormayr to develop a plan for a similar institution. The moving spirit behind the project was one of the region's most committed advocates of the Enlightenment, Count Johann Nepomuk von Mittrowský (1770–1842). He and his colleagues hoped to further not only the well-being of their province through a greater understanding of natural phenomena, but the progress of all humankind. Disseminating news of ongoing developments in science and technology was crucial to this effort. This mission, however, could only be completed when it was carried to a more literate and generally better-educated populace, a task most efficiently conducted in everyday languages.[68]

The purpose of these undertakings was 'patriotic' rather than 'national', that is, to heighten public awareness of the history, geography, and natural resources of the kingdom rather than to stress the connection of these subjects with any language community. Both Slavs and Germans were simply among the living topographical features of the kingdom's general landscape. Count Kinský proudly confessed himself to be a Slav and was a keen student of those languages' history, but he continued to write in German. Count Kolowrat, who with Counts Šternberk and Klebelsberk were the moving forces behind the founding of the Czech National Museum in 1818, were in and out of the ministerial cabinets of Francis I and his successor. Loyalty to the house of Habsburg among such men and a deep interest in the particularities of their homeland, including the Czech language, were still mutually consistent.[69]

The earliest scholars of Slavic languages also respected Habsburg rule. In the remote eastern regions of the monarchy, Polish Galicia and the Transcarpathian Ukraine, the monarchy's educational reforms encouraged both schooling in the local languages and improvement of the pedagogical facilities of the Greek Catholic and Orthodox confessions. The title of the Czech philologian Josef Dobrovský's address to Leopold II in 1791, 'On the Fidelity and Dependence of the Slavic Peoples toward the Arch[ducal] House of Austria' ('Über die Ergebenheit und Abhänglichkeit der slavischen Völker an das Erzhaus Österreich'), was hardly a summons to revolution. Bartholomäus Kopitar (1780–1844), a Slovene and the first director of the court library, would become a police censor, responsible for Greek, Slavic, and Rumanian. He thought that all Slavs were more or less one and had once called the Austrian lands their home. Believing that Old Church Slavonic developed somewhere in Carinthia/Pannonia, he concluded that Austria, and not Russia, was the natural guardian of Slavic peoples.[70]

It was not, however, necessary to accept the politics of noblemen such as Kinský and conservative scholars in order to further the larger cause they represented. Others less attached to the pan-Austrian nobility that had sustained itself through association with the dynasty enlisted as well, but did not subscribe to the idea of cultural communality in the Habsburg empire. Indeed the leap from the blandly patriotic to the enthusiastically national was effortless where the study of the Czech language was concerned. Bohemia between 1800 and 1848 was the scene of an explosion of linguistic and philological studies that found an enthusiastic response up and down the class ladder in the kingdom but particularly among the Czech-speaking middle classes in Prague.[71]

Even among relatively cautious academics, the renewal of the Czech language furthered notions of Czechs as a people apart from any other. Indeed, as they codified, and in many instances invented, the vocabulary to replace items that German, Latin, and other languages had once covered, scholars felt their personal sense of Czechness grow. Recreating their particular language nationalized them in the act. This feeling spilled over into the natural sciences to which eighteenth-century Bohemian academies were dedicated. An interest in rock formations does not in itself distinguish a Czech from a German. But inventing a specific vocabulary to make the natural world accessible to a specific language group gave the group a proprietary hold on the knowledge itself. One of the key Czech philologians of the time, Joseph Jungmann (1773–1847), quickly noted the process. World literature took on a Czech identification in translation as well. While leading intellectuals in Bohemia acknowledged the accomplishments of foreign authors, they became 'our Tasso' or 'our Sappho' once their works appeared in Czech.[72]

The One Now Many

The cultural commonality that had given to the Habsburg empire much of whatever coherence it had in the early modern era had thus come under serious attack by 1848. It had in large part been based upon the preference of both church and state for unreflected belief and non-literate indoctrination. By the middle of the eighteenth century, both institutions realized that these strategies had little relevance to the world in which they were operating, particularly when addressing economic problems. It was unfortunate for the Habsburg monarchy, but unavoidable, that necessary changes involved addressing language policy, thereby underscoring the particularity of the Habsburg peoples.

Language need not act as a marker between groups of people nor destroy commonality.[73] In theory, linguistically disparate peoples can acknowledge the same sovereign, be it a monarch or a written constitution. When groups do, however, define all categories of shared experience in terms of language, the possibility of cultural generality grows faint indeed. By 1848, most of the major regions of the Habsburg monarchy had begun this process, thereby reinforcing the political differences that appeared at the same time. Even the linguistically inclusive definitions of culture found in Hungary and in Poland, where dreams of return to an overarching Polish state still existed, challenged the notion of a cultural generality in the empire as a whole. That the aristocratic, even clerical elites of the Habsburg lands had played essential roles in this development only underscored the hollowed-out texture of the confessional and political hegemony that had once been the bedrock upon which the empire had rested.

A Summary Afterword

The administrative machinery and military prowess of the Habsburg empire, especially during its first two centuries, were far more imposing on paper than in practice. More subtle strategies kept the empire in place. One was the dynasty's readiness to cooperate with local elites, a skill cultivated in all of Europe's pre-modern and modern empires. The Habsburg imperial enterprise grew, indeed flourished, from the sixteenth to the middle of the eighteenth centuries in good part because the dynasty persuaded the lay aristocracy and high clergy of its lands that the house of Austria had something to offer them: the continuation of their many social, economic, and political privileges. For their part, the Habsburgs had a crucial stake in the natural and human resources that nobles and their ecclesiastical counterparts traditionally controlled.

Even when the balance of power tipped decidedly to the advantage of the territorial ruler in Bohemia and the Austrian lands after the Thirty Years War, estates still retained an active presence in fiscal affairs. Well into the nineteenth century, the several parties in this relationship renegotiated and redefined their positions many times, but always in the expectation that they would strike some modus vivendi anew. Even Hungary, an exceptionally intractable case, followed the pattern. That their empire was, by and large, not a product of outright conquest helped the Habsburg position in central and east central Europe considerably. The dynasty's unwanted role as Christendom's champion against the forces of Islam from Constantinople offset fears of Habsburg pre-eminence in central Europe; the recapture of Hungary was, for those exposed to Ottoman aggression, a war of liberation. Where the Habsburgs did engage in negotiated land awards – in northern Italy and Polish

167

Galicia – they were defending borders and not following grand expansionary designs.

Great empires are, however, also frequently energized and solidified by grand and lasting missions. Habsburg imperialism, more than most, harnessed its material trade-offs to a large and complex calling that had a spiritually universal dimension.[1] The spread of the house of Austria's rule coincided with two challenges to western Christendom, dominated for centuries by the Church of Rome. The first came from Islam; the second and, for contemporaries, more serious was the Protestant Reformation. Publicly, and in most cases inwardly, committed to the Catholic cause, the Habsburgs and their noble and clerical agents were instrumental in restoring Roman orthodoxy to great parts of central and east central Europe. With few exceptions, their subjects, noble and common alike, followed the institutional lead of their sovereigns, and not infrequently their spiritual examples.

Out of this program emerged not only what one modern historian has called 'an aristocratic–clerical commonwealth presided over by the Habsburgs', but a broader dynastic community as well, linked together by a species of hegemony that validated Habsburg rule among all classes of its subjects.[2] Taken individually, the Habsburg lands were linguistically, ethnically, economically, even institutionally, heterogeneous. Nevertheless, the firm allegiance of the dynasty's rulers to the religion and culture of the Catholic Counter-Reformation and their relentless pursuit of confessional uniformity wherever they reigned tempered these differences. The Habsburg peoples were one with their sovereigns in ways that contemporary European colonial empires, even that of their Spanish cousins, could not approach. All subjects in central and east central Europe, privileged and unprivileged alike, were part of a Catholic enterprise on the road to triumphant recovery from the publicly proclaimed menaces of Protestantism and Islam. Noble and commoner alike had a place in it, so long as they did not question Habsburg rule and its very few principles.

The dynasty's long and discriminating patronage of art, architecture, and music played a central role in this relationship; both the politics of the house of Habsburg and the aesthetic artifices with which it celebrated its position drew crucial inspiration from the ideals and convictions of Counter-Reformation Catholicism. Habsburg rule was therefore a cultural experience as much as a political one. Indeed, the two were operationally indistinguishable.

With very few exceptions, the house of Habsburg-Lorraine remained steadfastly Catholic to the collapse of its empire in 1918 and even afterward. It was also most at home with the noble elites of its realms, taken, at least, as individuals. But the world in which the Habsburgs formed these beliefs and the one in which they continued to hold them changed. As long as status and privilege remained the basis of social, material, and political advantage, and religious faith could persuade the empire's social orders that this arrangement was appropriate, the Habsburgs had found a way to keep otherwise disparate peoples together. By the eighteenth century, however, the dynasty's rulers, as well as members of their nobility and clergy, recognized the limitations of important aspects of this system. To maintain their political preeminence at home and their place in the international state system that had often rescued the empire from foreign aggression, the government in Vienna adopted economic, educational, and administrative policies that actively or potentially called into question the institutional foundations upon which the empire had been laid down. Even before the era of the French Revolution and Bonapartist imperialism, the Habsburgs were in serious conflict with aristocratic and clerical elements in their lands whose cooperation had been essential for the establishment and maintenance of Austrian rule in central Europe for almost 300 years.

The privileged elites of the empire did not welcome any form of ideological contamination from France. Nevertheless, by the beginning of the nineteenth century some among them had begun to find the dynasty wanting when more progressive policies in the interests of their homelands, particularly in economic matters, seemed needed. Status and privilege still very much concerned them, but the monarch no longer set all the terms of those qualities. Prosperity, even as some nobles had come to see it, was as much a by-product of economic development of scale as it was simple ownership of land. The wealthy aristocrat required a state organized to further the accumulation of capital, as well as to support the legal advantages that allowed him to maximize whatever profits he made. The behavior of the government in Vienna following the Napoleonic wars raised questions about the Habsburg commitment to both of these concerns.

The dynasty had also concluded that it had to cultivate the cooperation of the well-to-do members of the empire's middle classes, especially in the Austrian and Bohemian lands. This policy posed challenges all its own: while the empire's bourgeoisies were certainly open to such a rela-

tionship, their participation was shot through with practical and ideological ambiguities absent from the connections between the crown and
the privileged aristocracy. The sovereign created the noble, but economic
forces made the bourgeois entrepreneur what he was. So did other more
faceless processes such as education and intellectual independence. The
monarchy's need to control its peoples politically was at odds with these
values; to adapt to their implications successfully, Habsburg rulers had to
reject long-standing notions about government, rather than to modify
their behavior within traditional constitutions, as had been their response
to noble rebellions in the past. That noble and middle classes alike were
embarking on definitions of culture that pointed up the differences not
only between themselves and their rulers but between themselves as well,
also represented a serious breach with the cultural matrix that had
guided the behavior of Habsburg subjects since the end of the Thirty
Years War.

In 1848, the Habsburg empire had outlasted the British empire in
North America, the French colonial empire in the New World and in
Asia, and even much of the Spanish empire of its erstwhile parallel
branch. Less explicitly economic than any of these ventures, the dynasty
had manipulated local societies and their political systems to maintain a
presence in Europe quite out of proportion to its initial Alpine–
Danubian base in the Austrian lands. The revolutions of 1848 had
announced the challenges that future Habsburg monarchs could expect
to face. They had often asked for the loyalty of their peoples in trying
times, particularly in the face of foreign attack, and had received it. Their
next test was to devise ways of making those appeals in a world defined
by new notions of capital and increasingly particularistic understandings
of culture.

Notes

Introduction

1. D. Lieven, *Empire: The Russian Empire and Its Rivals* (London: John Murray, 2000), p. xiv.
2. B. S. Cohn, *Colonialism and Its Forms of Knowledge* (Princeton, NJ: Princeton University Press, 1993), pp. 4–5.
3. J. Bérenger, *A History of the Habsburg Empire, 1273–1700*, trans. C. A. Simpson (London: Longman, 1994), pp. 79–81.
4. Ibid., pp. 74–7.
5. V. Zimányi, 'Adel und Grundherrschaft in Ungarn in der Frühneuzeit', in H. Feigl and W. Rosner (eds), *Adel im Wandel* (Vienna: Niederösterreichisches Institut für Landeskunde, 1991), p. 40.
6. Bérenger, *Habsburg Empire*, pp. 39–40, 79.
7. On the importance of persuasion in the relations of imperial powers and subject elites, see generally R. Guha, *Dominance without Hegemony: History and Power in Colonial India* (Cambridge, MA: Harvard University Press, 1997). For the central statement on the role of collaboration in building and maintaining empires, see R. Robinson, 'Non-European Foundations of European Imperialism: Sketch for a Theory of Collaboration', in E. R. Owens and R. B. Sutcliffe (eds), *Studies in the Theory of Imperialism* (London: Longman, 1972), p. 18. See also P. Kennedy, 'Continuity and Discontinuity in British Imperialism, 1815–1914', in C. C. Eldridge (ed.), *British Imperialism in the Nineteenth Century* (London: Macmillan [now Palgrave Macmillan], 1984), p. 4, and J. Gallagher with R. Robinson, 'The Imperialism of Free Trade', in J. Gallagher with A. Seal (eds), *The Decline, Revival*

171

and Fall of the British Empire (Cambridge: Cambridge University Press, 1982), pp. 6–7. A useful recent commentary on the Habsburg empire is Solomon Wank, 'The Habsburg Empire', in K. Barkey and M. von Hagen (eds), *After Empire: Multiethnic Societies and Nation-Building* (Boulder, CO: Westview Press, 1997), pp. 49–50.

Chapter 1: The Pattern of Empire

1. Matthias von Neuenburg, *Chronik*, in *Quellenbuch zur Geschichte Österreichs*, ed. O. Frass, 4 vols (Vienna: Birkenverlag, 1956–67), vol. 1, p. 125.

2. C. F. Laferl, *Die Kultur der Spanier in Österreich unter Ferdinand I., 1522–1564* (Vienna: Böhlau, 1997), p. 38.

3. From Joseph Grünpeck, *Geschichte Friedrichs III*, in Frass, *Quellenbuch*, vol. 2, pp. 257–9. A good appraisal is A. Lhotsky, 'Friedrich III: Sein Leben und Seine Persönlichkeit', in A. Lhotsky, *Aufsätze und Vorträge*, 5 vols, ed. H. Wagner and H. Koller (Vienna: Verlag für Geschichte und Politik, 1971), vol. 2, pp. 119–63.

4. E. Bruckmüller, *Sozialgeschichte Österreichs* (Vienna: Herold, 1985), p. 156; V. Press, 'The System of Estates in the Austrian Hereditary Lands and in the Holy Roman Empire: A Comparison', in R. J. W. Evans and T. V. Thomas (eds), *Crown, Church and Estates: Central European Politics in the Sixteenth and Seventeenth Centuries* (New York: St. Martin's, 1991), p. 11.

5. M. Tanner, *The Last Descendant of Aeneas: The Hapsburgs and the Mythic Image of the Emperor* (New Haven, CT: Yale University Press, 1993), p. 124. A thoughtful overview of the Habsburg connection with music is K. Vocelka and L. Heller, *Die Lebenswelt der Habsburger: Kultur- und Mentalitätsgeschichte einer Familie* (Graz: Styria, 1997), pp. 52–66.

6. H. Wiesflecker, *Maximilian I.: Die Fundamente des habsburgischen Weltreiches* (Vienna: Verlag für Geschichte und Politik, 1991), pp. 365–75; H. Wiesflecker, *Kaiser Maximilian I.: Das Reich, Österreich und Europa an der Wende der Neuzeit*, 5 vols (Vienna: Verlag für Geschichte und Politik, 1986), vol. 5, p. 614.

7. H. G. Koenigsberger, 'The States-General of the Netherlands before the Revolt', in H. G. Koenigsberger (ed.), *Estates and Revolutions: Essays in Early Modern History* (Ithaca, NY: Cornell University Press, 1971), pp. 125–43.

8. Wiesflecker, *Maximilian I.*, vol. 5, pp. 530–45.
9. Wiesflecker, *Fundamente*, p. 310.
10. Ibid., pp. 311, 313.
11. Ibid., p. 312.
12. Bruckmüller, *Sozialgeschichte*, pp. 135–6.
13. Wiesflecker, *Fundamente*, pp. 296–7.
14. Ibid., pp. 296–310. A good overview of Burgundian administration is R. Vaughan, *Valois Burgundy* (London: Allen Lane/Penguin, 1975), pp. 95–113.
15. Frass, *Quellenbuch*, vol. 2, p. 25.
16. Laferl, *Spanier in Österreich*, pp. 66–75; S. Petrin, 'Die niederösterreichischen Stände im 16. und 17. Jahrhundert', in H. Knittler (ed.), *Adel im Wandel: Politik. Kultur. Konfession, 1500–1700* (Horn: Berger, 1990), p. 287.
17. A. Niederstätter, *1400–1522: das Jahrhundert der Mitte: an der Wende vom Mittelalter zur Neuzeit* (Vienna: Ueberreuter, 1996), p. 138.
18. Frass, *Quellenbuch*, vol. 1, pp. 263–4.
19. P. S. Fichtner, *Ferdinand I of Austria: The Politics of Dynasticism in the Age of the Reformation* (Boulder, CO: East European Monographs, 1982), p. 45.
20. V. Zimányi, *Economy and Society in Sixteenth- and Seventeenth-Century Hungary (1526–1650)* (Budapest: Akadémiai Kiadó, 1987), pp. 68–9.
21. Fichtner, *Ferdinand I*, p. 62.
22. Ibid., pp. 54–5.
23. Ibid., pp. 158–9; K. J. Dillon, *Kings and Estates in the Bohemian Lands, 1526–1564* (Brussels: Librairie Encyclopédique, 1976), pp. 133–42; J. Bahlcke, *Regionalismus und Staatsintegration im Wiederstreit: Die Länder der böhmischen Krone im ersten Jahrhundert der Habsburgerherrschaft (1526–1619)* (Munich: Oldenbourg, 1994), p. 166.
24. Fichtner, *Ferdinand I*, pp. 66–7; T. Fellner and H. Kretschmayr, *Die österreichische Zentralverwaltung*, 4 vols (Vienna: Holzhausen, 1907–25), vol. 1, pt 1, pp. 29–31.
25. See the tables in Fellner and Kretschmayer, *Zentralverwaltung*, vol. 1, pt 1, pp. 275–87.
26. P. S. Fichtner, *Emperor Maximilian II* (New Haven, CT: Yale University Press, 2001), pp. 80–3.
27. Ibid., p. 73.
28. T. Winkelbauer, 'Herren und Holden: Die niederösterreichischen Adeligen und ihre Untertanen im 16. und 17. Jahrhundert', in Knittler, *Adel im Wandel*, pp. 77–8.

29. P. S. Fichtner, 'Habsburg Household or Habsburg Government?: A Sixteenth-Century Administrative Dilemma', *Austrian History Yearbook*, 26 (1995), pp. 45–60.

30. Fichtner, *Maximilian II*, p. 79.

31. The classic work on this subject remains Stephen Fischer-Galati, *Ottoman Imperialism and German Protestantism, 1521–1555* (Cambridge, MA: Harvard, 1959).

32. G. Murdock, *Calvinism on the Frontier, 1600–1660: International Calvinism and the Reformed Church in Hungary and Transylvania* (Oxford: Clarendon Press, 2000), p. 22.

33. H. Louthan, *Johannis Crato and the Austrian Habsburgs: Reforming a Counter-Reform Court* (Princeton, NJ: Princeton Theological Seminary, 1994), p. 3.

34. František Černý (ed.), *Dějiny Ceského Divadla*, 4 vols (Prague: Československá Akademia Věd, 1968), vol. 1, pp. 134–7.

35. A. Edel, *Der Kaiser und Kurpfalz: Eine Studie zu den Grundelementen politischen Handelns bei Maximilian II. (1564–1576)* (Göttingen: Vandenhoeck and Ruprecht, 1997), pp. 307–8.

36. This picture is worked out in compelling detail by A. P. Luttenberger, *Kurfürsten, Kaiser, und Reich: Politische Führung und Friedenssicherung unter Ferdinand I. und Maximilian II.* (Mainz: Philip von Zabern, 1994).

37. R. J. W. Evans, *Rudolf II and his World: A Study in Intellectual History, 1576–1612* (Oxford: Clarendon Press, 1973), pp. 62–3; K. Vocelka, *Rudolf II und seine Zeit* (Vienna: Böhlau, 1985), p. 96.

38. Evans, *Rudolf II*, pp. 53–83.

39. Winkelbauer, 'Herren und Holden', pp. 78–9. See also V. Press, 'Adel in den österreichisch–böhmischen Erblanden und im Reich zwischen dem 15. und dem 17. Jahrhundert', in Knittler, *Adel in Wandel*, p. 24.

40. Frass, *Quellenbuch*, vol. 2, p. 98.

Chapter 2: An Empire Takes Hold

1. G. Mecenseffy, *Geschichte des Protestantismus in Österreich* (Graz: Böhlau, 1956), pp. 71–6.

2. R. Bireley, SJ, 'Confessional Absolutism in the Habsburg Lands in the Seventeenth Century', in C. W. Ingrao (ed.), *State and Society in Early*

Modern Austria (West Lafayette, IN: Purdue University Press, 1994), pp. 40–1; Fichtner, *Maximilian II*, p. 189.

3. Bireley, 'Confessional Absolutism', pp. 45–6; P. S. Fichtner, 'Habsburg State Building: The Incomplete Sixteenth Century', *Austrian History Yearbook*, 25 (1994), p. 152.

4. J. Franzl, *Ferdinand II.: Kaiser im Zwiespalt der Zeit* (Graz: Verlag Styria, 1978), pp. 43–5; Mecenseffy, *Protestantismus*, pp. 79–82; R. Bireley, SJ, *Religion and Politics in the Age of the Counterreformation: Emperor Ferdinand II, William Lamormaini, S.J., and the Formation of Imperial Policy* (Chapel Hill, NC: University of North Carolina Press, 1981), pp. 13, 17.

5. K. J. MacHardy, 'Cultural Capital and Noble Identity', *Past and Present*, 163 (May 1999), pp. 46–7, 68–71.

6. J. Bücking, *Frühabsolutismus und Kirchenreform in Tirol (1566–1665): Ein Beitrag zum Ringen zwischen 'Staat' und 'Kirche' in der frühen Neuzeit* (Wiesbaden: Steiner, 1972), pp. 115–222.

7. K. J. MacHardy, 'The Rise of Absolutism and Noble Rebellion in Early Modern Habsburg Austria, 1570–1620', *Comparative Studies in Society and History*, 34 (1992), pp. 410, 431–2; J. Van Horn Melton, 'The Nobility in the Bohemian and Austrian Lands, 1620–1780', in H. M. Scott and C. Storrs (eds), *The European Nobilities in the Seventeenth and Eighteenth Centuries*, 2 vols (London: Longman, 1995), vol. 2, pp. 111–13.

8. Bireley, 'Confessional Absolutism', pp. 38–9. See also J. Mears, 'The Thirty Years' War, the "General Crisis", and the Origins of a Standing Professional Army in the Habsburg Monarchy', *Central European History*, 21 (1988), pp. 122–41; A. Kraus, 'Das katholische Herrscherbild im Reich, dargestellt am Beispiel Kaiser Ferdinands II. und Kurfürst Maximilians I. von Bayern', in K. Repgen (ed.), *Das Herrscherbild im 17. Jahrhundert* (Münster: Aschendorff, 1991), p. 19.

9. Bireley, 'Confessional Absolutism', pp. 45–76; Fichtner, 'Habsburg State Building', p. 152.

10. H. Dollinger, 'Kurfürst Maximilian I. von Bayern und Justus Lipsius', *Archiv für Kulturgeschichte*, 66, nos. 2/3 (1964), pp. 229–33; Kraus, 'Katholische Herrscherbild', pp. 13, 16.

11. G. Reingrabner, *Protestanten in Österreich: Geschichte und Dokumentation* (Graz: Böhlau, 1981), p. 175; F. Schragl, *Glaubensspaltung in Niederösterreich* (Vienna: Dom-Verlag, 1973), p. 153.

12. K. J. MacHardy, 'Der Einfluß von Status, Konfession und Besitz auf das politische Verhalten des niederösterreichischen Ritterstandes,

1580–1620', in G. Klingenstein and H. Lutz (eds), *Spezialforschung und 'Gesamtgeschichte': Beispiele und Methodenfragen zur Geschichte der frühen Neuzeit* (Vienna: Verlag für Geschichte und Politik, 1981), pp. 69–73; A. Kohler, 'Bildung und Konfession: Zum Studium der Studenten in den habsburgischen Ländern an Hochschulen im Reich (1560–1620)', in G. Klingenstein, H. Lutz, and G. Stourzh (eds), *Bildung, Politik, und Gesellschaft* (Vienna: Verlag für Geschichte und Politik, 1978), p. 100.

13. Bireley, *Religion and Politics*, pp. 17–18; Vienna, Hofkammerarchiv (Court Treasury Archives) (hereafter HKA), *Gedenkbücher* (Memorandum Books), 333, fol. 26.

14. T. Winkelbauer, *Fürst und Fürstendiener: Gundaker von Liechtenstein, ein österreichischer Aristokrat des konfessionellen Zeitalters* (Vienna: Oldenbourg, 1999), pp. 24–46, 62–5; Melton, 'Nobility', in Scott/Storrs, *Nobilities*, vol. 2, pp. 114–15.

15. R. Endres, *Adel in der frühen Neuzeit* (Munich: Oldenbourg, 1993), pp. 79–80.

16. Bireley, 'Confessional Absolutism', pp. 41–3.

17. H. Rebel, *Peasant Classes: The Bureaucratization of Property and Family Relations under Early Habsburg Absolutism* (Princeton, NJ: Princeton University Press, 1981), pp. 6, 128–33.

18. Winkelbauer, *Fürst und Fürstendiener*, pp. 39–46.

19. A particularly clear study of the mutual benefits of Habsburg relations with the imperial knights to the very end of the Holy Roman Empire in 1804 is Berthold Sutter, 'Kaisertreue oder rationale Überlebensstrategie?: Die Reichsritterschaft als Habsburgische Klientel im Reich', in H. Duchhardt and M. Schnettger (eds), *Reichsständische Libertät und Habsburgisches Kaisertum* (Mainz: Philipp von Zabern, 1999), pp. 257–307. A good summary of the provisions of the Peace of Westphalia is H. Klueting, 'Das Reich und Österreich, 1648–1740', in W. Brauneder and L. Hobelt (eds), *Sacrum Imperium: Das Reich und Österreich, 996–1806* (Vienna: Almathea, 1996), pp. 171–7.

20. Klueting, 'Reich und Österreich', p. 164.

21. V. Press, 'The System of Estates in the Austrian Hereditary Lands and in the Holy Roman Empire: A Comparison', in Evans/Thomas, *Crown, Church and Estates*, p. 16.

22. G. Schmidt, 'Angst vor dem Kaiser?: Die Habsburger, die Erblande und die deutsche Libertät im 17. Jahrhundert', in Duchhardt/Schnettger, *Reichsständische Libertät*, pp. 342–3; Klueting, 'Reich und Österreich', p. 164.

23. M. Schnettger, 'Der Kaiser und die Bischofwahlen: Das Haus Österreich und die Reichskirche vom Augsburger Religionsfrieden bis zum Mittel des 17. Jahrhunderts', in Duchhardt/Schnettger, *Reichständische Libertät*, pp. 218–19, 229–32, 238, 252.

24. Klueting, 'Reich und Österreich', p. 202; J. P. Spielman, *Leopold I of Austria* (New Brunswick, NJ: Rutgers, 1977), p. 103.

25. V. Press, 'Die Erblande und das Reich von Albrecht II. bis Karl VI. (1438–1740)', in R. A. Kann and F. Prinz (eds), *Deutschland und Österreich: Ein bilaterales Geschichtsbuch* (Vienna: Jugend und Volk, 1980), pp. 78–83. Václav Eusebius Lobkovic, at one point chief adviser to Leopold I, was the single richest man in the kingdom of Bohemia by the end of the seventeenth century. Melton, 'Nobility', in Scott/Storrs, *Nobilities*, vol. 2, p. 115.

26. Klueting, 'Reich und Österreich', p. 190.

27. Especially useful for a summary of the provisions of the Peace of Westphalia is ibid., pp. 171–7.

28. Press, 'Estates', pp. 11–12, and V. Press, 'The Imperial Court of the Habsburgs: From Maximilian I to Ferdinand III, 1493–1657', in R. G. Asch and A. M. Birke (eds), *Princes, Patronage, and the Nobility: The Court at the Beginning of the Modern Age, c. 1450–1650* (London: Oxford, 1991), p. 303.

29. J. P. Spielman, *The City and the Crown: Vienna and the Imperial Court, 1600–1740* (West Lafayette, IN: Purdue University Press, 1993), pp. 32, 45–6, 58; Spielman, *Leopold I*, pp. 89–90.

30. J. P. Spielman, 'Status as Commodity: The Habsburg Economy of Privilege', in Ingrao, *State and Society*, pp. 114–15.

31. Ibid., p. 117.

32. Press, 'Estates', pp. 11–12; Press, 'Imperial Court', p. 303.

33. Spielman, *City and Crown*, pp. 185–7.

34. Klueting, 'Reich und Österreich', p. 208.

35. W. Kessler, 'Die Siebenbürger Sachsen im habsburgischen Gesamtstaat, 1688–1790', in M. Csáky and R. Hagelkrys (eds), *Vaterlandsliebe und Gesamtstaatsidee im österreichischen 18. Jahrhundert* (Vienna: Verein der wissenschaftlichen Gesellschaften Österreichs, 1989), pp. 65–8; J. Bérenger, 'L'Idée de nation dans la hongrie du XVIIe siècle', *XVIIe Siècle*, 44 (1992), p. 357.

36. T. Winkelbauer, 'Grundherrschaft, Sozialdisziplinierung und Konfessionalisierung in Böhmen, Mähren, und Österreich im 16. u. 17. Jahrhundert', in J. Bahlcke and A. Strohmeyer (eds), *Konfessionalisierung in Ostmitteleuropa* (Stuttgart: Steiner, 1999), pp. 307–38; Péter

Pázmány, 'Antwort auf das Buch des Predigers von Sárvár, István Magyari . . .', in J. von Farkas (ed.), *Ungarns Geschichte und Kultur in Dokumenten* (Wiesbaden: Harrassowitz, 1955), pp. 54–6, 58.

37. Schimert, 'Hungarian Nobility', in Scott/Storrs, *Nobilities*, vol. 2, pp. 144–6, 150–1, 153–4, 158, 168.

38. MacHardy, 'Cultural Capital', p. 50.

39. K. Benda, 'Habsburg Absolutism and the Resistance of the Hungarian Estates in the Sixteenth and Seventeenth Centuries', in Evans/Thomas, *Crown, Church and Estates*, pp. 126–7.

40. Ibid., pp. 123–4; R. Okey, *Eastern Europe, 1740–1985: Feudalism to Communism*, 2nd edn (London: Hutchison, 1986), p. 26.

41. Schimert, 'Hungarian Nobility', in Scott/Storrs, *Nobilities*, vol. 2, pp. 144–5; Okey, *Eastern Europe*, p. 26.

42. Schimert, 'Hungarian Nobility', in Scott/Storrs, *Nobilities*, vol. 2, p. 155; Bérenger, 'Idée', pp. 351–3.

43. Press, 'Imperial Court', pp. 310–11.

44. Bérenger, 'Idée', p. 350.

45. Ibid., pp. 359–60; Spielman, *Leopold I*, pp. 50–3, 61–72, 83–9.

46. Spielman, *Leopold I*, p. 97.

47. Mears, 'Professional Army', p. 136; T. Barker, *Double Eagle and Crescent: Vienna's Second Turkish Siege and Its Historical Setting* (Albany, NY: State University of New York Press, 1967), p. 300.

48. Mears, 'Professional Army', pp. 123–6, 134, 137–9; Barker, *Double Eagle*, p. 375.

49. F. Bosbach (ed.), 'Princeps in Compendio', in Repgen, *Herrscherbild*, pp. 109–10.

50. Spielman, *Leopold I*, pp. 99, 115 and 214, ch. 9 n. 5.

51. C. W. Ingrao, *The Habsburg Monarchy, 1618–1815* (Cambridge: Cambridge University Press, 1994), p. 84.

52. Ibid., pp. 94–5.

53. Spielman, *Leopold I*, pp. 114, 116, 119–22.

54. Florin and gulden were interchangeable terms in seventeenth-century central Europe.

55. Ingrao, *Habsburg Monarchy*, p. 85.

56. H. M. Scott and C. Storrs, 'Introduction: The Consolidation of Noble Power in Europe, c. 1600–1800', in Scott/Storrs, *Nobilities*, vol. 1, pp. 24, 31.

57. HKA, *Hofzahlamtsbücher* nos. 133 (1688), fols. 25, 60, 138.

58. Ingrao, *Habsburg Monarchy*, pp. 84–8.

59. F. Rákóczi, excerpt from 'Das Bekenntnis eines Sünders', in Farkas (ed.), *Ungarns Geschichte*, p. 80.

60. On peasant–landlord problems, see Á. Várkonyi, 'Rákóczi's War of Independence and the Peasantry', in J. M. Bak and B. K. Király (eds), *From Hunyadi to Rákóczi: War and Society in Late Medieval and Early Modern Hungary* (Boulder, CO: Social Science Monographs, 1982), pp. 379–81.

61. J. Van Horn Melton, *Absolutism and the Eighteenth-Century Origins of Compulsory Schooling in Prussia and Austria* (Cambridge: Cambridge University Press, 1988), pp. 63–4.

62. For a thoughtful discussion of the interplay of Austrian culture with the Baroque, see M. P. Steinberg, *The Meaning of the Salzburg Festival: Austria as Theater and Ideology, 1890–1938* (Ithaca, NY: Cornell University Press, 1990), pp. 1–8. On matters of architectural consistency see, above all, T. D. Kaufmann, *Court, Cloister, and City: The Art and Culture of Central Europe, 1450–1800* (Chicago: University of Chicago Press, 1995), esp. ch. 14.

63. P. R. Magocsi, *A History of Ukraine* (Toronto: University of Toronto Press, 1996), p. 388.

64. R. W. J. Evans, *The Making of the Habsburg Monarchy, 1550–1700* (Oxford: Clarendon Press, 1979), pp. 419–32; M. Dietrich, 'Aufführung und Dramaturgie', in Johann Bernhardt Staudt, *Mulier Fortis*, ed. W. Pass and F. Niiyama-Kalicki, Denkmäler der Tonkunst in Österreich, vol. 152 (Graz: Akademische Druck- und Verlagsanstalt, 2000), pp. viii, xvii; W. Pass and F. Niiyama-Kalicki, 'Die musikalische Gestaltung', in ibid., p. xiii.

65. Murdock, *Calvinism*, p. 301.

66. H. Sturmberger, *Adam Graf Herberstorff* (Munich: Oldenbourg, 1976), pp. 159–259.

Chapter 3: Creating a State

1. Ingrao, *Habsburg Monarchy*, pp. 105–8.

2. Ibid., p. 115.

3. J. Whaley, 'Die Habsburgermonarchie und das Heilige Römische Reich im 18. Jahrhundert', in Brauneder/Hobelt, *Sacrum Imperium*, p. 293.

4. G. Mraz, 'Das Kaisertum Österreich: Die Vollendung der Gesamt-staatsidee', in G. Mraz, H. Mraz and G. Stangler (eds), *Kaisertum Österreich, 1804–1848* (Vienna: Amt der niederösterreichischen Landesregierung, 1996), p. 5.

5. Ingrao, *Habsburg Monarchy*, p. 121.

6. Ibid., p. 183.

7. R. Browning, *The War of the Austrian Succession* (New York: St. Martin's, 1993), pp. 38–9, 70.

8. Eduard Maur, 'Der böhmische und mährische Adel vom 16. bis zum 18. Jahrhundert', in Feigl/Rosner, *Adel im Wandel*, p. 32. An instructive insight into just how much the position of the Bohemian nobility at the Habsburg court changed relative to Italians, Spaniards, Hungarians, and Germans, including those from the Habsburg Austrian lands, is to be drawn from HKA, *Hofzahlamtsbücher*, no. 138 (1693), fols. 1–69; no. 144 (1702), fols. 6–59; no. 152 (1710), fols. 6–60; no. 165 (1763–8), fols. 3–23. See also Melton, 'Nobility', in Scott/Storrs, *Nobilities*, vol. 2, pp. 136–7.

9. T. C. W. Blanning, *Joseph II* (London: Longman, 1994), p. 35; Melton, 'Nobility', in Scott/Storrs, *Nobilities*, vol. 2, pp. 136–7.

10. Browning, *Austrian Succession*, pp. 66–8.

11. Whaley, 'Habsburgermonarchie', p. 298.

12. Ingrao, *Habsburg Monarchy*, pp. 150–8; Whaley, 'Habsburger Monarchie', p. 298.

13. F. A. J. Szábó, *Kaunitz and Enlightened Absolutism, 1753–1780* (Cambridge: Cambridge University Press, 1994), pp. 267–8.

14. C. Duffy, *The Army of Maria Theresa: The Armed Forces of Imperial Austria, 1740–1780* (North Pomfret, VT: David & Charles, 1977), pp. 170–205 *passim.*

15. J. Kunisch, 'Der Aufstieg neuer Großmächte im 18. Jahrhundert und die Aufteilung der Machtsphären in Ostmitteleuropa', in G. Klingenstein and F. A. J. Szábó (eds), *Staatskanzler Wenzel Anton von Kaunitz-Rietberg, 1711–1794: Neue Perspektive zu Politik und Kultur der europäischen Aufklärung* (Graz: Schneider, 1996), pp. 77, 83–4; Ingrao, *Habsburg Monarchy*, pp. 193–4; Blanning, *Joseph II*, p. 34.

16. B. Mazohl-Wallnig, *Österreichischer Verwaltungsstaat und administrative Eliten im Königreich Lombardo-Venetien, 1815–1859* (Mainz: Philipp von Zabern, 1993), p. 295.

17. C. A. Macartney (ed.), *The Habsburg and Hohenzollern Dynasties in the Seventeenth and Eighteenth Centuries* (New York: Harper & Row, 1970), pp. 99–100; J. Komlos, *Nutrition and Economic Development in the*

Eighteenth-Century Habsburg Monarchy: An Anthropomorphic History (Princeton, NJ: Princeton University Press, 1989), pp. 119, 121, 123–4.

18. H. M. Scott, 'Reform in the Habsburg Monarchy, 1740–1790', in H. M. Scott (ed.), *Enlightened Absolutism: Reformed and Reformers in Later Eighteenth-Century Europe* (Basingstoke, UK: Macmillan [now Palgrave Macmillan], 1990), p. 154.

19. E. Wangermann, *The Austrian Achievement, 1700–1800* (New York: Harcourt, Brace, Jovanovich, 1973), pp. 60–3.

20. Scott, 'Reform', p. 155.

21. Endres, *Adel*, p. 81; C. Duffy, 'Count Kaunitz-Rietberg, Military Strategist, 1756–1763', in Klingenstein/Szábó, *Kaunitz*, p. 62; Karl Vocelka and Lynne Heller, *Die Lebenswelt der Habsburger: Kultur- und Mentalitätsgeschichte einer Familie* (Graz: Styria, 1997), pp. 213–14; Scott, 'Reform', p. 151.

22. Endres, *Adel*, p. 81.

23. HKA, *Hofzahlamtsbücher*, no. 165 (1763–8), fols. 3–23.

24. Klueting, 'Reich und Österreich', p. 213.

25. D. F. Good, *The Economic Rise of the Habsburg Empire, 1750–1914* (Berkeley, CA: University of California Press, 1984), pp. 28–32; Wangermann, *Achievement*, p. 66; Ingrao, *Habsburg Monarchy*, p. 213.

26. Komlos, *Nutrition*, pp. 125–7, 157.

27. Ibid., p. 130; Wangermann, *Achievement*, p. 64; Scott, 'Reform', p. 179.

28. Komlos, *Nutrition*, p. 129; Melton, *Absolutism*, pp. 137, 159–60, 164–6.

29. Scott, 'Reform', p. 180.

30. Komlos, *Nutrition*, pp. 153, 156, 158–9; Melton, *Absolutism*, p. 149; Wangermann, *Achievement*, p. 71.

31. R. Melville, 'Adel und Grundherrschaft in Böhmen an der Schwelle des bürgerlichen Zeitalters', in Feigl/Rosner, *Adel*, pp. 76–7, 80–1.

32. D. Uhlíř, 'Kaunitz und die böhmischen Länder', in Klingenstein/Szábó, *Kaunitz*, p. 488; R. J. W. Evans, 'Moravia and the Culture of the Enlightenment in the Habsburg Monarchy', in ibid., p. 386.

33. Melville, 'Adel', in Feigl/Rosner, *Adel*, pp. 77–8; Wangermann, *Achievement*, p. 63.

34. Wangermann, *Achievement*, pp. 77, 81; Scott, 'Reform', pp. 156–7.

35. Melton, *Absolutism*, pp. 82–3, 160; Komlos, *Nutrition*, pp. 125, 154.

36. Kunisch, 'Aufstieg', in Klingenstein/Szábó, *Kaunitz*, p. 87.

37. Wangermann, *Achievement*, p. 63; Scott, 'Reform', pp. 157–9; Melton, 'Nobility', in Scott/Storrs, *Nobilities*, vol. 2, p. 141.

182 NOTES

38. See, for example, HKA, *Hofzahlamtsbücher*, no. 165 (1763–8), fols. 3–23.
39. Evans, 'Moravia', in Klingenstein/Szábó, *Kaunitz*, p. 395.
40. Uhlíř, 'Kaunitz und die böhmischen Länder', in ibid., pp. 490–3.
41. Ibid., pp. 489–93.
42. H. Carl, 'Kaunitz und Ostfriesland: Aspekte adliger Familienpolitik im Hause Kaunitz', in Klingenstein/Szábó, *Kaunitz*, pp. 404–5, 407, 411–12.
43. Mazohl-Wallnig, *Österreichischer Verwaltungsstaat*, pp. 290–2.
44. Ibid., pp. 73, 300–1, 328–9.
45. Zimányi, 'Adel und Grundherrschaft', in Feigl/Rosner, *Adel*, pp. 42–3.
46. Cf. HKA, *Hofzahlamtsbücher*, nos. 138 (1693), fols. 1–69; 144 (1702), fols. 6–59; 152 (1710), fols. 6–60; 165 (1763–8), fols. 3–23. See also Ingrao, *Habsburg Monarchy*, p. 203.
47. Scott, 'Reform', pp. 162–3.
48. Wangermann, *Achievement*, pp. 78–83; Scott, 'Reform', p. 166.
49. Wangermann, *Achievement*, pp. 74–88.
50. Klaus Epstein, *The Genesis of German Conservatism* (Princeton, NJ: Princeton University Press, 1966), esp. pp. 496–502.
51. D. Beales, *Joseph II*, vol. 1, *In the Shadow of Maria Theresa, 1741–1780* (Cambridge: Cambridge University Press, 1987), p. 16.
52. Ingrao, *Habsburg Monarchy*, p. 193.
53. On Joseph's education, see Beales, *Joseph II*, vol. 1, pp. 43–68; D. Beales, 'Christians and *philosophes*: The Case of the Austrian Enlightenment', in D. Beales and Geoffrey Best (eds), *History, Society and the Churches* (Cambridge: Cambridge University Press, 1985), p. 175; É. Balázs, *Hungary and the Habsburgs, 1765–1800*, trans. T. Wilkinson (Budapest: Central European Press, 1987), pp. 88–9.
54. Ingrao, *Habsburg Monarchy*, p. 182.
55. Beales, *Joseph II*, vol. 1, pp. 66, 252–5.
56. J. Haydn, 'Die Jahreszeiten', libretto by G. van Swieten after J. Thomson, *The Seasons*, trans. Gottfried van Swieten (Berlin/DDR: VEB Deutsche Schallplatte, 3 records, 1971), side 4.
57. R. W. J. Evans, 'Maria Theresa and Hungary', in Scott, *Enlightened Absolutism*, p. 205.
58. Komlos, *Nutrition*, p. 131.
59. Wangermann, *Achievement*, pp. 112–13.
60. C. Donati, 'The Italian Nobilities in the Seventeenth and Eighteenth Centuries', in Scott/Storrs, *Nobilities*, vol. 1, p. 262.

61. W. Heindl, *Gehorsame Rebellen: Bürokratie und Beamte in Österreich, 1780 bis 1848* (Vienna: Böhlau, 1990), p. 119.

62. Macartney, *Habsburg and Hohenzollern*, p. 109; Heindl, *Rebellen*, pp. 22–3, 28–9, 33, citation, p. 22.

63. Press, 'Adel', in Knittler, *Adel im Wandel*, p. 28; P. G. M. Dickson, 'Monarchy and Bureaucracy in Late 18th Century Austria', *English Historical Review*, 110 (1995), pp. 324, 328, 335, 337.

64. Heindl, *Rebellen*, pp. 142–56; Balázs, *Hungary*, p. 291. See also Dickson, 'Monarchy', p. 345.

65. M. J. Levy, *Governance and Grievance: Habsburg Policy and Italian Tyrol in the Eighteenth Century* (West Lafayette, IN: Purdue University Press, 1988), pp. 46–63.

66. Scott, 'Reform', p. 185; Ingrao, *Habsburg Monarchy*, p. 205.

67. Ingrao, *Habsburg Monarchy*, p. 205.

68. A. M. Drabek, 'Der Nationsbegriff in Böhmen an der Grenze von Aufklärung und "nationaler Wiedergeburt"', in Csáky/Hagelkrys, *Vaterlandsliebe*, pp. 43–4.

69. Ibid., pp. 53–4.

70. G. Kókay, 'György Bessenyi', in Csáky/Hagelkrys, *Vaterlandsliebe*, pp. 36–41; B. K. Király, *Hungary in the Late Eighteenth Century: The Decline of Enlightened Despotism* (New York: Columbia University Press, 1969), pp. 108–9, 147–70, 180–1, 268; C. A. Macartney, *Hungary: A Short History* (Chicago: Aldine, 1962), pp. 124–5; D. Mervyn Jones, *Five Hungarian Writers* (Oxford: Oxford University Press, 1966), p. xx.

71. Blanning, *Joseph II*, pp. 147–51.

Chapter 4: Holding the Center

1. E. Cochrane, *Florence in the Forgotten Centuries, 1527–1800: A History of Florence and the Florentines in the Age of the Grand Dukes* (Chicago: University of Chicago Press, 1973), pp. 257–9, 428, 450–1.

2. Ibid., pp. 487–500.

3. P. S. Fichtner, 'Viennese Perspectives on the American War of Independence', in Béla K. Király and George Barany (eds), *East Central European Perceptions of Early America* (Lisse: Peter De Ridder, 1977), pp. 20–1.

4. Király, *Hungary*, pp. 190–5.

5. Ingrao, *Habsburg Monarchy*, pp. 210–11; P. R. Magocsi, *A History of Ukraine* (Toronto: University of Toronto Press, 1996), pp. 329–402.

6. Wangermann, *Achievement*, p. 169.
7. G. Pajkossy, 'Das Kaisertum Österreich und Ungarn, 1804–1848', in Mraz/Mraz/Stangler, *Kaisertum Österreich*, p. 44; Blanning, *Joseph II*, p. 4.
8. Pajkossy, 'Österreich und Ungarn', pp. 44–5.
9. Excerpts from Leopold's Hungarian Declaration in P. S. Fichtner, *The Habsburg Empire: From Dynasticism to Multinationalism* (Malabar, FL: Krieger, 1997), pp. 128–9; Pajkossy, 'Österreich und Ungarn', p. 41; Király, *Hungary*, pp. 177, 181, 183, 235.
10. Wangermann, *Achievement*, pp. 170–1.
11. Ibid., pp. 171–3.
12. Levy, *Governance and Grievance*, p. 142; Wangermann, *Achievement*, pp. 174–5.
13. Ingrao, *Habsburg Monarchy*, p. 221.
14. Ibid.
15. Blanning, *Joseph II*, p. 4. Ingrao, *Habsburg Monarchy*, pp. 212–15 gives a good summary analysis.
16. Wangermann, *Achievement*, pp. 175–6.
17. E. Sagarra, 'Benign Authority and its Cultivation in the Biedermeier', in I. F. Roe and J. Warren (eds), *The Biedermeier and Beyond* (Bern: Peter Lang, 1999), p. 74.
18. Wangermann, *Achievement*, p. 177; Ingrao, *Habsburg Monarchy*, p. 224.
19. Wangermann, *Achievement*, pp. 180–1; Pajkossy, 'Österreich und Ungarn', p. 46.
20. Wangermann, *Achievement*, pp. 182–4; Ingrao, *Habsburg Monarchy*, p. 225.
21. A good summary of Napoleon's military encounters with the Habsburgs is J. Black, 'Revolutionary and Napoleonic Warfare', in J. Black (ed.), *European Warfare, 1453–1815* (Basingstoke, UK: Macmillan [now Palgrave Macmillan], 1999), pp. 232–9.
22. W. D. Gruner, 'Österreich zwischen altem Reich und deutschem Bund (1789–1816)', in Brauneder/Hobelt, *Sacrum Imperium*, pp. 336–41.
23. Klueting, 'Reich und Österreich', p. 254.
24. Pajkossy, 'Österreich und Ungarn', pp. 41, 46; J. Bérenger, *Histoire de l'empire des Habsbourg, 1273–1918* (Paris: Fayard, 1990), pp. 538, 542.
25. Pajkossy, 'Österreich und Ungarn', p. 46; Macartney, *Hungary*, pp. 127–9; Ingrao, *Habsburg Monarchy*, p. 224.

26. M. Csáky, *Von der Aufklärung zum Liberalismus: Studien zum Frühliberalismus in Ungarn* (Vienna: Verlag der österreichischen Akademie der Wissenschaften, 1981), pp. 93, 95 n. 1.

27. Macartney, *Hungary*, p. 137.

28. Bérenger, *Histoire*, pp. 537–8.

29. V.-L. Tapié, *The Rise and Fall of the Habsburg Monarchy*, trans. S. Hardman (New York: Praeger, 1971), pp. 246–7.

30. C. Magris, *Der habsburgische Mythos in der österreichischen Literatur* (Salzburg: Müller, 1988 [1969]), pp. 45, 47–50.

31. H. Rössler, *Graf Johann Philipp Stadion: Napoleons deutscher Gegenspieler*, 2 vols (Vienna: Herold, 1966), vol. 1, p. 293; R. Erickson, 'Vienna in Its European Context', in R. Erickson (ed.), *Schubert's Vienna* (New Haven, CT: Yale University Press, 1997), pp. 15–16.

32. Rössler, *Stadion*, vol. 1, pp. 297–8.

33. Ibid., pp. 295–6.

34. G. Barany, 'From Fidelity to the Habsburgs to Loyalty to the Nation: The Changing Role of the Hungarian Aristocracy before 1848', *Austrian History Yearbook*, 23 (1992), pp. 46–7; H. L. Agnew, 'The Noble *Natio* and the Modern Nation: The Czech Case', *Austrian History Yearbook*, 23 (1992), pp. 61–3, 65.

35. H. Haider-Pregler, 'Der Wienerische Weg zur k. k. Hof- und Nationalschaubühne', in R. Bauer and J. Wertheimer (eds), *Das Ende des Stegreifspiels: Die Geburt des Nationaltheaters* (Munich: Fink, 1983), p. 32.

36. Rössler, *Stadion*, vol. 1, pp. 302–3.

37. Blanning, *Joseph II*, p. 8.

38. P. Schroeder, *The Transformation of European Politics, 1763–1848* (Oxford: Clarendon Press, 1994), p. 505; E. Kraehe, *Metternich's German Policy*, 2 vols (Princeton, NJ: Princeton University Press, 1963–83), vol. 2, p. 397.

39. Rössler, *Stadion*, vol. 1, pp. 297–8.

40. Ingrao, *Habsburg Monarchy*, p. 238.

41. Schroeder, *Transformation*, pp. 89, 91.

42. Ibid., pp. 495–509; Ingrao, *Habsburg Monarchy*, p. 238; Enno Kraehe, 'The Congress of Vienna', in Erickson, *Schubert's Vienna*, p. 61.

43. Kraehe, 'Congress of Vienna', pp. 56–7, 71.

44. Ibid., pp. 64–6.

45. Schroeder, *Transformation*, pp. 541, 546–7.

46. Ibid., p. 530.

47. Ibid., pp. 547, 558–9; Kraehe, 'Congress of Vienna', p. 73.

48. E. Bruckmüller, 'Biedermeier und österreichische Identität', in Roe/Warren, *Biedermeier and Beyond*, p. 22.

Chapter 5: Revolution: Text and Subtext

1. Fichtner, *Habsburg Empire*, p. 32.
2. Bruckmüller, *Sozialgeschichte*, pp. 287–90.
3. P. Judson, *Exclusive Revolutionaries: Liberal Politics, Social Experience, and National Identity in the Austrian Empire, 1848–1914* (Ann Arbor, MI: University of Michigan Press, 1996), pp. 14–16 and n. 9; Heindl, *Rebellen*, pp. 211–16.
4. Good, *Economic Rise*, pp. 61–73.
5. Bruckmüller, *Sozialgeschichte*, pp. 341–2.
6. Ibid., pp. 284, 286.
7. Good, *Economic Rise*, pp. 67–8.
8. Ibid., p. 39; S. Z. Pech, *The Czech Revolution of 1848* (Chapel Hill, NC: University of North Carolina Press, 1969), p. 42.
9. Schroeder, *Transformation*, p. 777.
10. G. Frodl, 'Viennese Biedermeier Painting', in Erickson, *Schubert's Vienna*, p. 175.
11. S. P. Scheichl, 'Die vaterländischen Balladen des österreichischen Biedermeier: Bausteine des habsburgischen Mythos. Zu Ludwig August Franks "Habsburgerlied"', in Roe/Warren, *Biedermeier and Beyond*, pp. 45–61; P. S. Fichtner, 'History, Religion, and Politics in the Austrian *Vormärz*', *History and Theory*, 10 (1971), pp. 43–5.
12. J. Marx, *Österreichs Kampf gegen die liberalen, radikalen und kommunistischen Schriften, 1835–1848* (Vienna: Böhlau, 1969), pp. 10–11.
13. Judson, *Exclusive Revolutionaries*, pp. 17–22.
14. Ibid., pp. 23–4.
15. A. J. P. Taylor, *The Habsburg Monarchy, 1809–1918* (London: Hamish Hamilton, 1947), p. 24; Pech, *Czech Revolution*, p. 7.
16. Bruckmüller, *Sozialgeschichte*, pp. 302–6, 311–19.
17. Ibid., pp. 300–1, 343, 345.
18. Csáky, *Aufklärung*, pp. 112–13.
19. Ibid., pp. 114, 116–17.
20. Ibid., pp. 95, 105; Macartney, *Hungary*, p. 129.
21. Cf. Lieven, *Empire*, p. 49.
22. Agnew, 'Noble *Natio*', pp. 62–4, citation p. 63.

23. M. Csokonai, 'Das Wiedererwachen der ungarischen Sprache', in Farkas, *Ungarns Geschichte*, p. 93; G. Szekfű, *Magyar Történet: A Tizenkilencedik és Huszadik Század*, in B. Hóman and G. Szekfű, *Magyar Történet*, 8 vols (Budapest: Royal Hungarian University Press, n.d.), vol. 7, pp. 14, 16.

24. Macartney, *Hungary*, p. 136.

25. Ibid., p. 138; Schroeder, *Transformation*, p. 776.

26. Csáky, *Aufklärung*, p. 106.

27. Mazohl-Wallnig, *Österreichischer Verwaltungsstaat*, pp. 314, 318–19, 325 and n. 50.

28. W. D. Gruner, 'Italien zwischen Revolution und Nationalstaatsgründung, 1789–1861', in W. D. Gruner and G. Trautmann (eds), *Italien in Geschichte und Gegenwart* (Hamburg: Krämer, 1991), pp. 133–4.

29. Mazohl-Wallnig, *Österreichischer Verwaltungsstaat*, pp. 92–5, 103–6, 109, 155–84; Schroeder, *Transformation*, pp. 595–6, 606–7; D. Beales, *The Risorgimento and the Unification of Italy* (London: Allen & Unwin, 1971), pp. 39–41.

30. Beales, *Risorgimento*, p. 48.

31. Schroeder, *Transformation*, pp. 595–6.

32. Ibid., pp. 608–9, 611–14, 622.

33. Beales, *Risorgimento*, p. 60.

34. A. J. Reinerman, *Austria and the Papacy in the Age of Metternich*, 2 vols (Washington, DC: Catholic University Press, 1979–89), vol. 2, pp. 187–200.

35. Schroeder, *Transformation*, pp. 595–6, 692–3, 695.

36. Ibid., p. 623.

37. Okey, *Eastern Europe*, p. 84.

38. Judson, *Exclusive Revolutionaries*, pp. 25–6.

39. A. Sked, *The Decline and Fall of the Habsburg Empire* (London: Longman, 1989), p. 61.

40. Beales, *Risorgimento*, pp. 51, 63–5.

41. Okey, *Eastern Europe*, p. 84; Agnew, 'Noble *Natio*', p. 65.

42. J. F. Zacek, 'Nationalism in Czechoslovakia', in P. F. Sugar and I. Lederer (eds), *Nationalism in Eastern Europe* (Seattle: University of Washington Press, 1969), pp. 176–82.

43. Barany, 'Fidelity', p. 41; I. Deák, 'Progressive Feudalists: The Hungarian Nobility in 1848', in I. Banac and P. Bushkovitch (eds), *The Nobility in Russia and Eastern Europe* (New Haven, CT: Yale Concilium on International and Area Studies, 1983), p. 124.

44. Macartney, *Hungary*, pp. 151–4; B. K. Király, *Ferenc Deák* (Boston, MA: Twayne, 1975), pp. 111–14.
45. A. Freifeld, *Nationalism and the Crowd in Liberal Hungary, 1848–1914* (Washington, DC: Woodrow Wilson Center Press, 2000), p. 56.
46. B. Jelavich, *The Habsburg Empire in European Affairs, 1814–1918* (Chicago: Rand McNally, 1969), pp. 60–5.
47. O. Urban, 'Czech Society, 1848–1918', in M. Teich (ed.), *Bohemia in History* (Cambridge: Cambridge University Press, 1998), pp. 203–4; Macartney, *Hungary*, pp. 131–2, 138; S. Pavlowitch, *A History of the Balkans* (London: Longman, 1999), pp. 67–70.
48. J. Polišenský, *Aristocrats and the Crowd in the Revolutionary Year 1848: A Contribution to the History of Revolution and Counter-Revolution in Austria*, trans. Frederick Snider (Albany, NY: State University of New York Press, 1980), pp. 138–40.
49. Magocsi, *Ukraine*, pp. 409–11; P. S. Wandycz, *The Lands of Partitioned Poland, 1795–1918* (Seattle, Wash.: University of Washington Press, 1974), pp. 146–7.
50. Pech, *Czech Revolutions*, pp. 139–66.
51. Beales, *Risorgimento*, pp. 52–3, 65.
52. Macartney, *Hungary*, pp. 149–50.
53. On Haynau's character and impact, see Freifeld, *Nationalism*, pp. 92–3, 100.
54. Urban, 'Czech Society', p. 203.
55. In general on this theme see Bruckmüller, 'Identität', in Roe/ Warren, *Biedermeier and Beyond*, pp. 21–44. See also Judson, *Exclusive Revolutionaries*, pp. 16 and 17, n. 11, and Heindl, *Rebellen*, pp. 179–200, 225–43.
56. Magocsi, *Ukraine*, p. 418.
57. Sked, *Decline and Fall*, p. 58; Deák, 'Progressive Feudalists', pp. 128–9.
58. F. Grillparzer, 'Feldmarschall Radetzky', in F. Grillparzer, *Sämtliche Werke*, 4 vols (Darmstadt: Wissentschaftliche Buchgesellschaft, 1969), vol. 1, p. 328.

Chapter 6: From One to Many

1. Pázmány, 'Antwort', in Farkas, *Ungarns Geschichte*, pp. 57–8.
2. W. M. Johnston, *The Austrian Mind: An Intellectual and Social History* (Berkeley, CA: University of California Press, 1972), p. 14. Cf. Steinberg, *Salzburg Festival*, p. 7.

3. H. Fielding, *The History of the Adventures of Joseph Andrews and his Friend Mr. Abraham Adams* (New York: New American Library, n.d.), pp. 41–2.

4. J. W. O'Malley, *The First Jesuits* (Cambridge, MA: Harvard University Press, 1993), pp. 39–41; Melton, *Absolutism*, p. 64; D. Kosáry, *Culture and Society in Eighteenth Century Hungary*, trans. Z. Béres with the assistance of C. Sullivan (Budapest: Corvina, 1987), pp. 191–2; W. Michal, 'Die Darstellung der Affekten auf der Jesuitenbühne', in G. Holthus (ed.), *Theaterwesen und dramatische Literatur: Beiträge zur Geschichte des Theaters* (Tübingen: A. Francke, 1987), pp. 234–5.

5. Ignatius Loyola, *The Spiritual Exercises of St. Ignatius*, trans. A. Mottola (Garden City, NY: Image Books, 1964), p. 54.

6. 'Hier ... lies nicht, sondern schau.' Cited in M. Dietrich, 'Aufführung und Dramaturgie', in Staudt, *Mulier Fortis*, p. xix.

7. Staudt, *Mulier Fortis*, p. xlii; Dietrich, 'Aufführung und Dramaturgie', p. xix.

8. H. S. Waldeck [pseud.] (ed.), *Lese aus Abraham A Sancta Clara* (Brixlegg, Tirol: Heimat-Verlag, 1938), p. 38. Trans. P. S. Fichtner.

9. In Farkas, *Ungarns Geschichte*, p. 64.

10. Melton, *Absolutism*, pp. 63–4.

11. Kosáry, *Culture and Society*, pp. 203–4.

12. Melton, *Absolutism*, pp. 66–7, 70.

13. M. Cesnaková-Michalcová, 'Humanistické a reformační divadlo v období z novu upevnění feudalismu', in Černý, *Dějiny*, vol. 1, pp. 135–6; *Magyar Színház Történet*, 2 vols, ed. G. Székely (Budapest: Akadémiai Kiadó, 1990), vol. 1, pp. 22, 26.

14. Cesnaková-Michalcová, 'Divadlo', in Černý, *Dějiny*, vol. 1, pp. 135–6.

15. Dietrich, 'Aufführung und Dramaturgie', p. xx.

16. *Magyar Színház*, vol. 1, plate 5 and p. 28; Pass and Niiyama-Kalicki, 'Musikalische Gestaltung', in Staudt, *Mulier Fortis*, p. xiii. See also ibid., p. xii.

17. Evans, *Habsburg Monarchy*, pp. 311–30.

18. J. Storey, *An Introduction to Cultural Theory and Popular Culture*, 2nd edn (London: Prentice Hall, 1997 [1993]), pp. 17–18.

19. Evans, *Habsburg Monarchy*, pp. 343–4, 375, 446.

20. Ibid., pp. 402–3, 406, 408–10.

21. Johnston, *Austrian Mind*, p. 274.

22. A. Seigfried, 'Die Dogmatik im 18. Jahrhundert unter dem Einfluß von Aufklärung und Jansenismus', in E. Kovács (ed.), *Katholische*

Aufklärung und Josephinismus (Munich: Oldenbourg, 1979), pp. 254–5; E. Turczynski, 'The Role of the Orthodox Church in Adapting and Transforming the Western Enlightenment in Southeastern Europe', *East European Quarterly*, 9 (1975), p. 433; P. Barton, *Ignatius Aurelius Feßler: Vom Barockkatholizismus zur Erweckungsbewegung* (Vienna: Böhlau, 1969), pp. 30, 49.

23. Melton, *Absolutism*, p. 83.

24. J. Kroupa, 'The Alchemy of Happiness: The Enlightenment in the Moravian Context', in Teich, *Bohemia in History*, p. 175.

25. L. Bodi, *Tauwetter in Wien: Zur Prose der österreichischen Aufklärung, 1781–1795* (Frankfurt: S. Fischer, 1977), p. 106; D. S. Luft, 'Austria as a Region of German Culture', *Austrian History Yearbook*, 23 (1992), p. 140; R. Bauer, 'Österreichische Literatur oder Literatur aus Österreich?', in Kann/Prinz, *Deutschland und Österreich*, p. 269.

26. Bodi, *Tauwetter*, p. 64.

27. Melton, *Absolutism*, pp. 83, 93; R. J. W. Evans, 'Joseph II and Nationality in the Habsburg Lands', in Scott, *Enlightened Absolutism*, p. 211; Kosáry, *Culture and Society*, pp. 102–3; D. Sayer, *The Coasts of Bohemia: A Czech History*, trans. A. Sayer (Princeton, NJ: Princeton University Press, 1998), pp. 68–9, 72.

28. Wangermann, *Achievement*, p. 117.

29. Ibid., p. 118.

30. Bodi, *Tauwetter*, p. 103. On the fate of the Gottschedian reforms in Vienna, see Melton, *Absolutism*, pp. 84–9.

31. Bodi, *Tauwetter*, pp. 102–3, 108–13.

32. Quoted from Pezzl's *Sketch of Vienna* (*Skizze aus Wien*) in Bodi, *Tauwetter*, p. 116.

33. Bauer, 'Österreichische Literatur', in Kann/Prinz, *Deutschland und Österreich*, pp. 264–6, 270, 273.

34. J. Haider, *Die Geschichte des Theaterwesens im Benediktinerstift Seitenstetten im Barock und Aufklärung*, Theatergeschichte Österreichs, vol. 4, no. 1 (Vienna: Verlag der Akademie der Wissenschaften, 1973), pp. 78–9, 131, 146, 149–50.

35. W. T. Elwert, 'Die europäische Rolle der Commedia dell'arte', in Holthus, *Theaterwesen*, p. 192; Melton, *Absolutism*, pp. 72–4.

36. P. Nettl, *W. A. Mozart, 1756–1791* (Frankfurt: Fischer, 1955), pp. 55–6.

37. Erickson, 'Vienna', in Erickson, *Schubert's Vienna*, pp. 22–3.

38. Magris, *Habsburgermythos*, pp. 87–8.

39. F. Raimund, 'Der Verschwender', in Raimund, *Sämtliche Werke* (Munich: Winkler, 1960), p. 583. Trans. P. S. Fichtner. See also Magris, *Habsburgische Mythos*, pp. 80, 82–3.

40. In J. Nestroy, *Nestroys Werke*, pt 1, *Volksstücke und Possen*, ed. O. Rommel (Berlin: Bong & Co., 1908?), p. 170. Trans. P. S. Fichtner.

41. Steinberg, *Salzburg Festival*, p. 7; J. Boyer, *Political Radicalism in Late Imperial Vienna: Origins of the Christian Social Movement, 1848–1897*, 2 vols (Chicago: University of Chicago Press, 1981–95), vol. 1, p. 116.

42. Sagarra, 'Benign Authority', in Roe/Warren, *Biedermeier and Beyond*, p. 67.

43. Grillparzer, *Werke*, vol. 1, pp. 1036–7. On Grillparzer's emotional bond with the Austrian lands, see Magris, *Habsburgermythos*, p. 97.

44. Magris, *Habsburgermythos*, pp. 87–8; Bauer, 'Österreichische Literatur', p. 272.

45. Bodi, *Tauwetter*, p. 116.

46. K. A. Schroeder, 'Kunst als Erzählung: Theorie und Ästhetik der Genremalerei', in G. Frodl and K. A. Schroeder (eds), *Malerei zwischen Wiener Kongreß und Revolution* (Munich: Prestel, 1992), pp. 9–34; W. Häusler, 'Biedermeier oder Vormärz?: Anmerkungen zur österreichischen Sozialgeschichte in der Epoche der bürgerlichen Revolution', in ibid., pp. 35–45.

47. W. Heindl, 'People, Class Structure, and Society', in Erickson, *Schubert's Vienna*, pp. 41–2; Frodl, 'Viennese Biedermeier Painting', in ibid., pp. 176–9.

48. Bodi, *Tauwetter*, pp. 65, 434; Magris, *Habsburgermythos*, pp. 94–7.

49. Cited in Levy, *Governance*, p. 39. See also p. 38.

50. E. P. Noether, *Seeds of Italian Nationalism* (New York: Columbia University Press, 1951), p. 118.

51. Ibid., pp. 115–16.

52. Ibid., pp. 109, 112 n. 6.

53. Ibid., pp. 133–4.

54. Beales, *Risorgimento*, p. 58; S. Pellico: *My Prisons: Le Mie Prigioni*, trans. I. G. Capaldi, SJ (London: Oxford, 1963), p. 198.

55. Noether, *Seeds*, pp. 145–9; Beales, *Risorgimento*, pp. 32, 100–2, 109.

56. D. M. Smith, *Mazzini* (New Haven, CT: Yale University Press, 1994), pp. 3, 38.

57. Barany, 'Royal Absolutism', in Sugar, *Hungary*, p. 180; György Hölvényi, 'Katholische Aufklärung und Jansenismus in Ungarn', in Kovács, *Katholische Aufklärung*, p. 95; Freifeld, *Nationalism*, p. 25.

58. G. Barany, 'The Age of Royal Absolutism, 1790–1848', in P. Sugar (ed.), *A History of Hungary* (Bloomington, IN: Indiana University Press, 1990), p. 180; Jones, *Hungarian Writers*, pp. xx, xxiv; L. Wolff, *Inventing Eastern Europe: The Map of Civilization on the Mind of the Enlightenment* (Stanford, CA: Stanford University Press, 1994), pp. 306–7, 312.

59. R. J. W. Evans, 'Maria Theresa and Hungary', in Scott, *Enlightened Absolutism*, pp. 197–8, 203; Kosáry, *Culture and Society*, pp. 203, 208; Freifeld, *Nationalism*, p. 30.

60. In Farkas, *Ungarns Geschichte*, p. 93; Evans, 'Joseph II and Nationality', p. 210; Kosáry, *Culture and Society*, pp. 40, 108–9.

61. In Farkas, *Ungarns Geschichte*, p. 93.

62. Jones, *Hungarian Writers*, pp. xxiv, 120, 127.

63. Ibid., pp. 120, 127, 149, 154, 230–2, 234, 239, 268, 279; Barany, 'Royal Absolutism', pp. 182, 190.

64. Barany, 'Royal Absolutism', p. 181; Kosáry, *Culture and Society*, p. 59.

65. In Farkas, *Ungarns Geschichte*, pp. 108–9; Barany, 'Royal Absolutism', p. 183.

66. Sayer, *Coasts*, p. 50; Evans, *Habsburg Monarchy*, p. 383 and n. 5.

67. V. Macura, 'Problems and Paradoxes of the National Revival', in Teich, *Bohemia in History*, pp. 184, 187–8.

68. Kroupa, 'Alchemy', in ibid., pp. 173–4.

69. Sayer, *Coasts*, pp. 53–7, 62; Pech, *Czech Revolution*, pp. 29–31.

70. A. Moritsch, 'Der Austroslavismus – ein verfrühtes Konzept zur politischen Neugestaltung Mitteleuropas', in A. Moritsch (ed.), *Der Austroslavismus: ein verfrühtes Konzept zur politischen Neugestaltung Mitteleuropas* (Vienna: Böhlau, 1996), pp. 13–14; Magocsi, *Ukraine*, pp. 389–402; P. R. Magocsi, *The Shaping of a National Identity: Subcarpathian Rus', 1848–1948* (Cambridge, MA: Harvard University Press, 1978).

71. On this question generally, see M. Hroch, 'The Social Composition of the Czech Patriots in Bohemia, 1827–1848', in P. Brock and H. G. Skilling (eds), *The Czech Renaissance of the Nineteenth Century* (Toronto: University of Toronto Press, 1970), pp. 33–52. See also Pech, *Czech Revolution*, pp. 27–8, and Sayer, *Coasts*, pp. 69–83.

72. Macura, 'National Revival', in Teich, *Bohemia in History*, pp. 188–9, 192.

73. Ibid., pp. 184–6.

Afterword

1. Lieven, *Empire*, p. xiv.
2. R. W. J. Evans, 'Introduction', in Evans/Thomas, *Crown, Church and Estates*, p. xxix. See also generally Evans, *Habsburg Monarchy*. Cf. Ingrao, *Habsburg Monarchy*, pp. 1–2.

Bibliography

1. Archival Sources

Hofkammer Archiv, Vienna (HKA)
Gedenkbücher, 333 (1621–5)
Hofzahlamtsbücher, 133 (1688); 138 (1693); 144 (1700); 165 (1763–8).

2. Source Collections

Farkas, J. von. *Ungarns Geschichte und Kultur in Dokumenten* (Wiesbaden: Harrassowitz, 1995).

Fielding, H. *The History of the Adventures of Joseph Andrews and his Friend Mr. Abraham Adams* (New York: New American Library, n.d.).

Frass, O. (ed.) *Quellenbuch zur österreichischen Geschichte*, 4 vols (Vienna: Birken-Verlag, 1956–67).

Grillparzer, F. *Sämtliche Werke*, 4 vols (Darmstadt: Wissenschaftliche Buchgesellschaft, 1969).

Haydn, J. *Die Jahreszeiten* (Berlin/DDR: VEB Deutsche Schallplatte, 3 records, 1971).

Loyola, Ignatius. *The Spiritual Exercises of St. Ignatius*, trans. A. Mottola (Garden City, NY: Image Books, 1964).

Macartney, C. A. (ed.) *The Habsburg and Hohenzollern Dynasties in the Seventeenth and Eighteenth Centuries* (New York: Harper & Row, 1970).

Nestroy, J. *Nestroys Werke*, pt 1: *Volksstücke und Possen*, ed. O. Rommel (Berlin: Bong & Co., 1908?).

Waldeck, H. S. [pseud.] (ed.) *Lese aus Abraham A Sancta Clara* (Brixlegg, Tirol: Heimat-Verlag, 1938).

3. Literature

Agnew, H. L. 'Noble *Natio* and the Modern Nation: The Czech Case', *Austrian History Yearbook*, 23 (1992), pp. 50–71.

Asch, R. G. and A. M. Birke (eds) *Princes, Patronage, and the Nobility: The Court at the Beginning of the Modern Age, c. 1450–1650* (London: Oxford University Press, 1991).

Bahlcke, J. *Regionalismus und Staatsintegration im Widerstreit: Die Länder der böhmischen Krone im ersten Jahrhundert der Habsburgerherrschaft (1526–1619)* (Munich: Oldenbourg, 1994).

Bak, J. and B. K. Király (eds) *From Hunyadi to Rákóczi: War and Society in Late Medieval and Early Modern Hungary* (Brooklyn, NY: Brooklyn College Press, 1982).

Balázs, É. *Hungary and the Habsburgs, 1765–1800*, trans. T. Wilkinson (Budapest: Central European Press, 1987).

Banac, I. and P. Bushkovitch (eds) *The Nobility in Russia and Eastern Europe* (New Haven, CT: Yale Concilium on International and Area Studies, 1983).

Barany, G. 'The Age of Royal Absolutism, 1790–1848', in P. Sugar (ed.), *A History of Hungary* (Bloomington, IN: Indiana University Press, 1990), pp. 174–208.

———. 'From Fidelity to the Habsburgs to Loyalty to the Nation: The Changing Role of the Hungarian Aristocracy before 1848', *Austrian History Yearbook*, 23 (1992), pp. 36–49.

Barker, T. *Double Eagle and Crescent: Vienna's Second Turkish Siege and Its Historical Setting* (Albany, NY: State University of New York Press, 1967).

Barton, P. *Ignatius Aurelius Feßler: Vom Barockkatholizismus zur Erweckungsbewegung* (Vienna: Böhlau, 1969).

Bauer, R. 'Österreichische Literatur oder Literatur aus Österreich?', in R. A. Kann and F. Prinz (eds), *Deutschland und Österreich: Ein beilaterales Geschichtsbuch* (Vienna: Jugend und Volk, 1980), pp. 264–87.

——— and J. Wertheimer (eds) *Das Ende des Stegreifspiels: Die Geburt des Nationaltheaters* (Munich: Fink, 1983).

Beales, D. 'Christians and *philosophes*: The Case of the Austrian Enlightenment', in D. Beales and G. Best (eds), *History, Society and the Churches* (Cambridge: Cambridge University Press, 1985), pp. 169–94.

———. *Joseph II*, vol. 1, *In the Shadow of Maria Theresa* (Cambridge: Cambridge University Press, 1987).

———. *The Risorgimento and the Unification of Italy* (London: Allen & Unwin, 1971).

Benda, K. 'Habsburg Absolutism and the Resistance of the Hungarian Estates in the Sixteenth and Seventeenth Centuries', in R. J. W. Evans and T. V. Thomas (eds), *Crown, Church and Estates: Central European Politics in the Sixteenth and Seventeenth Centuries* (New York: St. Martin's, 1991), pp. 123–8.

Bérenger, J. *Histoire de l'empire des Habsbourg, 1273–1918* (Paris: Fayard, 1990).

——. *A History of the Habsburg Empire, 1273–1700*, trans. C. A. Simpson (London: Longman, 1994).

——. 'L'Idée de nation dans la hongrie du XVIIe siècle', *XVIIe Siècle*, 44 (1992), pp. 345–61.

Bireley, R., SJ. 'Confessional Absolutism in the Habsburg Lands in the Seventeenth Century', in C. W. Ingrao (ed.), *State and Society in Early Modern Austria* (West Lafayette, IN: Purdue University Press, 1994), pp. 36–53.

——. *Religion and Politics in the Age of the Counterreformation: Emperor Ferdinand II, William Lamormaini, S.J., and the Formation of Imperial Policy* (Chapel Hill, NC: University of North Carolina Press, 1981).

Black, J. 'Revolutionary and Napoleonic Warfare', in J. Black (ed.), *European Warfare, 1453–1815* (Basingstoke, UK: Macmillan [now Palgrave Macmillan], 1999), pp. 224–46.

Blanning, T. C. W. *Joseph II* (London: Longman, 1994).

Bodi, L. *Tauwetter in Wien: Zur Prosa der österreichischen Aufklärung, 1781–1795* (Frankfurt: S. Fischer, 1977).

Bosbach, F. (ed.) 'Princeps in Compendio', in K. Repgen (ed.), *Das Herrscherbild im 17. Jahrhundert* (Münster: Aschendorff, 1991), pp. 79–114.

Boyer, J. *Political Radicalism in Late Imperial Vienna: Origins of the Christian Social Movement, 1848–1897*, 2 vols (Chicago: University of Chicago Press, 1981–95).

Brauneder, W. and L. Hobelt (eds) *Sacrum Imperium: Das Reich und Österreich, 996–1806* (Vienna: Almathea, 1996).

Brock, P. and H. G. Skilling (eds) *The Czech Renaissance of the Nineteenth Century* (Toronto: University of Toronto Press, 1970).

Browning, R. *The War of the Austrian Succession* (New York: St. Martin's, 1993).

Bruckmüller, E. 'Biedermeier und österreichische Identität', in I. F. Roe and J. Warren (eds), *The Biedermeier and Beyond* (Bern: Peter Lang, 1999), pp. 21–44.

——. *Sozialgeschichte Österreichs* (Vienna: Herold, 1985).

Bücking, J. *Frühabsolutismus und Kirchenreform in Tirol (1566–1665): Ein Beitrag zum Ringen zwischen 'Staat' und 'Kirche' in der frühen Neuzeit* (Wiesbaden: Steiner, 1972).

Capra, Carlos, 'Kaunitz and Austrian Lombardy', in G. Klingenstein and F. A. J. Szábó (eds), *Staatskanzler Wenzel Anton von Kaunitz-Rietberg, 1711–1794: Neue Perspektive zu Politik und Kultur der europäischen Aufklärung* (Graz: Schneider, 1996), pp. 245–60.

Carl, H. 'Kaunitz und Ostfriesland: Aspekte adliger Familienpolitik im Hause Kaunitz', in G. Klingenstein and F. A. J. Szábó (eds), *Staatskanzler Wenzel Anton von Kaunitz-Rietberg, 1711–1794: Neue Perspektive zu Politik und Kultur der europäischen Aufklärung* (Graz: Schneider, 1996), pp. 401–15.

Černý, F. (ed.) *Dějiny Českého Divadla*, 4 vols (Prague: Československá Akademie Věd, 1968).

M. Cesnaková-Michalová, 'Humanistické a reformační divadlo v období znovuupevněvní feudalismu', in F. Černy (ed.), *Dějiny Českého Divadla*, 4 vols (Prague: Československá Věd, 1968), pp. 99–152.

Cochrane, E. *Florence in the Forgotten Centuries, 1527–1800: A History of Florence and the Florentines in the Age of the Grand Dukes* (Chicago: University of Chicago Press, 1973).

Cohn, B. *Colonialism and Its Forms of Knowledge* (Princeton, NJ: Princeton University Press, 1996).

Csáky, M. *Von der Aufklärung zum Liberalismus: Studien zum Frühliberalismus in Ungarn* (Vienna: Verlag der österreichischen Akademie der Wissenschaften, 1981).

—— and R. Hagelkrys (eds) *Vaterlandsliebe und Gesamtstaatsidee im österreichischen 18. Jahrhundert* (Vienna: Verband der wissenchaftlichen Gesellschaften Österreichs, 1989).

Davies, N. *God's Playground: A History of Poland*, 2 vols (New York: Columbia University Press, 1982).

Deák, I. 'Progressive Feudalists: The Hungarian Nobility in 1848', in I. Banac and P. Bushkovitch (eds), *The Nobility in Russia and Eastern Europe* (New Haven, CT: Yale Concilium on International and Area Studies, 1983), pp. 123–35.

Dickson, P. G. M. 'Monarchy and Bureaucracy in late 18th Century Austria', *English Historical Review*, 110 (1995), pp. 323–67.

Dietrich, M. 'Aufführung und Dramaturgie', in Johann Bernhardt Staudt, *Mulier Fortis*, ed. W. Pass and F. Niiyama-Kalicki, Denkmäler der Tonkunst in Österreich, 152 (Graz: Akademische Druck und Verlagsanstalt, 2000), pp. xvii–xxi.

Dillon, K. J. *King and Estates in the Bohemian Lands, 1526–1564* (Brussels: Librairie Encyclopédique, 1976).

Dollinger, H. 'Kurfürst Maximilian I. von Bayern und Justus Lipsius', *Archiv für Kulturgeschichte*, 66, nos. 2/3 (1964), pp. 227–308.

Donati, C. 'The Italian Nobilities in the Seventeenth and Eighteenth Centuries', in H. M. Scott and C. Storrs (eds), *The European Nobilities in the Seventeenth and Eighteenth Centuries*, 2 vols (London: Longman, 1995), vol. 1, pp. 237–68.

Drabek, A. M. 'Der Nationsbegriff in Böhmen an der Grenze von Aufklärung und "nationaler Wiedergeburt"', in M. Csáky and R. Hagelkrys (eds), *Vaterlandsliebe und Gesamtstaatsidee im österreichischen 18. Jahrhundert* (Vienna: Verband der wissenchaftlichen Gesellschaften Österreichs, 1989), pp. 43–62.

Duchhardt, H. and M. Schnettger (eds) *Reichständische Libertät und Habsburgisches Kaisertum* (Mainz: Philipp von Zabern, 1999).

Duffy, C. *The Army of Maria Theresa: The Armed Forces of Imperial Austria, 1740–1780* (North Pomfret, VT: David & Charles, 1977).

——. 'Count Kaunitz-Rietberg, Military Strategist 1756–1763', in G. Klingenstein and F. A. J. Szábó (eds), *Staatskanzler Wenzel Anton von Kaunitz-Rietberg, 1711–1794: Neue Perspektive zu Politik und Kultur der europäischen Aufklärung* (Graz: Schneider, 1996), pp. 57–69.

Edel, A. *Der Kaiser und Kurpfalz: Eine Studie zu den Grundelementen politischen Handelns bei Maximilian II. (1564–1576)* (Göttingen: Vandenhoeck and Ruprecht, 1997).

Eldridge, C. C. *British Imperialism in the Nineteenth Century* (London: Macmillan, 1984).

Elwert, W. T. 'Die europäische Rolle der Commedia dell'arte', in G. Holtus (ed.), *Theaterwesen und dramatische Literatur: Beiträge zur Geschichte des Theaters* (Tübingen: A. Francke, 1987), pp. 181–94.

Endres, R. *Adel in der frühen Neuzeit* (Munich: Oldenbourg, 1993).

Epstein, K. *The Genesis of German Conservatism* (Princeton, NJ: Princeton University Press, 1966).

Erickson, R. (ed.) *Schubert's Vienna* (New Haven, CT: Yale University Press, 1997).

——. 'Vienna in Its European Context', in R. Erickson (ed.), *Schubert's Vienna* (New Haven, CT: Yale University Press, 1997), pp. 3–35.

Evans, R. J. W. and T. V. Thomas (eds) *Crown, Church and Estates: Central European Politics in the Sixteenth and Seventeenth Centuries* (New York: St. Martin's, 1991).

——. 'Joseph II and Nationality in the Habsburg Lands', in H. M. Scott (ed.), *Enlightened Absolutism: Reform and Reformers in Later Eighteenth-Century Europe* (Basingstoke, UK: Macmillan [now Palgrave Macmillan], 1990), pp. 209–19.

——. *The Making of the Habsburg Monarchy, 1550–1700* (Oxford: Clarendon Press, 1979).

——. 'Maria Theresa and Hungary', in H. M. Scott (ed.), *Enlightened Absolutism: Reform and Reformers in Later Eighteenth-Century Europe* (Basingstoke, UK: Macmillan [now Palgrave Macmillan], 1990), pp. 189–207.

——. 'Moravia and the Culture of Enlightenment in the Habsburg Monarchy', in G. Klingenstein and F. A. J. Szabó (eds), *Staatskanzler Wenzel Anton von Kaunitz-Rietberg, 1711–1794: Neue Perspektive zu Politik und Kultur der europäischen Aufklärung* (Graz: Schneider, 1996), pp. 383–99.

——. *Rudolf II and His World: A Study in Intellectual History, 1576–1612* (Oxford: Clarendon, 1973).

Feigl, H. and W. Rosner (eds) *Adel im Wandel* (Vienna: Niederösterreichischen Institut für Landeskunde, 1991).

Fellner, F. 'Alfons Huber: Werk und Wirken im Umfeld der zeitgenössischen Geschichtswissenschaft', in G. Barth-Scalmani and H. J. W. Kuprian (eds), *Alfons Huber (1834–1898): Ein Gelehrter aus dem Zillertal. Österreichische Geschichtswissenschaft im Spannungsfeld zwischen Region und Nation* (Innsbruck: Universitätsverlag Wagner, 2000), pp. 8–21.

Fellner, T. and H. Kretschmayr. *Die österreichische Zentralverwaltung*, 4 vols (Vienna: Holzhausen, 1907–25).

Fichtner, P. S. *Emperor Maximilian II* (New Haven, CT: Yale University Press, 2001).

——. *Ferdinand I of Austria: The Politics of Dynasticism in the Age of the Reformation* (Boulder, CO: East European Monographs, 1982).

——. *The Habsburg Empire: From Dynasticism to Multinationalism* (Malabar, FL: Krieger, 1997).

——. 'Habsburg Household or Habsburg Government?: A Sixteenth-Century Administrative Dilemma', *Austrian History Yearbook*, 26 (1995), pp. 45–60.

——. 'History, Religion, and Politics in the Austrian *Vormärz*', *History and Theory*, 10 (1971), pp. 35–48.

——. 'Viennese Perspectives on the American War of Independence', in B. K. Király and G. Barany (eds), *East Central European Perceptions of Early America* (Lisse: Peter De Ridder, 1977), pp. 19–32.

Fischer-Galati, S. *Ottoman Imperialism and German Protestantism, 1521–1555* (Cambridge, MA: Harvard, 1959).

Franzl, J. *Ferdinand II.: Kaiser im Zwiespalt der Zeit* (Graz: Styria, 1978).

Freifeld, A. *Nationalism and the Crowd in Liberal Hungary, 1848–1914* (Washington, DC: Woodrow Wilson Center Press, 2000).

Frodl, G. 'Viennese Biedermeier Painting', in R. Erickson (ed.), *Schubert's Vienna* (New Haven, CT: Yale University Press, 1997), pp. 174–82.

—— and K. A. Schroeder (eds) *Malerei zwischen Wiener Kongreß und Revolution* (Munich: Prestel, 1992).

Gallagher, J. with R. Robinson, 'The Imperialism of Free Trade', in J. Gallagher, *The Decline, Revival and Fall of the British Empire*, ed. A. Seal (Cambridge: Cambridge University Press, 1982), pp. 1–18.

—— and——. 'The Partition of Africa', in J. Gallagher, *The Decline, Revival and Fall of the British Empire*, ed. A. Seal (Cambridge: Cambridge University Press, 1982), pp. 19–72.

Good, D. F. *The Economic Rise of the Habsburg Empire, 1750–1914* (Berkeley, CA: University of California Press, 1984).

Gruner, Wolf D. 'Italien zwischen Revolution und Nationalstaatsgründung, 1789–1861', in W. D. Gruner and G. Trautmann (eds), *Italien in Geschichte und Gegenwart* (Hamburg: Krämer, 1991), pp. 105–56.

——. 'Österreich zwischen altem Reich und deutschem Bund (1789–1816)', in W. Brauneder and L. Hobelt (eds), *Sacrum Imperium: Das Reich und Österreich, 996–1806* (Vienna: Almathea, 1996), pp. 319–60.

Guha, R. *Dominance Without Hegemony: History and Power in Colonial India* (Cambridge, MA: Harvard University Press, 1997).

Haider, J. *Die Geschichte des Theaterwesens im Benediktinerstift Seitenstetten im Barock und Aufklärung*, Theatergeschichte Österreichs, 4, no. 1 (Vienna: Verlag der österreichischen Akademie der Wissenschaften, 1973).

Haider-Pregler, H. 'Das Wienerische Weg zur k.k. Hof- und National-schaubühne', in R. Bauer and J. Wertheimer (eds), *Das Ende des Stegreifspiels: Die Geburt des Nationaltheaters* (Munich: Fink, 1983), pp. 24–37.

Häusler, W. 'Biedermeier oder Vormärz?: Anmerkungen zur österreichischen Sozialgeschichte in der Epoche der bürgerlichen Revolution', in G. Frodl and K. A. Schroeder (eds), *Malerei zwischen Wiener Kongreß und Revolution* (Munich: Prestel, 1992), pp. 35–45.

Heindl, W. *Gehorsame Rebellen: Bürokratie und Beamte in Österreich, 1780 bis 1848* (Vienna: Böhlau, 1990).

——. 'People, Class Structure, and Society', in R. Erickson (ed.), *Schubert's Vienna* (New Haven, CT: Yale University Press, 1997), pp. 36–54.

Hölvenyi, G. 'Katholische Aufklärung und Jansenismus in Ungarn', in E. Kovács (ed.), *Katholische Aufklärung und Josephinismus* (Munich: Oldenbourg, 1979), pp. 93–100.

Holtus, G. (ed.), *Theaterwesen und dramatische Literatur: Beiträge zur Geschichte des Theaters* (Tübingen: A. Francke, 1987).

Hóman, B. and G. Szekfű. *Magyar Történet*, 8 vols (Budapest: Royal Hungarian University Press, n.d.).

Hroch, M. 'The Social Composition of the Czech Patriots in Bohemia, 1827–1848', in P. Brock and H. G. Skilling (eds), *The Czech Renaissance of the Nineteenth Century* (Toronto: University of Toronto Press, 1969), pp. 33–52.

Ingrao, C. W. *The Habsburg Monarchy, 1618–1815* (Cambridge: Cambridge University Press, 1994).

—— (ed.) *State and Society in Early Modern Austria* (West Lafayette, IN: Purdue University Press, 1994).

Jelavich, B. *The Habsburg Empire in European Affairs, 1814–1918* (Chicago: Rand McNally, 1969).

Johnston, W. M. *The Austrian Mind: An Intellectual and Social History, 1848–1938* (Berkeley, CA: University of California Press, 1972).

Jones, D. M. *Five Hungarian Writers* (Oxford: Oxford University Press, 1966).

Judson, P. M. *Exclusive Revolutionaries: Liberal Politics, Social Experience, and National Identity in the Austrian Empire, 1848–1914* (Ann Arbor, MI: University of Michigan Press, 1996).

Kann, R. A. and F. Prinz (eds) *Deutschland und Österreich: Ein bilaterales Geschichtsbuch* (Vienna: Jugend und Volk, 1980).

Kaufmann, T. D. *Court, Cloister, and City: The Art and Culture of Central Europe, 1450–1800* (Chicago: University of Chicago Press, 1995).

Kennedy, P. 'Continuity and Discontinuity in British Imperialism, 1815–1914', in C. C. Eldridge (ed.), *British Imperialism in the Nineteenth Century* (London: Macmillan, 1984), pp. 20–38.

Kessler, W. 'Die Siebenbürger Sachsen im habsburgischen Gesamtstaat, 1688–1790', in M. Csáky and R. Hagelkrys (eds), *Vaterlandsliebe und Gesamtstaatsidee im österreichischen 18. Jahrhundert* (Vienna: Verband der wissenchaftlichen Gesellschaften Österreichs, 1989), pp. 63–70.

Király, B. K. *Ferenc Deák* (Boston, MA: Twayne, 1975).

——. *Hungary in the Late Eighteenth Century: The Decline of Enlightened Despotism* (New York: Columbia University Press, 1969).

202   BIBLIOGRAPHY

Klingenstein, G., H. Lutz and G. Stourzh (eds) *Bildung, Politik, und Gesellschaft* (Vienna: Verlag für Geschichte und Politik, 1978).

—— and H. Lutz (eds) *Spezialforschung und 'Gesamtgeschichte': Beispiele und Methodenfragen zur Geschichte der frühen Neuzeit* (Vienna: Verlag für Geschichte und Politik, 1981).

—— and F. A. J. Szábó (eds) *Staatskanzler Wenzel Anton von Kaunitz-Rietberg, 1711–1794: Neue Perspektive zu Politik und Kultur der europäischen Aufklärung* (Graz: Schneider, 1996).

Klueting, H. 'Das Reich und Österreich, 1648–1740', in W. Brauneder and L. Hobelt (eds), *Sacrum Imperium: Das Reich und Österreich, 996–1806* (Vienna: Almathea, 1996), pp. 162–287.

Knittler, H. (ed.) *Adel im Wandel: Politik. Kultur. Konfession, 1500–1700* (Horn: Berger, 1990).

Kohler, A. 'Bildung und Konfession: Zum Studium der Studenten in den habsburgischen Ländern an Hochschulen im Reich (1560–1620)', in G. Klingenstein, H. Lutz and G. Stourzh (eds), *Bildung, Politik, und Gesellschaft* (Vienna: Verlag für Geschichte und Politik, 1978), pp. 64–123.

Kókay, G. 'György Bessenyi', in M. Csáky and R. Hagelkrys (eds), *Vaterlandsliebe und Gesamtstaatsidee im österreichischen 18. Jahrhundert* (Vienna: Verband der wissenchaftlichen Gesellschaften Österreichs, 1989), pp. 35–41.

Komlos, J. *Nutrition and Economic Development in the Eighteenth-Century Habsburg Monarchy: An Anthropomorphic History* (Princeton, NJ: Princeton University Press, 1989).

Koenigsberger, H. G. *Estates and Revolutions: Essays in Early Modern European History* (Ithaca, NY: Cornell University Press, 1971).

Kosáry, D. *Culture and Society in Eighteenth Century Hungary*, trans. Z. Béres with the assistance of C. Sullivan (Budapest: Corvina, 1987).

Kovács, E. (ed.) *Katholische Aufklärung und Josephinismus* (Munich: Oldenbourg, 1979).

Kraehe, E. 'The Congress of Vienna', in R. Erickson (ed.), *Schubert's Vienna* (New Haven, CT: Yale University Press, 1997), pp. 55–76.

——. *Metternich's German Policy*, 2 vols (Princeton, NJ: Princeton University Press, 1963–83).

Kraus, A. 'Das katholische Herrscherbild im Reich, dargestellt am Beispiel Kaiser Ferdinands II. und Kurfürst Maximilians I. von Bayern', in K. Repgen (ed.), *Das Herrscherbild im 17. Jahrhundert* (Münster: Aschendorff, 1991), pp. 1–25.

Kroupa, J. 'The Alchemy of Happiness: The Enlightenment in the Moravian Context', in M. Teich (ed.), *Bohemia in History* (Cambridge: Cambridge University Press, 1998), pp. 164–81.

Kunisch, J. 'Der Aufstieg neuer Großmächte im 18. Jahrhundert und die Aufteilung der Machtsphären in Ostmitteleuropa', in G. Klingenstein and F. A. J. Szábó (eds), *Staatskanzler Wenzel Anton von Kaunitz-Rietberg, 1711–1794: Neue Perspektive zu Politik und Kultur der europäischen Aufklärung* (Graz: Schneider, 1996), pp. 70–90.

Laferl, C. F. *Die Kultur der Spanier in Österreich unter Ferdinand I., 1522–1564* (Vienna: Bohlau, 1997).

Levy, M. J. *Governance and Grievance: Habsburg Policy and Italian Tyrol in the Eighteenth Century* (West Lafayette, IN: Purdue University Press, 1988).

Lhotsky, A. *Aufsätze und Vorträge*, 5 vols (Munich: Oldenbourg, 1970–6).

Lieven, D. *Empire: The Russian Empire and Its Rivals* (London: John Murray, 2000).

Louis, W. R. 'Historians I Have Known', *Perspectives*, 39, no. 5 (2001), pp. 15–20.

Louthan, H. *Johannis Crato and the Austrian Habsburgs: Reforming a Counter-Reform Court* (Princeton, NJ: Princeton Theological Seminary, 1994).

Luft, D. S. 'Austria as a Region of German Culture: 1900–1938', *Austrian History Yearbook*, 23 (1992), pp. 135–48.

Luttenberger, A. P. *Kurfürsten, Kaiser und Reich: Politische Führung und Friedenssicherung unter Ferdinand I. und Maximilian II.* (Mainz: Philip von Zabern, 1994).

MacHardy, K. J. 'Cultural Capital, Family Strategies and Noble Identity in Early Modern Habsburg Austria, 1579–1620', *Past and Present*, 163 (May 1999), pp. 36–75.

——. 'Der Einfluß von Status, Konfession und Besitz auf das politische Verhalten des niederösterreichischen Ritterstandes, 1580–1620', in G. Klingenstein and H. Lutz (eds), *Spezialforschung und 'Gesamtgeschichte': Beispiele und Methodenfragen zur Geschichte der frühen Neuzeit* (Vienna: Verlag für Geschichte und Politik, 1981), pp. 56–83.

——. 'The Rise of Absolutism and Noble Rebellion in Early Modern Habsburg Austria', *Comparative Studies in Society and History*, 34 (1992), pp. 407–39.

——. 'Social Mobility and Noble Rebellion in Early Modern Habsburg Austria', *History and Society in Central Europe/Medium AEvum Quotidianum*, 2/29 (1994), pp. 97–139.

Macartney, C. A. *Hungary: A Short History* (Chicago: Aldine, 1962).

Macura, V. 'Problems and Paradoxes of the National Revival', in M. Teich (ed.), *Bohemia in History* (Cambridge: Cambridge University Press, 1998), pp. 182–97.

Magocsi, P. R. *A History of Ukraine* (Toronto: University of Toronto Press, 1996).

——. *The Shaping of a National Identity: Subcarpathian Rus', 1848–1948* (Cambridge, MA: Harvard University Press, 1978).

Magris, C. *Der habsburgische Mythos in der österreichischen Literatur* (Salzburg: Müller, 1988 [1969]).

Magyar Színház Történet, 2 vols, ed. G. Székely (Budapest: Akadémiai Kiadó, 1990).

Marx, J. *Österreichs Kampf gegen die liberalen, radikalen und kommunistischen Schriften, 1835–1848* (Vienna: Böhlau, 1969).

Maur, E. 'Der böhmische und mährische Adel vom 16. bis zum 18. Jahrhundert', in H. Feigl and W. Rosner (eds), *Adel im Wandel* (Vienna: Niederösterreichischen Institut für Landeskunde, 1991), pp. 17–37.

Mazohl-Wallnig, B. *Österreichischer Verwaltungsstaat und administrative Eliten im Königreich Lombardo-Venetien, 1815–1859* (Mainz: Philipp von Zabern, 1993).

Mears, J. 'The Thirty Years' War, the "General Crisis" and the Origins of a Standing Professional Army in the Habsburg Monarchy', *Central European History*, 21 (1988), pp. 122–41.

Mecenseffy, G. *Geschichte des Protestantismus in Österreich* (Vienna: Böhlau, 1956).

Melville, R. 'Adel und Grundherrschaft in Böhmen an der Schwelle des bürgerlichen Zeitalters, 1780–1850', in H. Feigl and W. Rosner (eds), *Adel im Wandel* (Vienna: Niederösterreichischen Institut für Landeskunde, 1991), pp. 75–90.

Melton, J. Van Horn. *Absolutism and the Eighteenth-Century Origins of Compulsory Schooling in Prussia and Austria* (Cambridge: Cambridge University Press, 1988).

——. 'The Nobility in the Bohemian and Austrian Lands, 1620–1780', in H. M. Scott and C. Storrs (eds), *The European Nobilities in the Seventeenth and Eighteenth Centuries*, 2 vols (London: Longman, 1995), vol. 2, pp. 110–43.

Michal, W. 'Die Darstellung der Affekten auf der Jesuitenbühne', in G. Holtus (ed.), *Theaterwesen und dramatische Literatur: Beiträge zur Geschichte des Theaterwesens* (Tübingen: A. Francke, 1987), pp. 233–51.

Moritsch, A. (ed.) *Der Austroslavismus: Ein verfrühtes Konzept zur politischen Neugestaltung Mitteleuropas* (Vienna: Böhlau, 1996).

——. 'Der Austroslavismus – ein verfrühtes Konzept zur politischen Neugestaltung Mitteleuropas', in A. Moritsch (ed.), *Der Austroslavismus: Ein verfrühtes Konzept zur politischen Neugestaltung Mitteleuropas* (Vienna: Böhlau, 1996), pp. 11–23.

Mraz, G., H. Mraz and G. Stangler (eds) *Kaisertum Österreich, 1804–1848*, Kataloge des niederösterreichischen Landesmuseums, N.F. 387 (Vienna: Amt der niederösterreichischen Landesregierung, 1996).

——. 'Das Kaisertum Österreich: Die Vollendung der Gesamtstaatsidee', in G. Mraz, H. Mraz and G. Stangler (eds), *Kaisertum Österreich, 1804–1848*, Kataloge des niederösterreichischen Landesmuseums, N.F. 387 (Vienna: Amt der niederösterreichischen Landesregierung, 1996), pp. 1–24.

Murdock, G. *Calvinism on the Frontier, 1600–1660: International Calvinism and the Reformed Church in Hungary and Transylvania* (Oxford: Clarendon, 2000).

Nettl, P. *W. A. Mozart, 1756–1791* (Frankfurt: Fischer, 1955).

Niederstätter, A. *1400–1522: das Jahrhundert der Mitte: an der Wende vom Mittelalter zur Neuzeit* (Vienna: Ueberreuter, 1996).

Noether, E. P. *Seeds of Italian Nationalism* (New York: Columbia University Press, 1951).

Okey, R. *Eastern Europe, 1740–1985: Feudalism to Communism*, 2nd edn (London: Hutchison, 1986).

O'Malley, J. W. *The First Jesuits* (Cambridge, MA: Harvard University Press, 1993).

Owen, E. R. J. and R. B. Sutcliffe. *Studies in the Theory of Imperialism* (London: Longman, 1972).

Pajkossy, G. 'Das Kaisertum Österreich und Ungarn, 1804–1848', in G. Mraz, H. Mraz and G. Stangler (eds), *Kaisertum Österreich, 1804–1848*, Kataloge des niederösterreichischen Landesmuseums, N.F. 387 (Vienna: Amt der niederösterreichischen Landesregierung, 1996), pp. 41–54.

Pass, W. and F. Niiyama-Kalicki, 'Die Musikalische Gestaltung', in Johann Bernhardt Staudt, *Mulier Fortis*, ed. W. Pass and F. Niiyama-Kalicki, Denkmäler der Tonkunst in Österreich, 152 (Graz: Akademische Druck- und Verlagsanstalt, 2000), pp. xiii–xiv.

Pavlowitch, S. *A History of the Balkans* (London: Longman, 1999).

Pech, S. Z. *The Czech Revolution of 1848* (Chapel Hill, NC: University of North Carolina Press, 1969).

Pellico, S. *My Prisons: Le Mie Prigioni*, trans. I. G. Capaldi, SJ (London: Oxford, 1963).

Petrin, S. 'Die niederösterreichischen Stände im 16. und 17. Jahrhundert', in H. Knittler (ed.), *Adel im Wandel: Politik. Kultur. Konfession, 1500–1700* (Horn: Berger, 1990), pp. 285–306.

Polišenský, J. *Aristocrats and the Crowd in the Revolutionary Year 1848: A Contribution to the History of Revolution and Counter-Revolution in Austria*, trans. F. Snider (Albany, NY: State University of New York Press, 1980).

Press, V. 'Adel in den österreichisch–böhmischen Erblanden und im Reich zwischen dem 15. und dem 17. Jahrhundert', in H. Knittler (ed.), *Adel im Wandel: Politik. Kultur. Konfession, 1500–1700* (Horn: Berger, 1990), pp. 19–31.

——. 'Die Erblande und das Reich von Albrecht II. bis Karl VI. (1438–1740)', in R. A. Kann and F. Prinz (eds), *Deutschland und Österreich: Ein bilaterales Geschichtsbuch* (Vienna: Jugend und Volk, 1980), pp. 44–88.

——. 'The System of Estates in the Austrian Hereditary Lands and in the Holy Roman Empire: A Comparison', in R. J. W. Evans and T. V. Thomas (eds), *Crown, Church and Estates: Central European Politics in the Sixteenth and Seventeenth Centuries* (New York: St. Martin's, 1991), pp. 1–22.

——. 'The Imperial Court of the Habsburgs from Maximilian I to Ferdinand III, 1493–1657', in R. G. Asch and A. M. Birke (eds), *Princes, Patronage, and the Nobility: The Court at the Beginning of the Modern Age, c. 1450–1650* (London: Oxford, 1991), pp. 289–312.

Reinerman, A. *Austria and the Papacy in the Age of Metternich*, 2 vols (Washington, DC: Catholic University of America Press, 1979–89).

Reingrabner, G. *Protestanten in Österreich: Geschichte und Dokumentation* (Graz: Böhlau, 1981).

Repgen, K. (ed.) *Das Herrscherbild im 17. Jahrhundert* (Münster: Aschendorff, 1991).

Robinson, R. 'Non-European Foundations of European Imperialism: Sketch for a Theory of Collaboration', in E. R. J. Owen and R. B. Sutcliffe (eds), *Studies in the Theory of Imperialism* (London: Longman, 1972), pp. 117–39.

Roe, I. F. and J. Warren (eds) *The Biedermeier and Beyond* (Bern: Peter Lang, 1999).

Rössler, H. *Graf Johann Philipp Stadion: Napoleons deutscher Gegenspieler*, 2 vols (Vienna: Herold, 1966).

Sagarra, E. 'Benign Authority and its Cultivation in the Biedermeier', in I. F. Roe and J. Warren (eds), *The Biedermeier and Beyond* (Bern: Peter Lang, 1999), pp. 63–73.

Sayer, D. *The Coasts of Bohemia: A Czech History*, trans. A. Sayer (Princeton, NJ: Princeton University Press, 1998).

Scheichl, S. P. 'Die vaterländischen Balladen des österreichischen Biedermeier: Bausteine des habsburgischen Mythos. Zu Ludwig August Frankls "Habsburgerlied"', in I. F. Roe and J. Warren (eds), *The Biedermeier and Beyond* (Bern: Peter Lang, 1999), pp. 45–61.

Schimert, P. 'The Hungarian Nobility in the Seventeenth and Eighteenth Centuries', in H. M. Scott and C. Storrs (eds), *The European Nobilities in the Seventeenth and Eighteenth Centuries*, 2 vols (London: Longman, 1995), vol. 2, pp. 144–82.

Schmidt, G. 'Angst vor dem Kaiser?: Die Habsburger, die Erblande und die deutsche Libertät im 17. Jahrhundert', in H. Duchhardt and M. Schnettger (eds), *Reichständische Libertät und Habsburgisches Kaisertum* (Mainz: Philipp von Zabern, 1999), pp. 329–48.

Schnettger, M. 'Der Kaiser und die Bischofswahlen: Das Haus Österreich und die Reichskirche vom Augsburger Religionsfrieden bis zur Mitte des 17. Jahrhunderts', in H. Duchhardt and M. Schnettger (eds), *Reichständische Libertät und Habsburgisches Kaisertum* (Mainz: Philipp von Zabern, 1999), pp. 213–56.

Schragl, F. *Glaubensspaltung in Niederösterreich* (Vienna: Dom-Verlag, 1973).

Schroeder, K. A. 'Kunst als Erzählung: Theorie und Ästhetik der Genremalerei', in G. Frodl and K. A. Schroeder (eds), *Malerei zwischen Wiener Kongreß und Revolution* (Munich: Prestel, 1992), pp. 9–34.

Schroeder, P. *The Transformation of European Politics, 1763–1848* (Oxford: Clarendon Press, 1994).

Scott, H. M. (ed.) *Enlightened Absolutism: Reformed and Reformers in Later Eighteenth-Century Europe* (Basingstoke, UK: Macmillan [now Palgrave Macmillan], 1990).

——. 'Reform in the Habsburg Monarchy, 1740–1790', in H. M. Scott (ed.), *Enlightened Absolutism: Reformed and Reformers in Later Eighteenth-Century Europe* (Basingstoke, UK: Macmillan [now Palgrave Macmillan], 1990), pp. 145–88.

—— and C. Storrs (eds) *The European Nobilities in the Seventeenth and Eighteenth Centuries*, 2 vols (London: Longman, 1995).

Seigfried, A. 'Die Dogmatik im 18. Jahrhundert unter dem Einfluß von Aufklärung und Jansenismus', in E. Kovács (ed.), *Katholische*

Aufklärung und Josephinismus (Munich: Oldenbourg, 1979), pp. 241–65.

Sked, A. *The Decline and Fall of the Habsburg Empire, 1815–1918* (London: Longman, 1989).

Smith, D. M. *Mazzini* (New Haven, CT: Yale University Press, 1994).

Spielman, J. P. *The City and the Crown: Vienna and the Imperial Court, 1600–1740* (West Lafayette, IN: Purdue University Press, 1993).

——. *Leopold I of Austria* (New Brunswick, NJ: Rutgers, 1977).

——. 'Status as Commodity: The Habsburg Economy of Privilege', in C. Ingrao (ed.), *State and Society in Early Modern Austria* (West Lafayette, IN: Purdue University Press, 1994), pp. 110–18.

Staudt, J. B. *Mulier Fortis*, ed. W. Pass and F. Niiyama, Denkmäler der Tonkunst in Österreich, 152 (Graz: Akademische Druck- und Verlagsanstalt, 2000).

Steinberg, M. P. *The Meaning of the Salzburg Festival: Austria as Theater and Ideology, 1890–1938* (Ithaca, NY: Cornell University Press, 1990).

Storey, J. *An Introduction to Cultural Theory and Popular Culture*, 2nd edn (London: Prentice Hall, 1997 [1993]), pp. 17–18.

Sturmberger, H. *Adam Graf Herberstorff* (Munich: Oldenbourg, 1976).

Sugar, P. (ed.) *A History of Hungary* (Bloomington, IN: Indiana University Press, 1990).

—— and I. Lederer (eds) *Nationalism in Eastern Europe* (Seattle: University of Washington Press, 1969).

Sutter, B. 'Kaisertreue oder rationale Überlebensstrategie?: Die Reichsritterschaft als habsburgische Klientel im Reich', in H. Duchhardt and M. Schnettger (eds), *Reichsständische Libertät und Habsburgisches Kaisertum* (Mainz: Philipp von Zabern, 1999), pp. 245–308.

Szábó, F. A. J. *Kaunitz and Enlightened Absolutism, 1753–1780* (Cambridge: Cambridge University Press, 1994).

Tanner, M. *The Last Descendant of Aeneas: The Hapsburgs and the Mythic Image of the Emperor* (New Haven, CT: Yale University Press, 1993).

Tapié, V.-L. *The Rise and Fall of the Habsburg Monarchy*, trans. Stephen Hardman (New York: Praeger, 1971).

Teich, M. (ed.) *Bohemia in History* (Cambridge: Cambridge University Press, 1998).

Turczynski, E. 'The Role of the Orthodox Church in Adapting and Transforming the Western Enlightenment in Southeastern Europe', *East European Quarterly*, 9 (1975), pp. 415–40.

Uhlíř, D. 'Kaunitz und die böhmischen Länder', in G. Klingenstein and F. A. J. Szábó (eds), *Staatskanzler Wenzel Anton von Kaunitz-Rietberg,*

1711–1794: Neue Perspective zu Politik und Kultur der europäischen Aufklärung (Graz: Schneider, 1996), pp. 485–95.

Urban, O. 'Czech Society, 1848–1918', in M. Teich (ed.), *Bohemia in History* (Cambridge: Cambridge University Press, 1998), pp. 198–214.

Várdy, S. B. *Historical Dictionary of Hungary* (Lanham, MD: Scarecrow, 1997).

Várkonyi, Á. 'Rákóczi's War of Independence and the Peasantry', in J. Bak and B. Király (eds), *From Hunyadi to Rákóczi: War and Society in Late Medieval and Early Modern Hungary* (Brooklyn, NY: Brooklyn College Press, 1982), pp. 369–92.

Vaughn, R. *Valois Burgundy* (London: Allen Lane Penguin, 1975).

Vocelka, K. *Rudolf II und seine Zeit* (Vienna: Böhlau, 1985).

—— and Lynne Heller, *Die Lebenswelt der Habsburger: Kultur- und Mentalitätsgeschichte einer Familie* (Graz: Styria, 1997).

Wandruszka, Adam. 'Leopold II', in B. Hamann (ed.), *Die Habsburger: Ein biographisches Lexikon* (Vienna: Ueberreuter, 1988), pp. 255–60.

Wandycz, P. S. *The Lands of Partitioned Poland, 1795–1918* (Seattle, Wash.: University of Washington Press, 1974).

Wangermann, E. *The Austrian Achievement, 1700–1800* (New York: Harcourt, Brace, Jovanovich, 1973).

Whaley, J. 'Die Habsburgermonarchie und das Heilige Römische Reich im 18. Jahrhundert', in W. Brauneder and L. Hobelt (eds), *Sacrum Imperium: Das Reich und Österreich, 996–1806* (Vienna: Almathea, 1996), pp. 288–318.

Wiesflecker, H. *Maximilian I.: Die Fundamente des habsburgischen Weltreiches* (Vienna: Verlag für Geschichte und Politik, 1991).

——. *Kaiser Maximilian I*, 5 vols (Vienna: Verlag für Geschichte und Politik, 1971–86).

Winkelbauer, T. *Fürst und Fürstendiener: Gundaker von Liechtenstein, ein österreichischer Aristokrat des konfessionellen Zeitalters* (Vienna: Oldenbourg, 1999).

——. 'Grundherrschaft, Sozialdisziplinierung und Konfessionalisierung in Böhmen, Mähren, und Österreich im 16. und 17. Jahrhundert', in J. Bahlcke and A. Strohmeyer (eds), *Konfessionalisierung in Ostmitteleuropa* (Stuttgart: Steiner, 1999), pp. 307–38.

——. 'Herren und Holden: Die niederösterreichischen Adeligen und ihre Untertanen im 16. und 17. Jahrhundert', in H. Knittler (ed.), *Adel im Wandel: Politik. Kultur. Konfession, 1500–1700* (Horn: Berger, 1990), pp. 73–9.

Wolff, L. *Inventing Eastern Europe: The Map of Civilization on the Mind of the Enlightenment* (Stanford, CA: Stanford University Press, 1994).

Zacek, J. F. 'Nationalism in Czechoslovakia', in P. Sugar and I. Lederer (eds), *Nationalism in Eastern Europe* (Seattle, Wash.: University of Washington Press, 1969), pp. 166–206.

Zimányi, V. 'Adel und Grundherrschaft in Ungarn in der Frühneuzeit', in H. Feigl and W. Rosner (eds), *Adel im Wandel* (Vienna: Niederösterreichischen Institut für Landeskunde, 1991), pp. 39–46.

Index

Roman page numbers in *italic* indicate maps
n = endnote (indexed only for background information, not simple citations)

211